up the Alabama river as far as Montgomery
as it was a much pleasanter mode of travelling
than by rail. The steamers all over this
continent are [illegible] splendid
~~affairs~~ vessels and we were very comfortable on
board our boat. The country through
which we passed was fertile and cultivated
and where ~~the river flowed through~~ there were high
"bluffs" as they call the hills ~~through~~ which
the river flows we remarked a singular ingenious contrivance for pitching
down cotton bales to the ~~waiting banks of the water side~~
and produces ~~a great deal~~ much
of cotton. ~~It is singular~~ I was not aware ~~that~~ the cultivation
of cotton in America is of comparatively
recent date. Colonel Deas told me that
in 1774 his grandfather who then resided
in England, ~~wrote~~ wrote out to his agents in
Charleston ~~to~~ and directed them to attempt
the cultivation of a sufficient amount
of cotton to supply the negroes on his
plantation with homespun. At that
time Tobacco ~~Indigo was~~ the great staple in the
Southern States was Indigo the cultivation of which is
now entirely discontinued ~~[illegible]~~
that ~~the naval uniform in the South is~~
~~grey like the~~ that they were not able to make
the naval uniform in the Confederacy blue,
as every one knows a naval uniform ought to

Cities and Camps of the Confederate States

UNIVERSITY OF ILLINOIS PRESS, URBANA, 1958

CITIES AND CAMPS OF THE CONFEDERATE STATES

BY FITZGERALD ROSS

EDITED BY
RICHARD BARKSDALE HARWELL

Manufactured in the United States of America
Library of Congress Catalog Card No. 58-9456

This book is for

Robert L. Talmadge, of Kansas, and
Robert L. Russell, of Georgia

EDITOR'S PREFACE

The freshness, the enthusiasm—even the naiveté—with which FitzGerald Ross wrote of his travels in the Confederate States have made editing his volume for a new audience an unusual pleasure. The reader deserves in any case a word as to how the editing has been conceived and undertaken.

Ross's *A Visit to the Cities and Camps of the Confederate States* is such an eminently straightforward account that it can be read either for instruction or entertainment without the impedimenta of scholarship. A fuller knowledge of the events of any book, however, adds to the enjoyment of it. The editor's purpose has been to elucidate Ross's narrative with parallel comments of his contemporaries on the same events. For the most part the editor's notes have been limited to comments of this type. He has further limited his notes to the events with which Ross had some direct relation. Much that Ross wrote referred to events outside his own observation and outside those which had any real bearing on his travels. Every paragraph, almost every sentence, could be annotated. But delimitation of some sort was necessary, and the broader facts of the course of the war can be followed in dozens of other volumes. Individuals below the rank of general have been identified in notes. (A few have remained unidentified.) Officers of field grade (including those who achieved it after Ross's mention of them) are not identified in notes, but their full names are given in the index. Names which Ross misspelled have been followed on their first occurrence with the correct form in brackets; subsequent occurrences have been corrected without comment.

It is always a pleasure to acknowledge the help of others that is so necessary to the writing, compilation, or editing of any book of history. Librarians, historians, collectors, publishers—all have piled in to help.

I am particularly indebted to Mr. James I. Robertson, Jr., of Decatur, Georgia, and Danville, Virginia, for help with many details. No worker in Confederate materials can fail to profit from the help and encouragement of Miss India Thomas and Miss Eleanor Brockenbrough at the Confederate Museum, Richmond. At the Emory University Library, Atlanta, I am more than ever in the debt of Miss Ruth Walling, Mrs. Mary Davis, Miss Esther Bergen, and Mr. Thomas E. Crowder. Miss Gertrude Ruhnka of the Henry E. Huntington Library, San Marino, California, has been eternally helpful and gracious. At the library of the University of Illinois, Urbana, Mr. Robert B. Downs, Miss Alice Appell, and Miss Helen Welch have helped in important ways.

I am indebted to the Henry E. Huntington Library for permission to reproduce illustrations from *The Illustrated London News,* and to Mr. Erwin F. Morkisch for his fine photography. For other illustrations, including that on the dust-jacket, I am under yet another obligation to the Confederate Museum.

For foreign records concerning FitzGerald Ross, I am indebted to Mr. F. H. Francis of the British Museum, Mr. J. S. Ritchie and Mr. J. R. Seaton of the National Library of Scotland, Dr. Oskar Regele and Mr. D. Kraus of the Österreichisches Staatsarchiv, Dr. M. Stickler of the Österreichische Nationalbibliothek, and to the firm of William Blackwood and Sons of Edinburgh.

Equally helpful have been Mr. Floyd M. Cammack and Miss Elaine Mitchell of the Association of College and Research Libraries, Mr. Beverly M. DuBose of Atlanta, Mr. Philip D. Sang of River Forest, Illinois, Mr. Donald Jackson of the University of Illinois Press, and Mr. Ralph Newman of Chicago.

To each and all I am grateful.

RICHARD BARKSDALE HARWELL

INTRODUCTION

This is FitzGerald Ross's book. *A Visit to the Cities and Camps of the Confederate States* is his own record of what he saw and learned of the South at war. As an honest (though over-sympathetic) picture of the Confederacy during the latter half of 1863 and the early months of 1864, it is one of the finest and most informative of the relatively few inclusive records left by outside observers of the Confederacy in its own time.

Ross saw the best of the Confederacy and became, consciously or not, one of its staunchest propagandists. His book gives, as one reviewer noted, "what a picture of power, prosperity, and even happiness, a rich country inhabited by brave men can present even in time of war." [1] *The Index* had commented earlier on *Cities and Camps:* "The writer is always vivacious, keenly observant of events, and his pictures of life and character are just." [2] At least they were just what the editor of *The Index,* a remarkable propagandistic journal published for the Confederates in London by Henry Hotze, wanted. There was

[1] *The Index* (London), v (1865), 75.

[2] *The Index,* IV (1864), 778.

another side, too. *The Athenaeum,* which disliked Ross's pro-slavery sentiments, therefore found the whole book bad. "It is thoroughly Austrian," wrote its reviewer, "and of course thoroughly illiberal. Speaking of Secession with enthusiastic admiration, the author seizes every occasion to hurl an insulting word at the people of the *old* Free States." [3] Accurate judgment doubtless lies in some middle ground. A traveler sees what he wants to see; a reader reads what he wants to read. If Ross's is not the whole story of the Civil War—and there are plenty of books in which to find other facets of that story—it is yet an honest and valid rendition of one man's observations. There is truth in *The Saturday Review's* appraisal: "Captain Ross is a shrewd observer; and, like many military men, he writes in a simple, agreeable, unaffected style, entirely free from that verbiage which is too common among authors by profession, and from that dreary ostentation of liveliness which has of late become fashionable. His unpretentious volume contrasts very favourably with the ponderous works of certain literary visitors to the Northern States, and will bear comparison even with the excellent narrative of Colonel Fremantle's expedition to the South." [4]

Ross's and Fremantle's books, in fact, comprise almost a unit. For Ross's *A Visit to the Cities and Camps of the Confederate States* is practically a continuation of, at least a sequel to, Colonel Sir Arthur James Lyon Fremantle's *Three Months in the Southern States, April–June 1863.*[5]

---

[3] *The Athenaeum* (London), May 13, 1865 (No. 1959), 646.

[4] *The Saturday Review* (London), XIX (1865), 545.

[5] (Edinburgh and London, 1863). Fremantle's account was published also in New York and in Mobile in 1864. It has more recently been republished (1954) as *The Fremantle Diary,*

Fremantle had entered the Confederacy at Brownsville, Texas, worked his way east with visits to the principal cities and camps along the way. Ross entered the Confederacy in the Northern Neck of Virginia in late May. Fremantle arrived in Richmond June 17, Ross June 18. From there, for the next three weeks, their itineraries were first similar, then identical. They met just before the Battle of Gettysburg and observed it together. Fremantle left the Confederacy on July 9. Ross headed south with the retreating Confederate army. He would remain as a military tourist in the Confederate States until the next April. Thus, the narratives of Ross and Fremantle both complement and supplement one another. Together they present accounts of nine of the eleven Confederate States (all except Arkansas and Florida). Together they cover a full year of the day-to-day history of the Confederacy. And they both report in detail the single most important battle of the war. They supplement, complement, and corroborate.

Both Fremantle and Ross espoused the cause of the South somewhat overzealously. They were not always, or often, able to discriminate between what was represented to them as good by their Southern hosts and what was actually good. Each allowed his predisposition to favor the Confederacy to be strengthened by the courtesies he met everywhere, both from soldiers and civilians. Ross's judgment of the Battle of Gettysburg is generally sounder than Fremantle's. Fremantle is usually more generous with names and details. Both had amazing opportunities to see the South at war—in its cities and its camps—and

---

with an introduction by Walter Lord. Also published in 1954 under the title *A Military Tourist* was a brief account of Colonel Fremantle, his Confederate travels, and his book, by the editor of the present volume.

to meet its influential figures. Their accounts are both good books.

Ross's observations of his year in America are all that secure him to fame. Outside of this year of adventure he seems to have lived the unostentatious, though interesting, life of a professional soldier, finally retiring into the obscurity of bachelor old age and leaving neither family papers nor so much as a record of his death at the office of the Registrar General in London.

What biographical facts remain survive largely in the Kriegsarchiv of the Österreichisches Staatsarchiv in Vienna and in Ross's own letters to his publisher in the National Library of Scotland, Edinburgh. He was born in 1825 at Little Bookham, Leatherhead, Surry, England, and christened Edward FitzGerald Turton Ross. Educated at the universities of Heidelberg and Göttingen, Ross joined the Austrian Hussars as a private soldier on January 16, 1850. He was promoted to second lieutenant May 20 of that year and to first lieutenant October 1, 1852. On July 10, 1861, he was promoted to captain of cavalry (second class). On October 13, 1862, while on duty at Krakow, he was placed in temporary retirement. He returned to Vienna and thence to England. After his year's trip to America, he traveled in Spain and lived a gentleman's life in London and at Little Bookham. He returned to the Hussars in April, 1868, apparently only for the purpose of *pro forma* status so that he could resign with his officer's rank. He effected that resignation April 28, 1868. The remainder of his life seems to have been spent in England, except the Austrian records note that on December 2, 1898, he was decorated with the *Jubiläumserinnerungs-Medaille.*

There is little to reveal personality in such a dossier, and Ross's Confederate companions left even less in the way of lively description of him. The Austrian records do comment that he was versed in languages: German, Hungarian, French, and English. A *Conduiteliste* of 1861 remarks that he "was of hardy constitution, solid character, and possessed many and outstanding talents. . . . He was rather a good rider and swimmer, very sociable, and sought good steady companionship."

It is not a complete biography, but an understanding of Ross's book, that is necessary here. Of his book he left a full record in his letters to his publisher, William Blackwood.[6] By the time of Ross's first letter to Blackwood October 22, 1864, *A Visit to the Cities and Camps of the Confederate States* was nearly completed.

"Sir," wrote Ross, "I have lately returned from America after spending nearly a year in the Confederate States. During that period I visited all the principal cities and armies in the field and was a witness of many interesting events—being present at Gettysburg, bombardment of Charleston, Chicamauga, etc.

"Leaving the Confederacy in April, after a short stay at Nassau and Havana, I also visited the Northern States and Canada.

"As my friends—especially those from the Southern Confederacy—think that a little account of my travels which I have written might interest the public generally, I take the liberty of offering it to you for publication.

"The narrative is no doubt very defective as I am quite unaccustomed to writing, but I believe that no one has had

[6] Ross's letters to Blackwood survive in the Blackwood Papers in the National Library of Scotland, Edinburgh.

such a favourable opportunity of becoming thoroughly acquainted with the Southern Confederacy, under its present aspects, as myself.[7]

"I may perhaps say at once that I have no pecuniary profit in view in offering my little work for your acceptance and that I am willing to bear any expense which the publication of it might entail.

"I enclose my card and am Sir your obedient servant

FitzGerald Ross"

Ross had good reason to believe Blackwood would be interested. Blackwood had already published, both in *Blackwood's Edinburgh Magazine* and as a book, Colonel Fremantle's narrative. The magazine had published a succession of articles sympathetic to the South, including Field-Marshal Wolseley's "A Month's Visit to the Confederate Headquarters." Blackwood was interested. Ross's manuscript was forwarded on October 29, 1864, and immediately accepted. He returned proof sheets for the first installment November 14 and by December 3 had received a check for his contribution and printed copies of the magazine.[8]

Immediately copies were forwarded his friends in the Confederacy by Captain Walker Fearn, agent of the Confederate State Department, who left London December 3 to

---

[7] In printing this letter as an introduction to Ross's narrative when it appeared in *Blackwood's,* the publishers ended it at this point and added the signature "A Cavalry Officer." Omitted in the printed version of the letter is the phrase qualifying "my friends" as "especially those from the Southern confederacy." *Blackwood's Edinburgh Magazine,* XCVI (1864), 645.

[8] Chapters I–VI appeared in *Blackwood's,* XCVI (1864), 645–670; chapters VII–IX in XCVII (1865), 26–48; and chapters X–XIII in XCVII (1865), 151–175. The rest of the narrative appeared for the first time in book form.

return to the South in the blockade runner *Maude Campbell.* Before leaving for Spain in the middle of the month, Ross instructed Blackwood that copies of the next issue should be sent to the Confederacy through the good offices of John R. Thompson, Richmond litterateur and librarian, recently come to London to serve on *The Index.* Thompson, wrote Ross, "will forward them to Dixie. He tells me they are so very hard up for reading now in Cousin Sally Ann's dominions that he will be very glad to send over 25 numbers." [9]

From Madrid, Ross was writing on January 25, 1865, suggesting that his articles be published in book form. "I suppose I should have to add a few chapters about the Northern States, Havana, Canada, etc., a task which I contemplate with a little dismay as I cannot help considering writing a[n] awful bore, at the same time I am ambitious of writing 'a book' for once in my life and shall most likely never have another opportunity." As soon as he returned to Little Bookham in mid-February, Ross completed the manuscript. "I found it very hard work to put together," he said in his letter of February 22, "and am afraid it is very stupid. However if you will have it printed in Capital letters, very wide apart[,] I dare say it will make a decent *sized* book."

He offered as illustrations for *Cities and Camps* portraits of a number of Confederate leaders, or "an original plan of Chicamauga and a Yankee one of Gettysburg," but Blackwood finally chose a map of the Southeastern states with Ross's route outlined on it.

Writing his preface gave Ross an uncommon bit of trouble. "I am afraid," he wrote Blackwood on March 24,

---

[9] Letter of December 14, 1864.

"I have made a mull of it but I can do no better though I have tried very hard. Is it the general experience of Authors that the preface is the most difficult part of the book to write?"

Ross's essays in *Blackwood's* had been printed as anonymous—as by "A Cavalry Officer." He demurred gently to signing his name to the book. "The only objection I have to putting my name to the book," he wrote February 15, "is that if this war lasts much longer and I should wish to pay another visit to Dixie and should pass through the North, I might get into trouble there as the Yankees seem to have established the rule that they might do as they please with anybody who is obnoxious to them. However if you think my name should be given to my child, by all means let it be so." Twelve days later he settled the matter: "I have no objection at all to putting my name to the book[;] indeed as I have said some sharp things about the Yankees I think it is much better that they should not be published anonymously."

After his return from Spain, Ross spent much of his time in London with two old Confederate friends, John R. Thompson and Heros von Borcke, the Prussian hero of General J. E. B. Stuart's staff. Ross was instrumental in directing von Borcke's memoirs (translated and, in fact, ghost-written by Thompson) to publication by Blackwood. "Are you tired of the Confederates or would you like to publish something more about them? Colonel von Borcke, whom I have mentioned in my journal as the distinguished officer who received the thanks of both houses of Congress, has just arrived in England on special service. He was Stuart's Inspector General & was in all the battles from Fairoaks till the advance into Pennsylvania. He *kept a diary* & I want very much to persuade him to publish it. I am sure it would be intensely interesting."[10] *Memoirs of the Confederate War for Independence* began serially in *Blackwood's* later in 1865 and was published separately in two volumes in 1866. It is a classic among Confederate personal narratives.

The three confederates in London—Ross, "the Austrian," von Borcke, the Prussian; and Thompson, the Confederate—maintained a deep interest in the course of affairs in America. Incidental paragraphs in Ross's letters to Blackwood provide a commentary on the events of the last months of the war:

November 9, 1864: "I am glad to see how finely old Price is getting on in Missouri. You are probably aware that the northern portion of Missouri is staunchly Southern in sentiment[,] the cultivation of hemp by negro labor being as remunerative as cotton planting in the more Southern states. The great mining districts in the south of the state—employing a great deal of Yankee capital & labor—are supposed still to sympathise with the North, though not nearly as much as at the beginning of the war. Price must now be getting an enormous amount of recruits and if he only has ammunition enough will be able to maintain himself in the rich country he now occupies."

February 15, 1865: "People here [in England] seem to me to attach a great deal to[o] much importance to the run of luck the Yankees have lately had. In my humble opinion the having to hold such a long line of coast, whilst they of course have to supply their armies from the North by sea, will be of more harm than use to the Yankees."

February 27, 1865: "The Yankees have just hanged a very fine fellow, [John Yates] Beall, who had been given

---

10 Letter of February 22, 1865.

up to them by the Canadians. He had gone to Canada under a commission from President Davis to attempt the release of the Confederate prisoners on Johnson's island in Lake Erie. In my humble opinion the Canadians have acted very shamefully in giving up the Confederate 'raiders' under the pretence of their being felons."

March 24, 1865: "We are all convinced here [Ross, Thompson, and von Borcke in London] that Sherman has been 'whipped.' "

May 12, 1865: "We are all dreadfully distressed here at the sudden collapse of the Confederacy, still I do not think the affair is over yet and shall be surprised if Texas and the West does not hold out.

"I conscientiously believe that it was Johnson who had Lincoln assassinated just as he had General van Dorn assassinated 2 years ago. As for the man who was shot the other day and secretly buried being Wilkes Booth that is a story 'for the Marines.' No one would have tried to escape in that direction except a Confederate prisoner from Point Lookout which the victim probably was. The only surprise is that for the money given, 150 thousand dollars, not half a dozen Wilkes Booths have been shot. Everybody seems to believe the story however and undoubtedly Johnson and Stanton have managed their affair very cleverly. They will probably succeed too in getting up a sort of Titus Oakes conspiracy and laying the blame on the South. Johnson is unprincipled enough for anything & Stanton is almost as bad."

Ross fretted at the turn of events in the South he had learned to love during his brief residence there. But he was pleased with his own handiwork, his book about the Confederacy. "I am," he wrote Blackwood in his letter of May 12, "quite jealous of the outward appearance of the book which everybody admires immensely and praises exclusively so that I get no credit for my part of the performance."

Ross's report of Confederate life was reasonably well received. But it had, because of the end of the war, gone stale before its time; it could not receive the acclaim or exert the influence that Fremantle's quicker account did. It has therefore suffered in comparison and is less well known than it deserves to be. "The present moment," noted the May 6, 1865, review of *Cities and Camps* in *The Saturday Review,* "is hardly favourable to the success of a book which was written while the Confederate cause still seemed prosperous; and which, although it contains some curious information respecting matters imperfectly understood and incidents comparatively unknown in this country, throws no light on the circumstances which disappointed the hopes so long and so confidently entertained, and brought the final catastrophe to pass so much more suddenly and decisively than ordinary observers could have expected. Till now, the strong interest felt in everything that could elucidate the recent events of the war, and assist us to understand the past vicissitudes and future prospects of the contest, ensured to everyone who could tell us anything new concerning the armies, people, and circumstances of the South an eager and attentive audience; and the papers in *Blackwood's Magazine* which are reprinted in this volume were read with extreme interest by all who wished to know what an intelligent professional observer could gather, in a hasty visit, about the military situation and operations of the Confederacy. When the fate of the Southern people is finally decided, and their gallant struggle has become nothing more than a recent and deeply moving episode of history, books of this class will have another and a more melancholy interest. But at this conjuncture we do not need them. As testimonies to the character and spirit of the defeated nation, we do not need them; as evidence of the apparent strength and prospects of a cause now fallen, and anticipations of the issue of a conflict now rapidly approaching a most unlooked-for conclusion, they have lost their value; and the time is not yet come when we can take them up simply as contributions to the history of the American war." [11]

The time has come when Captain Ross's comments and observations have an increased value and interest as contributions to the history of the Civil War. Increased awareness of the importance of the American past has made any contribution to an understanding of that past of very real interest and importance. Captain Ross's honest and straightforward representation of the Confederacy—however betrayed by his over-optimism and over-conviction for its cause—is a positive contribution to a full comprehension of that "most deeply moving episode of history."

[11] *The Saturday Review,* XIX (1865), 545.

Cities and Camps of the Confederate States

CONTENTS

Chapter I. 9–30
The Major
Hiding in church
Aid and comfort
Hospitality under difficulties
Country fare
Christopher Columbus
European news
Friendly invitation
Taking a drink
The gunboat
Secessia reached
Yankee devastation
Southern hospitality
Richmond
Stonewall Jackson
Advance of Confederates
Reception at Richmond
Yankee rapacity
Captain Lee
The Richmond
President Davis
Richmond to Staunton
Staunton to Winchester
Capture of Winchester
Federals astonished
Enormous captures

Chapter II. 31–45
Winchester to Martinsburg
Treatment of slaves
Southern cavalry
Soldiers' equipments
Pennsylvanian spoil
Confederate teetotalism
March into Pennsylvania
March by night
Dutch and Germans
Pennsylvanian Dutch
Chambersburg
Union sentiment
The Southern yell
Procuring supplies
Horrors of war
Lee's headquarters
Lost order
M'Clellan's report
Longstreet's headquarters

Chapter III. 46–54
Advance on Gettysburg
Glorious news
Morning before the battle
The battle-field
Discipline of the army
Campaigning
Colonel Walton
Confederate sacrifices
Opening of the attack
Longstreet leading the charge
Lee's report

Chapter IV. 55–62
Return from the field
Preparations for renewing the fight
Our view of the battle
Assault of Pickett's division
Failure of supporting division
Pickett's division repulsed
Severe loss of the enemy
Losses of Longstreet's corps
The thief in the night
General Pendleton

Chapter V. 63–74
Bream's tavern
Noble bearing of the wounded
Torrents of rain
Luxurious pillow
Shocking state of the roads
Hagerstown
The "fine gentleman"
Advantages of the campaign
Prisons North and South
Healthy state of Belle Isle
A Yankee *jeu d'esprit*

Chapter VI. 75–86
Conversation with General Lee
General Stuart
Delay in forwarding supply-trains
Probable results of success
Colonel Wickham
Mr Lincoln's finger and thumb
Our happy ignorance of danger
General Pettigrew killed
American cavalry
"Trading" a boot
Our negro cook "Jeff"
Attachment of slaves to their masters
Poor "free niggers"

Chapter VII. 87–92
The Federal doodle
Rumours of victory at Richmond
High spirits of the soldiers
Picturesque encampments
Forced marches
Virginian hospitality
Skirmish at Chester Gap
The signal corps
Discovering the enemy's alphabet

Chapter VIII. 93–112
Richmond
Money matters
Petersburg
Wilmington
Charleston
The great fire in 1862
The "Battery"
Fort Sumter
Advantage of sand forts
Conversion by fire
Ashley Hall
Scuppernong grapes
Bombardment of Sumter
Precarious condition of the fort
The shore batteries
The science of arson
Shelling the city
Greek fire
The "fair warning"
A "mean Yankee trick"
The "swamp-angel" burst
Treatment of negroes
Yankee "liberation"
Cruelty of wholesale emancipation
Prohibition of the slave-trade
Spurious philanthropy

Chapter IX. 113–143
Evacuation of Fort Wagner
Attempt to storm Fort Sumter
Augusta
General Jenkins
A lady captain
The "Gate City"
Ingenious mode of recruiting
Forrest and his "calvary"
The field of battle
Arrival at headquarters
Narrow escape of General M'Laws

Largesses to servants
Gallant Mississippian
The last man running
General Buckner
General Wheeler
"Brag is a good dog"
"I wish he had lost a thousand"
"Bull of the woods"
Lookout Mountain
Fine horses
Western generals
Crowded quarters
Confederate artillery
Superior field-ammunition
Massing artillery
Artillery staff organisation
Small-arms
Telescopic rifles
Medical matters
North American Indians
John Ross
"Jeff's" dignity
Yankees not worth killing
Somebody's chairs
Afternoon concert
Napoleon's courtesy before battle
Yankee dead still unburied
Inclement weather
Lord John Russell
Hungry travellers
Powder-mills at Augusta
Powder-magazines
Enormous grains of powder
The Blakely guns
Mild climate

Chapter X. 144–165
Major Pringle
Fort Sumter
Summerville
Middleton Place
Northern creditors
John Locke
Railroad accident
Buried for nothing
General Whiting
Successful blockade-runners
Fort Fisher
Loss of the Ceres
Bragg's resignation
Battle of Missionary Ridge
Officers throwing stones
Sherman's corps "whipped"
Joe Hooker repulsed
Return to Richmond
Gambling put down
Corporal punishment
Oriental Saloon
Bill of fare
Starvation in the South
Profusion and waste
Negro rations
Libby Prison
Tredegar Ironworks
Kidnapping negroes
Colonel Sothern
Escape across the lines

Chapter XI. 166–185
General Stuart
Christmas eve
General Jimmy J. E. B. Stuart, junior
General Lee
Christmas fare
Garlands of flowers
Egg-nogg
"My name's M'Gregor"
Colonel St Leger Grenfell
"Only seventy-seven"
Confederate scouts
New Year's Day
General Morgan
Guerillas
Major Von Borcke
Not "dearest," but "nearest"
English engineer officer
Seward and Chase
States' rights
Ball at Fredericksburg
Battle-field
Sunken road
Burnside's retreat
Dr Moore

General Wade Hampton
Farewell dinner to L.

Chapter XII. 186–192
Petersburg
General Whiting
Shelling of Charleston
Blakely guns
The soldier's home
Savannah
General Beauregard
General Bragg
Provisions abundant

Chapter XIII. 193–206
Mobile
Wedding-party and ball
The forts
Down the bay
Fort Morgan
Re-enlistments
The field of Chicamauga
Dog River bar
Ships of war for Brazil
Appreciation of English sympathy
The shell road
Faithful slave
Improvident marriages
Magnificent steamer
Reinforcements returning
Farewell to the South
The Hansa
Nassau
Fishing party

Chapter XIV. 207–213
Havana
"Dos duros"
Volantes
Blockade-running
Chinese coolies
The theatre
Enterprising Yankees
Havana cigars
Smoking allowed everywhere
The fish-market

Chapter XV. 214–222
Yankee expeditions
Glorious victories
Excitement in Wall Street
Luxury at New York
Everybody satisfied
Frightful losses of the Yankees
Discontent in the Yankee army
Prisoners at Lookout Point
The Continental Hotel
Philadelphia propriety
Saving appearances
Lee in his last ditch
Commissariat whisky

Chapter XVI. 223–225
Spurious proclamation
Story of the "mob" at Richmond
Yankee untruthfulness

Chapter XVII. 226–233
Tour in the country
An assistant provost-marshal
Niagara Falls
Kentucky refugees
The rebellion of 1837 in Canada
Murder and arson
Yankee sympathisers
Threats of Seward and General Dix
The right of asylum
Montreal
Bad accommodation for troops
The green cliffs of old Ireland

Appendix. 234–237

EXTRACT FROM APPLETON'S GUIDE-BOOK.

Slaves in South Carolina
Bridal festivities
Softened feudal life
"Go 'way, Sambo"
Rich soil

PREFACE

The kind reception which was accorded to the Author's narrative of his adventures in the Southern States of America, upon their first appearance in 'Blackwood's Magazine,' has been the occasion of its present republication.

A few chapters relating to a short sojourn in the Northern States and in Canada have been added.

To the great interest which is taken by all Englishmen, without reference to party, in the events of the war in America, more than to any especial merit in the narrative itself, the Author attributes the degree of favour which was extended to his Sketches on their first appearance; and he ventures to hope that the same indulgence may be granted to them in their present collected and enlarged form.

3 CLIFFORD STREET, *March 1865.*

CHAPTER I

I came into this neighbourhood, which, by way of distinction, I will call a station on the Underground Railway from Yankeeland to Secessia, some time in the month of May 1863, and stopped at a road and river side inn, where I found four gentlemen, with whom I linked my fortunes for the nonce.[1]

[1] Frank Vizetelly, wartime correspondent for *The Illustrated London News,* entered the Confederate States in the same fashion and by approximately the same route in June, 1862. In an unsigned article, "Underground to Richmond," in *All the Year Round* (London), February 16, 1867 (XVII, 172–78) he commented (p. 172): "This term of 'Underground Route' may appear to signify some tubular arrangement for tunnelling beneath the waters of the Potomac, but does no more than typify the secret way in which Southern sympathisers were conveyed, during the recent civil war in The States, from the shores of Maryland to the Virginia banks of the Potomac."

I could not tell you their names, even if I chose to do so; they all go by false ones, as they have informed me, with a promise to disclose their true patronymics when we reach the other side. I cannot tell you where this neighbourhood is to be found, lest I should get my friends into trouble.

The one of them of whom I see most, and with whom I chiefly associate, is called the Major. He is very agreeable and well-informed, has travelled a great deal in his own country, and seems to know everybody. I believe him to be a Virginian country gentleman, who has been run off his plantation by the Yankees. Of course he hates them most cordially.

Two others are young Marylanders going to join the army; and the fourth is, I think, going to run the blockade for commercial purposes.

I brought the latest newspapers with me, which were immediately seized, and the Major read them aloud with amusing comments.

Most Northern newspapers make it a rule never to tell the truth if they can help it, and it requires a great deal of ingenuity and practice to interpret them correctly.

The Major did so, I thought, very successfully. The reading over, we took "a drink" all round, according to the custom of the country. Conversation ensued, and it was late before we retired; the Major and the two soldiers to a deserted church near at hand, and the commercial blockade-runner and myself to our beds at the inn.

The next morning the Major pumped me a little, and finding me, I suppose, "all right," he promised me his protection and services, for which I was very grateful, and indeed they proved invaluable in the sequel. I found the day tediously long, as we got up soon after daylight, and the Major left after breakfast to make some arrangement for obtaining a boat to cross the water. He returned in the evening, having purchased a boat, in which we shall embark as soon as the weather permits. I had to shut myself up in my room for some time during the day, as a Federal officer came to the inn to look at our landlord's whisky, and see that he had not too much of it—rather a strange piece of duty, I thought, for a commissioned army officer. I understand that innkeepers are not allowed to keep more than a certain store of whisky, for fear they should sell it to the rebels over the water, and thereby "aid and comfort" them. This is a very out-of-the-way place. Fancy in this "Excelsior" "go-ahead" country your being seven or eight miles from the nearest post-office, and even there the post coming in only once a-week!

Still we thought ourselves not safe from observation, and "concluded" to part company, and lie about amongst the farmers and planters in the neighbourhood whilst making our preparations. I stuck to the Major, and we have been living at different houses with all sorts of people ever since.

They are all kind, hospitable, good fellows, a little depressed by the bad times, and at being obliged to keep their political sentiments entirely to themselves; for I need not say that in this part of the world all are violent Secessionists, and have forfeited all their political rights, as they will not take an oath of allegiance to the administration. They run no small risk in harbouring us too. If found out, it would go very hard with their persons, and their estates would almost certainly be confiscated. Only a few days ago, the family of a gentleman of large property in Maryland entertained two relations, soldiers in the Southern army, at their house during the absence of the owner himself. They were found out; the gentleman, who knew nothing of the matter, was sent to Fort Warren; his property was confiscated, and the ladies of the family were sent South without being allowed to take anything with them.*

Yet I never discovered the slightest hesitation on the part of the sturdy planters and farmers down here as to receiving us into their houses, and giving us the best entertainment they could afford.

This kind of life is very instructive and entertaining, as far as giving one a thorough insight into the American mode of living in the country; but it is rather hard work to get up at daylight every morning, and breakfast at half-past four or five. During the day-time we occupy ourselves with walking or riding, or boating and fishing, or we visit a neighbour who invites us to make his house our next quarters.

We never stop more than two nights at the same place.

Dinner is generally before twelve, and by nine in the evening we are in bed and asleep. There is always a great profusion at every meal of salt meat, fish, terrapins, hot cakes, eggs, bacon, butter, &c.; but fresh meat is very rare. I do not believe that a butcher exists nearer than the county town, twenty miles off. There are no markets anywhere except in large cities—not even in the county town, where I spent two days before I came to this part of the country.

A company of Federal soldiers were stationed there, but the "citizens" are all ardently Southern in their sentiments.

I sat one evening with a party of them before the door of the hotel, and they were talking red-hot "Secesh" poli-

* They subsequently earned their living by needlework at Gordonsville.

tics. All regretted that the American colonies had ever separated from England; and though they professed to admire Washington personally, yet they heartily wished he had never been born. One went so far as to d—— Christopher Columbus—"What business on earth," he said, "had he to come and discover this God-forsaken country?"[2]

"Yes, sir," said another, addressing himself to me, "it was a Yankee trick, sir: they cheated us, as they have done ever since. We didn't want to quarrel with England, but they did, because they had been kicked out of the country, with their Mayflower and their Puritans. D—— them, I wish they'd all been drowned at the bottom of the sea. And they didn't want to fight, sir; Yankees never do, sir; and we Southerners, like fools, went and fought it out for them, just as they're making them Dutch and Irishmen fight for them now, sir! No Yankee is ever killed in battle, sir—not at least to speak of," he added, in modification of this rather untenable proposition.

---

[2] Ross wrote his publisher, William Blackwood, December 14, 1864: "I find that my Southern friend was not singular in his want of appreciation of Columbus' magnificent 'diskivery.' Says Artemus Ward in his report of his interview with 'Prints' Napoleon: 'It cost Columbus twenty thousand dollars to fit out his explorin expedition. If he had bin a sensible man he'd hav put the money in a hoss railroad or a gas company, and left this magnificent continent to intelligent savages, who when they got hold of a good thing knew enuff to keep it, and who wouldn't have seceded, nor rebelled nor knocked Liberty in the head with a slungshot. Columbus wasn't much of a feller, after all. It would hav bin money in my pocket if he'd staid to home. Chris ment well, but he put his foot in it when he saled for America." Ross was quoting "Interview with Prince Napoleon" in Charles Farrar Browne's *Artemus Ward His Book* (New York, 1862), p. 229.

I believe I added to the geographical knowledge of many persons there, by explaining to them the relative position of Vienna and Berlin, dissipating the idea of Prussia being governed by an emperor, &c. &c. At the same time, I have myself learnt several "facts" of which I was previously ignorant.

It seems that the Austrian Field-Marshal Giulay, after losing the battle of Magenta, was cashiered, and then re-entered the army as a private soldier, and was killed at Solferino fighting like a hero.

There was once a famine threatening to break out amongst the tailors of Paris in consequence of want of work. Upon this the Emperor Louis Napoleon suddenly appeared in a totally new and original costume, and all the fashionable young men of Paris following his example, the tailors got plenty to do, and were saved.

I made great friends with several of the unsophisticated natives of that quaint little county town; and one of them said to me as we shook hands at parting—"I hope, sir, when you are here again, I'll see you at the jail."

I suppose I looked rather startled at his suggesting such a contingency, which, under the circumstances, was not quite an improbable one; for he then added in explanation that he himself was the guardian of that county institution: "I am the jailer, you know, sir." He seemed to be a very intelligent fellow, and I hope will live to be a judge.

I mentioned before that there are no markets in this country, except in large cities; but they have a substitute for them in the shape of periodical meetings of planters and farmers in fixed places on stated days. Such a reunion takes place weekly at ——; and thither I betook myself one day, having ascertained that there would be none but "right" people about.

A long line of one-horse buggies and a good many saddle-horses were fastened up to the stake-fences on one side of the road, and their owners were at the store or the wayside-inn, or walking about, buying and selling, and bargaining or talking (politics, of course), or—and that very frequently—"taking a drink." This national custom never takes a solitary form, nor is it indulged in for the purpose of satisfying your thirst. To take a drink with any one, is to accept or proffer a compliment; to refuse one would give grave offence.[3]

Your friend takes you to the bar, and the "liquor" is concocted. Probably several of your friend's friends are there. "Mr So-and-so, will you join us? Mr So-and-so, allow me to introduce you to my friend, Mr Blank." "Mr Blank, I am very happy to meet you, sir" (an American always repeats your name, and treasures it up in his memory); "I hope you are in good health, Mr Blank." You go through the ceremony with all the friends, and in the mean time the drink is ready. Then you bow all round, saying, "My regards, gentlemen," and swallow it gravely, pretending to like it, and trying not to make a grimace. Of course all the drinks here are made of very bad whisky; and I did think it very nasty at first, but one gets used to everything.

After spending nearly a fortnight in this neighbour-

---

[3] "I have," wrote another military tourist from England, "now become comparatively accustomed to the necessity of shaking hands and drinking brandy with every one." Sir Arthur James Lyon Fremantle, *Three Months in the Southern States, April–June 1863* (Edinburgh and London, 1863), p. 22.

hood, the wind and weather suddenly became favourable, and it was determined that we should be off at dark.[4]

There was no time to lose. It was five o'clock, and we had to collect our party, which had been increased by two gentlemen from Washington (father and son) and a young doctor. However, by ten o'clock we were on board our little boat, and were fairly off.

We passed one guardship without being perceived, and nothing disturbed us till near daylight. As it dawned, a big dark object suddenly loomed up in the distance. We strained our eyes looking through the twilight. Could it be? Yes, it was—yes, it was certainly—there could be no mistake—it was a gunboat. I was excessively disgusted: if she saw us we were lost—Fort Lafayette instead of a campaign with Lee. Horrible thought!

Still she came nearer and nearer, whilst we scudded away as fast as we could. But what chance had our little boat against steam? Bigger and bigger the monster became, till hope dawned within us as we saw her swing round and turn her black broadside towards us. She had not perceived our little cockle-shell. Away she steamed in an opposite direction, and as her ugly black hulk gradually receded, and began to look smaller and smaller in the distance, we recovered our spirits and laughed at our "scare." The Major proposed "a drink," and I thought the whisky this time really delicious.

We ran safely into a little creek on the Virginia shore, and then we soon discovered that it was all for the best

---

[4] Describing his similar trip, Vizetelly wrote: "Leonard's Town was the point selected for embarkation, and there the river could not have been less than nine or ten miles in width, with an additional inlet of some seven miles to navigate before reaching the river itself." *All the Year Round,* XVII (1867), 175.

that we had been detained so long. We landed in the midst of a deserted Yankee camp, and its occupants had only left this part of the country two days before, after having dispossessed the inhabitants of all the property they could lay their hands on.

Negroes, horses, mules, cattle, had been carried off; corn and hay, and even agricultural implements, had been burnt and destroyed. The poor people were in a state of despair.

This part of the country, I must remark, is entirely removed from the seat of war, and the Yankee raid had been made solely for the purpose of plundering and destroying the property of the poor unoffending inhabitants.[5]

---

[5] Ross apparently landed on the shores of Westmoreland County, Virginia. His own map of his travels begins at Fredericksburg (to avoid revelation of his route into the Confederacy). J. B. Jones, clerk in the Confederate War Department, commented on the Yankee raids into northern Virginia in his diary entry for June 9, 1863: "The people in the 'Northern Neck' have been much harassed by the incursions of the invaders. I clip the following account from the *Whig* of this date: 'Nearly every house was visited, and by deceptive artifices, such as disguising themselves in Confederate gray clothes, stolen, or otherwise surreptitiously obtained, they imposed themselves upon our credulous and unsuspecting people; excited their sympathies by pretending to be wounded Confederate soldiers—won their confidence, and offered to hide their horses and take care of them for them, to prevent the Yankees from taking them, who, they said, were coming on. They thus succeeded in making many of our people an easy prey to their rapacity and cunning. In this foray, they abducted about 1000 negroes, captured from 500 to 700 horses and mules, a large number of oxen, carriages, buggies and wagons—stole meat, destroyed grain, and robbed gentlemen, in the public road, of gold watches and other property. There are some instances related of personal indignity and violence. They returned with their spoils to camp, after a week devoted by them in the Northern

Landed in this desolate place, it is hard to say what we all should have done without the Major; but he, who knew everybody, of course was acquainted with the principal proprietor in the neighbourhood, and through his influence we obtained a yoke of oxen which had been hidden in the woods during the raid, and a cart on which our baggage was put.

The Major's friend drove him over in his buggy, and we marched some fifteen miles to the banks of a river, where we met another friend of the Major's, who took us in, lodged, and fed us.

Neck, among our unhappy people, to the highly civilized, brave, and chivalrous exploits of theft, robbery, and almost every species of felony committed upon a defenseless, unarmed, and helpless population—chiefly consisting of women and children! It was an easy achievement—a proud conquest—the more glorious to the noble and heroic Yankee, because stained with crime and won without danger to his beastly carcass.'

"This is but a fair specimen of their conduct whenever they have been permitted to devastate the country with impunity." John Beauchamp Jones, *A Rebel War Clerk's Diary at the Confederate States Capital* (Philadelphia, 1866), I, 343–44.

Official Federal reports of the operations on the Northern Neck appear in *The War of the Rebellion: A Compilation of the Official Records of the Union and Confederate Armies* (Washington, 1880–1901), Ser. I, XXV, pt. I, 1111–16. General Alfred Pleasonton, commanding the First Cavalry Division of the Army of the Potomac, reported: "The Eighth Illinois Cavalry are coming from their raid. They destroyed 50 boats, and broke up the underground trade pretty effectually, having destroyed some $30,000 worth of goods in transit. They bring back with them 800 contrabands [slaves], innumerable mules, horses, &c., and have captured between 40 and 50 prisoners, including a captain and lieutenant. The amount of damage done the enemy is thought to be nearly $1,000,000." P. 1112.

Clearly there was military purpose in a raid which could break

Next morning early we had engaged a boat, and had a most charming sail up the river. At three o'clock we landed on the other side; and after a delicious bath, walked on to the house of another of the Major's friends, where again we were hospitably received, and slept the next night.

Fresh troubles about a conveyance for baggage—for the Yankees had been here too, robbing and destroying; but the Major was once more successful in getting a waggon, and, moreover, found here two horses which he had left behind some time back. They had fortunately escaped the Yankee raid, much to his satisfaction—and mine too, as for the rest of the road I had a mount.

It was a very pleasant ride through a beautiful country

---

up the contraband trade with Maryland and eliminate blockade running across the Potomac. But even a principal Federal officer in the expedition (Henry A. Morrow, Colonel of the Twenty-Fourth Michigan Volunteers) supported the allegations of the *Whig*. "Everywhere," he wrote, "I found a majority of the people bitterly opposed to the [Federal] Government, which they charged with sending among them cavalry to rob and plunder them. In several instances I was assured by intelligent men and women that the wholesale plunder and pillage of our cavalry had done more to weaken the affection of the people for the Government than all other causes combined, and, in fact, the cavalry have left the inhabitants very little cause to respect them as men and soldiers. They have robbed and plundered all that came in their way. These men, pretending to be the representatives of our Government, and to act under and by virtue of its orders, have stripped helpless women and children of their last horse, and in many instances of their last article of food, and have then grossly insulted them for complaining." P. 1115.

If Ross was correct in dating his arrival two days after the Yankee raiders had left, he came into the Confederacy May 28, 1863.

with magnificent trees. We got along slowly, as most of the party had to walk the whole way.

Wherever we stopped we were kindly and hospitably welcomed; you could not even ask for a glass of water at any house without their sending out a lump of ice in it, and asking you to dismount and sit in the shady porch. The country-houses are chiefly built of wood—*frame-houses* they call them—and all have a porch along the whole of one side, which in hot weather is the general resort of the inmates when at home.

On the last day of our journey, I rode into a yard where there were two little boys at play. They looked up, and one cried out, "Have you heard the news?" Then he looked a little frightened at my outlandish appearance, for Stoneman's cavalry had been near lately, during the battle of Chancellorsville.[6]

"You're not a Yankee, are you?"

I reassured him on this point, and he went on eagerly—

"Well, Ewell has taken Winchester, and whipped Milroy, and taken him prisoner with all his folk." Then the little fellow ran up with a "Won't you get down? Pap's indoors; he's got the paper and all about it."

Pap soon came out with a hearty welcome and confirmed the news. Of course he knew the Major, who came up just then, and insisted on our stopping to take some refreshment and feed our horses, which we were glad to do, as it was an overpoweringly hot day.[7]

---

[6] The reports of General George Stoneman's raid of April 29–May 7 appear in the *Official Records,* XXV, pt. 1, 1057–99.

[7] The reports of the engagement at Winchester, June 13–15, appear in the *Official Records,* XXVII, *passim.* On the day that Ross reached Richmond, diarist Jones gleefully wrote of the Con-

At ten in the evening of Thursday, June 18th, we reached Richmond, it having taken us five days to travel not more than seventy miles, owing to the devastation of the country we had passed through. Here, then, I was at length safe in the Confederate capital, and had reached it at one of the most critical periods of the war.

It will be remembered that little more than a month previously, in the beginning of May (1863), a great battle had been fought at Chancellorsville, sixty miles to the north of Richmond.

General Hooker had crossed the Rapidan not far from Fredericksburg, and a series of battles had been fought during three days, ending in the complete rout of the Federal army, with a loss of thirty thousand men. Lee's loss on this occasion had been comparatively very small, but his triumph had been dearly purchased by the death of the brave General "Stonewall" Jackson, who was accidentally killed by a shot from one of his own men.

Shattered as it was, the Federal army had nevertheless succeeded in recrossing the Rapidan and the Rappahannock, and occupied a position on the north bank of the latter river sufficiently strong to make it disadvantageous to attack, and the Confederate commander determined upon a march into the enemy's country, in order to draw

---

federate success at Winchester: "From Winchester we have many accounts in the absence of official reports (Gen. Lee being too busy in the saddle to write), which have exalted our spirits most wonderfully. . . . The whole valley is doubtless in our possession —the Baltimore and Ohio Railroad—and the way is open into Maryland and Pennsylvania. It is believed Hooker's army is utterly demoralized, and that Lee is *going on.* This time, perhaps, no Sharpsburg will embarrass his progress, and the long longed-for day of retributive invasion may come at last." Jones, 1, 352.

General Hooker away from his position. The motives which induced General Lee to take this step are stated by himself in an official despatch addressed to the Adjutant-General of the Confederate army.

He wrote as follows:—

"The position occupied by the enemy opposite Fredericksburg being one in which he could not be attacked to advantage, it was determined to draw him from it. The execution of this purpose embraced the relief of the Shenandoah Valley from the troops that had occupied the lower part of it during the winter and spring, and, if practicable, the transfer of the scene of hostilities north of the Potomac. It was thought that the corresponding movements on the part of the enemy, to which those contemplated by us would give rise, might offer a fair opportunity to strike a blow at the army therein, commanded by General Hooker, and that in any event that army would be compelled to leave Virginia, and possibly to draw to its support troops destined to operate against other parts of the country.

"In this way it was supposed that the enemy's plan of campaign for the summer would be broken up, and part of the season of active exertions be consumed in the formation of new combinations, and the preparations they would require.

"In addition to these advantages, it was hoped that other valuable results might be attained by military success."

This advance of the Confederate army had commenced on June 3, a fortnight before my arrival, and had been thus far very successful. The Shenandoah Valley had been cleared of the enemy; General Milroy had fled from Winchester, leaving the greater part of his division prisoners in the hands of the Confederates, besides a large amount of military stores and artillery; and the day before

I reached Richmond (June 17th), the vanguard of the Confederate army had entered Maryland.[8]

On the morning after my arrival I delivered my introductions, which were chiefly in the shape of photographs, letters being considered too compromising.[9] I met with the kindest and most cordial reception from each and all of them.

Major Norris, Chief the Signal Corps, Mr Joynes, Under-Secretary of War, and Mr Harrison, the Presi-

---

[8] A British impression of Richmond at about this time appeared in a weekly periodical published there, reprinting an anonymous piece from *The Cornhill Magazine* entitled "Richmond and Washington During the War": "The idleness and business of war [in Richmond] are instanced, on the one hand, by the belted and spurred braggarts who lounge about the hotels; the closed shops, the schools that keep perpetual holiday, the old men that gather in the shady side walks to gossip and bewail, and the negro women that scream delightedly at the peals of music. On the other, by the thousands of workmen that frame oddly-constructed floating batteries at the waterside, and forge great guns at the Tredegar works; the medley of transportation teams that rumble over the bridges and file along the turnpike roads; the gangs of negro men that are marched under guard to work at entrenchments and government buildings; the regiments in homespun gray and 'butternut,' that trail dustily through the high streets to swell distant camps. War looks at you from hospital churches and through the bright eyes of fever; it thrills you in the limp of cripples that beg at the wayside; it whispers sadly in the rustle of crape, and shouts its discontent in the yells of newsboys." *The Record* (Richmond), I (1863), 41–42.

[9] This seems to have been a usual practice. Vizetelly wrote of his arrangements for identifying his guide on his trip into the Confederacy: "My appearance had been accurately described to him, and his photograph had been sent to me." *All the Year Round,* XVII (1867), 175.

dent's private secretary,[10] were especially obliging, and furnished me with letters of introduction to their friends in the army. In the evening I called on Mr Benjamin, the Secretary of State, and was fortunate in finding him at home and alone. We had a long, and, I need hardly say, a most interesting conversation. We talked about the war and the foreign prospects of the Confederacy, and the atrocities which the Yankees seem to delight in committing wherever they have a chance.

"If they had behaved differently," Mr Benjamin remarked—"if they had come against us observing strict discipline, protecting women and children, respecting private property, and proclaiming as their only object the putting down of armed resistance to the Federal Government, we should have found it perhaps more difficult to prevail against them. But they could not help showing their cruelty and rapacity; they could not dissemble their true nature, which is the real cause of this war. If they had been capable of acting otherwise, they would not have been Yankees, and we should never have quarrelled with them."

Next day I went down to Drewry's Bluff with a letter from Major Norris to Captain Lee, brother of the Gen-

---

[10] William Norris, Edward S. Joynes, Burton N. Harrison. Joynes was not "Under-Secretary of War" but principal clerk in the Bureau of War of the War Department. In September, 1863, R. G. H. Kean, chief of that Bureau, wrote in his diary: "I find an imbroglio in my office between the principal clerk and Mr. Seddon [Secretary of War]. It is not yet fully developed but must result in Joynes's leaving the Department." Robert Garlick Hill Kean, *Inside the Confederate Government* . . . (New York, 1957), p. 104.

eral, who is in command there.[11] "The Major," my travelling companion, and a friend of his, accompanied me.

Captain Lee kindly showed us over the fortifications, which are very formidable, and would effectually bar the passage up the river against any number of ironclads or gunboats.

Drewry's Bluff is the same place as Fort Darling, where the Yankee gunboats were repulsed last summer. At that time only three guns were there, and those not particularly large ones; but now the place is really very strong, and much more heavily armed.

After Captain Lee had shown us the fort we sat down in front of his house, and had a long conversation whilst waiting for the steamer to return to Richmond.

I thought Captain Lee spoke rather despondently about the coming campaign. He dwelt a good deal upon the difficulties General Lee has to contend with—his want of mechanical appliances, pontoons, &c.; no organised corps

---

[11] Drewry's Bluff was a heavily fortified eminence on the west side of the James River, some six to eight miles below Richmond. At a strategic bend in the river and providing a point for firing down on attacking gunboats, it was a vital defense spot. The naval installation was under command of Captain Sydney Smith Lee, a brother of General Robert E. Lee. Drewry's Bluff was also the station of the *CSS Patrick Henry,* the schoolship which served as the Confederate Naval Academy. On the land side it was the headquarters and chief training post of the Confederate Marine Corps.

Sir Arthur James Lyon Fremantle, Lieutenant-Colonel of the Coldstream Guard, arrived in Richmond on the day after Ross. On June 19 (the day before Ross did so) Fremantle visited Drewry's Bluff. His trip there is described in his *Three Months in the Southern States,* pp. 221–23.

of engineers; the danger of exposing Richmond if he gets too far away. He gave us some interesting details of their extraordinary difficulties at the commencement of the war, which they began without any material for carrying it on except men, and without the means of supplying their most urgent necessities.

But things have greatly improved since then.

Now they manufacture their own guns, small-arms, gunpowder, clothing, and almost everything they want. The blockade-runners easily supply the rest.

He told us how little they thought at Washington that it would come to war, till the Administration treacherously, and against their repeated promises, attempted to reinforce Fort Sumter, adding, "But by God's mercy, the fleet was detained by contrary winds, and Beauregard then took the fort before they could get there."

Before we left Drewry's Bluff we went on board the Richmond, or Merrimac No. 2, as she used to be called. She is built on the same principle as the Merrimac No. 1, and is very heavily armed. A banded "Brooke" gun was especially pointed out to us as a great beauty and triumph of art.[12]

In the evening Mr Harrison took me to see the President, who was very courteous in his reception, and conversed some time with me.

I mentioned the devastations of the country I had passed through on my journey, and he observed, "It is the same everywhere, I am sorry to say; they are not behaving well to us."

---

[12] "A Captain Maury took me on board the Richmond ironclad, in which vessel I saw a 7-inch treble-banded Brook[e] gun, weighing, they told me, 21,000 lb., and capable of standing a charge of 25 lb. of powder." Fremantle, pp. 222–23.

1. Sir Arthur James Lyon Fremantle in the clothes in which he toured the Confederacy. (A list of sources for illustrations precedes the Index.)

2. "Opening Spring Campaign."

3. “Quaker Battery.” A salient in the defenses of Charleston.

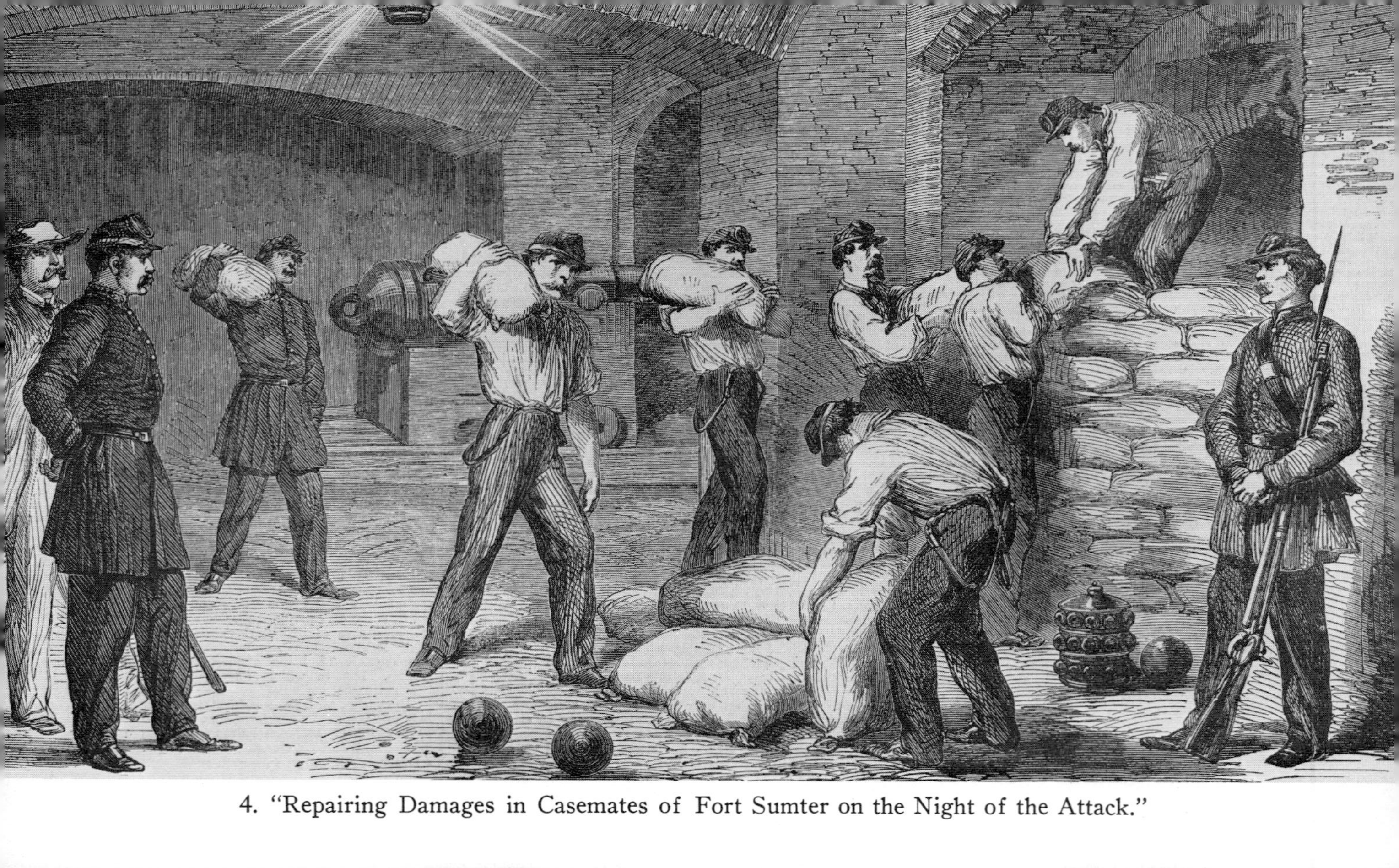

4. "Repairing Damages in Casemates of Fort Sumter on the Night of the Attack."

5. "The Interior of Fort Sumter, After a Continuous Bombardment by the Federal Batteries on Morris Island."

6. General James Longstreet.

7. General J. E. B. Stuart.

8. "General Stuart's Head-Quarters on the Rapidan."

9. "Confederates Sinking Torpedoes [Mines] by Moonlight in the Harbour Channel, Charleston."

10. "The Defences of Charleston, Looking Seaward." The view is from Fort Johnson, looking toward Fort Sumter.

11. "Fort Fisher, Commanding the New Inlet Entrance to Cape Fear River.— The British Steamer Hansa Running the Blockade Under the Guns of the Fort."

12. "Confederate Sharpshooters Firing on a Federal Supply-Train on the Tennessee River."

13. "Unloading Cotton from Blockade-Runners at Nassau, New Providence."

14. "Battle of Chicamauga — The Confederate General Hood, Wounded."

15. "Enlisting Irish and German Emigrants on the Battery at New York."

16. "Camp of Federal Prisoners on Belle Isle, Richmond."

17. Confederate soldiers at Mobile in the spring of 1865, as seen by an unknown photographer.

18. "The Federals Shelling the City of Charleston. . . ."

I had also an interview with Mr Seddon, the Secretary of War, who kindly wrote me a pass to the army, so that I was now all ready to start.[13]

Major Norris was particularly obliging in making all arrangements for my journey, which was to be by rail to Staunton, and thence by stage to Winchester, where I should learn the whereabouts of General Lee. Nobody at Richmond seemed to know anything about his movements.

Major Carrington[14] telegraphed to Staunton to secure me a place on the *stage,* and gave me a letter to the quartermaster there. He came down to the train to see me off at six o'clock in the morning, and got me a seat in the ladies' car, and told the conductor to take care of me. Everybody seems to take pleasure in doing all they possibly can to oblige a stranger. It is enough to know that you are a foreigner, and all will do their utmost to assist you.

We rattled along a very good railroad, up hill and down hill—the steepness of the grades rather astonishing me—through a beautiful country, till we reached Staunton in the afternoon.

The little town was crowded with all sorts of people "hurrying up" to the army, and I thought myself fortunate in getting a room to myself in the hotel.

I had made the acquaintance of several officers on the road, and we strolled about the little pleasant place, and passed away the time agreeably enough till supper and an early bedtime.

---

[13] Fremantle passed through much the same routine in Richmond as Ross. His interviews with Benjamin, Davis, and Seddon are recounted in his book, pp. 210–14.

[14] Charles S. Carrington.

It was lucky that my place on the stage had been taken by telegraph, or I should not have got off next morning. The coach was crowded both inside and out, and many who wanted to go on with us were left behind. It was not particularly pleasant travelling, as we sat squeezed up on top of the coach amongst sharp-edged boxes and baggage, with scarcely room to turn round; but we were only too glad to get on at all.

We reached Woodstock that night, and slept there, going supperless to bed, as the landlord's provisions had been exhausted before we arrived.

In the afternoon of the next day we reached Winchester. There was no room to be had at the hotel; but a young Baltimorean, Mr Crane, who had been a very pleasant companion during our uncomfortable journey from Staunton, immediately took me under his protection, and brought me to a very comfortable boardinghouse, where a number of officers were boarding. My next care was to try and find some further means of conveyance towards the front; and I began to feel some misgivings on this score, when I discovered that several of my travelling companions, amongst whom was a member of General Lee's staff, had already applied in vain to the quartermaster for assistance.

When I presented myself with my passport for the same purpose, Captain Thomson soon relieved my apprehensions, and, welcoming me cordially, placed a Government waggon at my entire disposal, which I might keep as long as I liked till I reached General Lee's headquarters.

The evening passed very pleasantly; also there were some very agreeable young ladies, who told us of their sufferings under Yankee rule, and hoped and prayed they might never return. The officers talked of the late battle and capture of Winchester.

It seems the Yankees were taken entirely by surprise. They had built a strong fort outside the town, towards Martinsburg, which they flattered themselves was impregnable, and which was intended to overawe Winchester, and keep the whole valley of the Shenandoah in subjection. Well, one fine morning there was some skirmishing in the valley, and the garrison of the fort, from which there is an extensive view, turned out upon the ramparts to see what was happening. Suddenly General Early opened upon them from some higher ground behind, which they had overlooked when they built their fort, and began knocking the place about their ears in a very disagreeable way. A Federal account of what passed that day describes the scene as follows:—

"Away down the valley in front heavy skirmishing was going on. Every eye was turned that way, when, on a sudden, came a boom of cannon and a rush of shell, as if hell itself had burst its bolts and bars, and was bringing fire and tempest on the world. Every eye was turned west. Twenty rebel cannon were throwing shot and shell into the regular battery. In less than five minutes the roar of cannon was exchanged for the sharp rattle of musketry, and we saw the fort stormed, taken, and the rebel flag floating over it. If an angel had descended from heaven, and told us of this five minutes before, we should not have believed it," &c. &c.

They held out in the other works till nightfall, and then, the same writer continues,—

"Every one knows what followed—the retreat in the darkness of the night, with everything left behind except men and animals; hundreds of waggons, immense commissary and

Government stores, all the private baggage, books, and papers of both officers and men; in a word, provisions enough to feed ten thousand men for two months, and clothing enough for the same number for six months."

General Ewell captured, besides this, a large number of guns, an enormous amount of ammunition, and nearly all General Milroy's "folk."

CHAPTER II

The following morning I left Winchester in a neat Pennsylvania spring-waggon, which had just been sent down from the advance of the army. As companion I had a young fellow carrying despatches to General Longstreet. The driver was a German Jew.

When we reached Martinsburg we found the hotel crowded, and there was no hope of getting any accommodation there for man or beast. I had not time to lament the circumstance, however; for a gentleman immediately stepped up, and, introducing himself as Captain Ehrhardt, Chief Quartermaster to General Ewell,[1] offered to take me to Colonel Faulkner,[2] whose residence is just outside Martinsburg.

---

[1] Here Ross is in error. Ewell's chief quartermaster was Major J. A. Harman. *Official Records,* Ser. I, XXVII, pt. 2, 452.

[2] Charles J. Faulkner.

Colonel Faulkner is Chief of the Staff to General Ewell, as he formerly was to Stonewall Jackson. Under Buchanan's administration he was ambassador at Paris.

The Colonel received me very kindly; and as I was advised not to attempt to get on to Hagerstown that night, the road being blocked up by Ewell's waggon-trains, I accepted his hospitable offer of staying till the next morning. I was duly presented to Mrs Faulkner, and spent a very pleasant afternoon.

One remark of Colonel Faulkner's struck me as not quite in accordance with the view of the treatment of slaves which Abolitionists indulge in.

He assured me that though he was a large slaveholder himself, and always lived amongst slaveholders, yet he had never in the course of his life even heard of a grown-up slave being whipped. He said, too, that a man guilty of cruelty towards his slaves would incur such odium as he would never survive.

He spoke very feelingly of Jackson, and with great admiration of his high qualities. He attributed his death, not so much to his unfortunate wounds, as to a severe attack on the lungs, brought on by exposure on the night of Friday.[3]

---

[3] Francis Lawley wrote a personal report to Secretary Seddon of a visit to Jackson's bedside between the time of the wounding of the General and his death: "You will probably have heard," he said, "of the serious anxiety entertained by Dr. Maguire [Hunter McGuire] in regard to General Jackson's health. Nothing could be more satisfactory than the General's condition up to 2 o'clock yesterday morning. He then woke, restless and with much pain in the side. Yesterday Dr. Maguire (with whom I had a long conversation) pronounced that pneumonia had attacked one lung & proceeded to cup & I believe to leech his already depleted patient. I cannot deny that the Doctor's appre-

Next morning I continued my journey, and crossed the Potomac into Maryland at Williamsport.

The road was getting very lively. Hundreds of soldiers on foot and on horseback, in large and small parties and squads, were hurrying up towards the front, each in a costume of his own, anything but uniform. Some of the horsemen had sabres, some pistols, and all of them some sort of rifle, long or short. The cavalry here is very differently organised from the same branch of the service in Europe. They are, in fact, mounted infantry. Every man's horse is his own property, and that may be one reason why they prefer fighting on foot, as if a man loses his horse, and cannot get another, he has forthwith to join the infantry. Besides, there has been no time to put them through a regular cavalry drill, and teach the efficient use of the sabre—the true arm of real cavalry—whilst with the use of the rifle they have been familiar from their earliest youth. To handle a rifle efficiently, of course, a man must dismount. On the whole, I think they have acted judiciously in taking their men as they found them, and not trying to establish the European system. Besides, the country is so wooded and broken up with high fences that opportunities for a regular cavalry-charge on a large scale seldom occur. Their horses are generally good, some exceedingly so, but not large. I understand they are very enduring, and will go through any amount of rough work.

The men's shoes are good, and so are their clothes, though they look very coarse, being made of a yellowish-

---

hensions about the General's life were of the gravest order. He is lying at a farm house close to Guinea's Station, attended by 2 Doctors & his wife who arrived yesterday." ALs, Richmond, May 8, 1863; private collection of Philip D. and Elsie O. Sang, River Forest, Illinois.

brown homespun. Very few carry a knapsack, but most of them have a haversack, and almost all a blanket. Many of the blankets are made out of old carpets with very gay colours, and all have a hole in the middle, through which the man inserts his head when the weather is cool, or when it rains, as it has been doing occasionally to-day, and the effect is marvellously picturesque, especially when you see them lying or squatting down in groups round a fire cooking their meals.

Beyond Williamsport we stopped, and turned our horse out to graze in a field by the side of the road. A number of horsemen were committing the same trespass. Amongst them was a handsome jolly fellow, singing songs to his horse, whom he had christened "Abe Lincoln." We made friends with him, and when we went on he joined us and rode by the side of our waggon, singing songs and making all sorts of funny observations. Besides the soldiers going forward to the army, the road was crowded with waggons and horses and droves of cattle and sheep, the spoils of Pennsylvania—all being sent to the rear. Some of the waggons were of the most extraordinary size, drawn by six or eight horses. Our merry companion remarked on one of them, "Why, I thought somebody told me Noah's ark had been broken up and burnt long ago, but here it is." "How many horses do you mean to get in Pennsylvania?" we asked. "Oh, I shall only taken one, sir. I intend to trade equal. I mean to take one and keep this one here that I've got." We offered him a "drink," which he refused—he was not going to drink any whisky again till the war was over. Teetotallers will rejoice to hear that none of the Confederate soldiers ever touch spirits, and they get on very well without. Wherever the army marches, the bar-rooms in the surrounding towns and villages are closed by the authorities, and no one is allowed to sell intoxicating liquors to the soldiers. Of course, a great many do drink whenever they can find an opportunity, but opportunities are very rare. I do not recollect ever to have seen a drunken private soldier in the South, though perhaps once or twice I may have seen an officer a little "tight." [4]

When we got to Hagerstown we found the shops all closed, and all the people were looking very glum. Lee left here yesterday, and it is said will be in Chambersburg to-day. The town is crowded with stragglers, amongst whom there is some little excitement, as five thousand Federal cavalry are said to have left Frederick City this morning with the intention of harassing Lee's rear.

The main army has now cast itself nearly loose from its base of supplies, carrying with it all that is absolutely necessary for the campaign, and intending to subsist chiefly on the country it passes through. There is some anxiety about an ammunition-train, I hear, which has not yet come up, and is of course of great importance.

It is surmised that the Yankees, reported on their march from Frederick, intend to attack this train; and the stragglers are, I believe, being organised in some sort of way to protect it. Altogether, there is a good deal of commotion. But of all places in the world, the rear of an army

---

[4] Here Ross's determination to show the Confederacy in the best possible light, down to the last detail, exceeds his trustworthiness as a reporter. Certainly his statement is belied by court-martial records. Fremantle, however, who was slightly more objective in seeing the Confederates, was also struck with the sobriety of the Confederate soldiers. "They are sober," he wrote, "of necessity, as there is literally no liquor to be got." Fremantle, p. 12.

is *the* place for all sorts of conjectures and rumours; and I daresay the five thousand Federal cavalry will turn out to be fifty, and marching in the opposite direction. We pushed on ourselves towards Greencastle, intending to sleep there. As soon as we got out of Maryland and into Pennsylvania the road became abominable, and we had to walk. We passed through several villages, where the inhabitants came out of their doors and stood and stared at the crowds of soldiers and waggons passing along. They were not in the least molested, of course, and seemed to have got over their first "scare" at the strange sight. All were ready to talk, and groups would gather together, especially around the wells and pumps, where the soldiers stopped to quench their thirst; and a good deal of civil conversation went on. One old fellow, however, who seemed to be half-crazy, was preaching in a very abusive style. He used Bible language, it is true, but they were words of wrath. The "rebel" soldiers only laughed, and *chaffed* him good-humouredly.

When we reached Greencastle reports were again rife of "Yankee" cavalry and "bushwhackers," and to our disgust it was determined that Ewell's waggon-train should move forward. That enormous train had *parked* on each side of the town, and we were in the middle of it, and had thus no choice but to move on too. So we tramped along. It was pitch dark, and by the side of the road innumerable fires were burning, surrounded each and all by groups of soldiers—a strange and picturesque sight. We marched several miles, for the road was too horribly bad for us to use the waggon; and at last halted again, and, finding a barn near at hand, we lay that night on the straw, and were comfortable. Next morning we went to a farmhouse close by, and persuaded the farmer's wife to give us some milk. The population of this part of the country is called Dutch, though neither they nor their ancestors ever had anything to do with Holland.

I find that when people mean to speak of a native of Holland, they call him an Amsterdam Dutchman; but when they speak of one of German race generally, they leave out the *Amster*. As most of the Germans of any education who come here were *Freiheits helden* at home, and left their country for their country's good, it is not surprising that they are considered a nuisance. There are quite enough demagogues already in this part of the world without any importations from "Fatherland."

The so-called Dutch, however, in this neighbourhood, are a simple race; they build enormous barns, in which their whole soul is wrapped up. I talked with the farmer's wife and her two daughters, and attempted to elicit from them what part of Germany they or their ancestors had emigrated from to this country. *"Mir seyn Pennsylvanisch Deutsch,"* was all the answer I could get. They knew nothing about their forefathers, and had evidently never heard of the "old country." Her grandfather had come here from Pennsylvania higher up. *"Mir seyn Pennsylvanisch Deutsch,"* she repeated, with utter disregard of German grammar; and she evidently thought me crazy for asking any further questions. Her accent in speaking German was decidedly Swabian, and both she and her daughters spoke very broken English.

We reached Chambersburg about mid-day, and here I was at last at the headquarters of the army. I drove out immediately to General Lee's camp, about a quarter of a mile from the town. The General was holding council with Longstreet, A. P. Hill, and others, but I was received in a most friendly way by his Staff, to several of whom I brought letters from Richmond. After staying some time, Captain Scheibert [5] of the Prussian army accompanied me back to the town, to assist me in getting quarters at the hotel there, where I should find L.,[6] whom I was particularly anxious to meet. After some trouble, and with the assistance of Colonel Allen,[7] who was acting as commandant of the place, we got inside the house, and here I found L. ill in bed.

Through his and Colonel Allen's intercession, and on my promising to pay liberally, and in greenbacks, the landlord was at last induced to receive me into his house, and gave me a very comfortable room.[8] I confess I was a little surprised to see how entirely this matter depended upon the goodwill and favour of the landlord. We manage these things differently in some parts of Europe, in war-times in an enemy's country. During the day numbers of troops passed through the town, amongst them the whole

[5] Justus Scheibert. In reporting this same visit to Lee's headquarters Scheibert quotes the General as declaring, "I strive to make my plans as good as human skill allows, but on the day of battle I lay the fate of my army in the hands of God; it is my generals' turn to perform their duty." Scheibert, *Der Bürgerkrieg in den Nordamerikanischen Staaten* (Berlin, 1874), p. 181.

[6] Francis Lawley. Lawley was a correspondent for the London *Times*. He had hitherto traveled, during this campaign, with Fremantle. He had been ill, and accommodations at the Franklin Hotel in Chambersburg had been found for him. This was June 28. Fremantle, p. 248.

[7] Robert C. Allen.

[8] ". . . our host became more and more surly when we [Lawley and Fremantle] stated our intention of remaining with him. However, the sight of *real gold* instead of Confederate paper, or even greenbacks, soothed him wonderfully, and he furnished us with some breakfast." Fremantle, p. 240.

of M'Laws's division. They seemed in high spirits, and, as they passed through the crowd of lookers-on, would treat them to a little chaff and badinage. The chief joke was about having "got back into the Union at last, you see." The Chambersburg public looked on with stolid equanimity. As long as their persons and property are left alone, they do not seem inclined to take much interest in either side. There are a large number of young fellows "loafing" about the town, who ought to be in the army, or in the "State militia" at least; which last-named body of defenders of the soil has been called out by the State Government, but does not seem likely to come. Our landlord professes entire neutrality, and asserts that, as the Administration at Washington has done nothing to defend their State, he can see no obligation for them to turn out for the defence of the Government. His son has stronger Union sentiments than the old man, and thinks that Hooker is quite sure to whip Lee, but is content to see it done without his personal assistance. A thick-headed young fellow, a staunch Unionist, with whom I conversed in the parlour, assures me that the South will be benefited by a reverse. "It is just like a bad boy, sir; a good sound whipping does him a world of good!" But he does not seem at all inclined to assist in performing the operation himself. There is a fine wooden statue of Franklin, boldly perched on the top of the county court-house, and painted to resemble marble. I am sorry to say that this great man excited the derision of the passing soldiers, who saluted him with that "terrible scream and barbarous howling," a real Southern yell, which rang along the whole line. I heard it that day for the first time. It was a very peculiar sound. By practice many have arrived at a high perfection, and can yell loud enough to be heard a mile off. They learnt it from the Indians, I believe.[9] Many of the regiments had little bands of three or four musicians, who played rather discordantly.[10] The Southerners are said to be extremely fond of music, though they seldom take the trouble to learn to play themselves, and seem not very particular as to whether the instruments they hear are in tune or not. The bandsmen are almost all Germans. I spent a pleasant evening at Colonel Allen's quarters, where there were a good many officers. Whilst I was there a sergeant reported that he had just come in from the country with a lot of horses, and we went out to look at them. There were about twenty big heavy animals, better adapted for draught than for the saddle. The parties sent out for supplies, horses, waggons, &c., give Confederate notes or receipts for everything they take, and the owners are thus sure of being paid eventually; as, if the Confederates do not pay them, they can, with a receipt in hand, easily prove their claim against their own Government for war damages, as indeed has since been done. Still they do not like the transaction, and hide their horses

[9] "The Southern troops, when charging, or to express their delight, always yell in a manner peculiar to themselves. The Yankee cheer is much like ours; but the Confederate officers declare that the rebel yell has a particular merit, and always produces a salutary and useful effect upon their adversaries. A corps is sometimes spoken of as a 'good yelling regiment.'" Fremantle, p. 265.

[10] In reporting the second day's fighting at Gettysburg, Fremantle remarked: "When the cannonade was at its height, a Confederate band of music, between the cemetery and ourselves, began to play polkas and waltzes, which sounded very curious, accompanied by the hissing and bursting of the shells." Fremantle, p. 266.

in the woods whenever they can, so that the scouting-parties have to exercise a good deal of ingenuity in finding them.* Next day L. was much better, and we breakfasted at the hotel. As none of the Confederate host were permitted to enter its sacred precincts, the guests at table were pretty free and outspoken in their opinion of passing events. One lady was especially indignant at the way in which the soldiers marching along had not kept to the

*A little account of this campaign by a Mr Jacobs, professor of mathematics at Gettysburg College, says of Ewell's "rebel" corps, which passed through Gettysburg going to Carlisle: "They did not do much damage in the town. In the country, however, they treated the farmers less gently. They there enacted their old farce of professing to pay for what they took by offering freely their worthless 'Confederate' scrip, which, they said, would in a few days be better than our own currency." I need hardly say here that the Yankees never enact the farce of professing to pay in greenbacks for what they take from the "rebels" when their opportunity comes.[11]

[11] Ross's reference is to Michael Jacob's *Notes on the Rebel Invasion of Maryland and Pennsylvania and the Battle of Gettysburg, July 1, 2 and 3, 1863* . . . (Philadelphia, 1864).

The Index (London) reported the Confederate occupation of Chambersburg in its issue for July 9 (III (1863), 161): "The Northerners are astonished at the orderly conduct of the Confederate troops. Referring to the occupation of Chambersburg, we are told, 'The rebels behaved themselves unusually well for soldiers.** The people are well satisfied that the raid brought with it only so few disadvantages. They did not expect the considerate treatment that they have received at the hands of the enemy; on the contrary, they were prepared to witness scenes of the wildest disorder. The town does not present an injured appearance. The streets are very dirty; but the general appearance of the whole place is about the same as it was before the raid.' "

road (a thing which it was almost impossible to do, as it was crowded with waggons, besides the mud being almost knee-deep). The bloodthirsty ruffians, she said, had actually marched through the fields by the side of the road, treading down the growing crops for about twenty yards on each side. The people here are, it seems, beginning to feel the horrors of war!

L. rather exasperated the company by showing them a twenty-dollar Confederate note, and saying that in a month it would be worth more than all their greenbacks in the North put together.

I went out to the camp again, and was presented to General Lee, who invited me to dinner. It was a frugal meal, and simply served. The General had little of the glorious pomp and circumstance of war about his person. A Confederate flag marks the whereabouts of his headquarters, which are here in a little enclosure of some couple of acres of timber. There are about half-a-dozen tents, and as many baggage-waggons and ambulances. The horses and mules from these, besides those of a small escort, are tied up to the trees, or grazing about the place. The General has a private carriage, or ambulance, as it is called, of his own, but he never uses it. It formerly belonged to the Federal General Pope. I remained some time at headquarters, and had a good deal of conversation with the officers of General Lee's Staff. Major Marshall mentioned to me, as one of the greatest misfortunes which has happened to them during the war (greater, he thought, than the fall of New Orleans), the accidental loss last year, through carelessness by a general of division, of a very important order of General Lee's. McClellan, who had been slowly and carefully feeling his way, totally ignorant of General Lee's plans, and the whereabouts of his main force, is said to have exclaimed, on finding this order, "Well, if I don't destroy Lee this time, you may call me what you like;" and he immediately pushed on as fast as he could march, and caught the Confederates before they were ready. The drawn battle of Sharpsburg, or Antietam Creek, followed; and Lee, not destroyed, but thwarted in the main object of his campaign, soon afterwards recrossed the Potomac. In the mean time, however, Jackson had captured Harper's Ferry, with its garrison of 12,000 men, and immense stores, so that Lee still reaped some advantage from his ably-conceived plan of campaign. McClellan alludes to this matter, in his evidence before Congress on the conduct of the war, in the following terms:—

"When at Frederick we found the original order issued to General D. H. Hill by direction of General Lee, which gave the orders of march for the whole army, and developed their intentions. The substance of the order was, that Jackson was to move from Frederick by the main Hagerstown road, and, leaving it at some point near Middleburg, to cross the Potomac near Sharpsburg, and endeavour to capture the garrison of Martinsburg, and cut off the retreat of the garrison of Harper's Ferry in that direction. General M'Laws was ordered, with his own command and the division of General Anderson, to move out by the same Hagerstown road, and gain possession of the Maryland heights, opposite Harper's Ferry. General Walker, who was then apparently somewhere near the mouth of the Monocacy, was to move through Lovettsville, and gain possession of Loudon's height, thus completing the investment of Harper's Ferry. General Longstreet was ordered to move to Hagerstown with Hill, to serve as a rearguard. Their reserve trains to Manassas, &c., were ordered to take a position either at Boonsboro' or Hagerstown, I have now forgotten which. It was directed in the same order, that after Jackson, Walker, M'Laws, &c., had taken Harper's Ferry, they were to rejoin the main army at Hagerstown or Boonsboro'. That order is important in another sense. It shows very plainly that the object of the enemy was to go to Pennsylvania, or at least to remain in Maryland. Upon learning the contents of this order I at once gave orders for a vigorous pursuit," &c.

Singularly enough, the same General lost an equally important order before the seven days' fighting around Richmond, and it was found on a prisoner who was captured at Gaines's Mill. Unaware, perhaps, of its importance, he had not sent it on to headquarters, or it would have done incalculable mischief.[12]

Next day we moved on a few miles on the road to Gettysburg, and encamped near a deserted saw-mill. General Longstreet's headquarters were, as usual, very near to General Lee's, so I walked over, and was introduced to the General and his Staff, to several members of which I had brought letters from Richmond. I dined there and spent the afternoon very pleasantly. Besides L., who is staying with Longstreet's medical staff, there was Colonel F. of the Coldstream Guards, who came to the Confederacy by Matamoros, in order not to run the blockade,

---

[12] Historians have generally charged General Hill with the responsibility for the famous "lost order" of the Maryland campaign. Hill defended himself against the charge in the columns of *The Land We Love* (Raleigh), IV (1868), 274 and the *Southern Historical Society Papers* (Richmond), XIII (1885), 420–21. There is no substantiation for Ross's story of a similar incident at the Battle of the Seven Days.

and had a most adventurous journey through the whole of the Southern States.[13]

---

[13] Actually Ross had met Fremantle on the evening of June 28 when the latter called at the Franklin Hotel to see Lawley. "In the evening," wrote Fremantle, "I called again to see Lawley, and found in his room an Austrian officer, in the full uniform of the Hungarian hussars. He had got a year's leave of absence, and had just succeeded in crossing the Potomac, though not without much trouble and difficulty. When he stated his intention of wearing his uniform, I explained to him the invariable custom of the Confederate soldiers, of never allowing the smallest peculiarity of dress or appearance to pass without a torrent of jokes, which, however good-humoured, ended in becoming rather monotonous." Fremantle, p. 249.

CHAPTER III

Early on the following morning, the 1st of July, the troops began to advance. The trains were enormously large in this army, as, being now separated from their base of supplies, they had to carry everything they wanted with them. Amongst other things, they carried their tents wherever they went, and the troops were never quartered in any village, nor allowed to enter houses on any account. Although this was the case with the Confederate army, I believe the Yankees are not so particular, at least when they are encamping in an enemy's country.

First came A. P. Hill's corps and waggon-train. After Hill's, Longstreet's corps, and in his train L. and myself occupied an ambulance. We got on but slowly, for we were crossing the South Mountains, and the roads were steep and crowded with waggons. Presently we heard cannonading, and news came from the front that Hill's corps was hotly engaged. Just as it was getting dusk we reached the crest of the mountains, whence we had a magnificent prospect of the country beyond us; but of the battle we could see nothing, as the town of Gettysburg, around which it had been raging, was still hidden from our sight. A mile or two farther on we reached our destination for that night. Of course we were excited and anxious to hear how things had been going; but it soon became pitch dark, and we could not move about, but had to wait patiently till some one should come in from the front. We lighted fires, tents were pitched, and presently the doctors Cullen, Maury, and Barksdale, of whose camp and mess I was henceforward to be a member, rode in and brought us the glorious news.[1] Ewell and Hill, after a stubborn fight, had routed the force opposed to them, driven them through Gettysburg, and taken from five to seven thousand prisoners. The Federal General Reynolds had been killed. Presently General Longstreet and his Staff came in and confirmed the news. The Yankees would probably make a stand to-morrow on the hills south and east of the town, as their position was strong, and a general action was pretty sure to take place. I had not been able to procure a horse for myself as yet, although I had luckily brought a saddle and bridle from Richmond; however, Major Walton,[2] of General Longstreet's Staff, very obligingly supplied me with one.

---

[1] J. S. Dorsey Cullen, Thomas F. Maury, and Randolph Barksdale. Fremantle had noted on June 27: "Lawley is to live with three doctors on the Headquarters Staff: their names are Cullen, Barksdale, and Maury; they form a jolly trio, and live much more luxuriously than their generals." Fremantle, p. 246.

[2] Thomas Walton.

Major Clarke[3] lent another to Colonel F., and L. had brought one from Richmond, so this important affair for us three strangers in camp was satisfactorily arranged. It was still dusk next morning when the sound of cannon aroused me from my sleep. "C'est le sanglant appel de Mars!" I sang out to my tent-mates. I went over to Longstreet's quarters, a few hundred yards off, "fixed" my saddle and bridle on the horse I was to ride, and then breakfasted with General Longstreet and his Staff.[4] We had to ride some five miles before we got to the front, where we halted at the top of a hill, from which there was a full view of the enemy's position. General Lee was there with his Staff, and we let our horses loose in an enclosed field close by, and lay about for some time looking through our glasses at the Yankees, who were near enough for us to distinguish every individual figure, gun, &c., and who were apparently engaged in the same occupation as ourselves.[5]

---

[3] John J. Clarke.

[4] In his entry for July 2, Fremantle recorded: "We all got up at 3.30 A.M., and breakfasted a little before daylight. Lawley insisted on riding, not withstanding his illness. Captain [Ross] and I were in a dilemma for horses; but I was accommodated by Major Clark[e] (of this [Longstreet's] Staff), whilst the stout Austrian was mounted by Major Walton. The Austrian, in spite of the early hour, had shaved his cheeks and *ciréd* his mustaches as beautifully as if he was on parade in Vienna." Fremantle, p. 262.

[5] "Colonel Sorrell [G. Moxley Sorrel], the Austrian, and I arrived at 5 A.M. at the same commanding position we were on yesterday, and I climbed up a tree in company with Captain Schreibert [Scheibert] of the Prussian army. Just below us were seated Generals Lee, Hill, Longstreet, and Hood, in consultation —the two latter assisting their deliberations by the truly American custom of *whittling* sticks. General Heth was also present." Fremantle, pp. 262–63.

As evidently a long time would elapse before Longstreet's corps, which was to do the chief fighting that day, could be placed in position, I determined meanwhile to ride into the town of Gettysburg with the doctors. We crossed the ground which had been fought over yesterday. The Confederate wounded had been removed and their dead buried, but there were still a large number of dead Yankees lying about and some of their wounded, especially in the cutting of a railroad where some of the fiercest fighting had taken place. I saw one man who had been entirely cut in two, his head and shoulders lying a couple of yards from the rest of his body—a horrible sight. The wounded men, too, who had lain there all night were ghastly to look at; and indeed a battle-field the day after the fight is anything but a pleasant place to come near.

Gettysburg is an insignificant little town, but contains some large buildings—county court-house, colleges, &c. —in and about the town. These have been turned into hospitals. At the end of one or two of the streets some sharpshooting was going on at the Federal position on the Cemetery Hill behind the town, and the Yankees were returning the fire, but without doing any mischief, as far as I could see. Still we did not take the trouble to go beyond the town in that direction.

We met General Chilton, Lee's Inspector-General, in the town.[6] He was riding about seeking whom he could devour in the shape of a depredator or illegal annexer of private property; but I do not think he found any. Indeed, the good behaviour and discipline of the men of this army is surprising to me, considering the way in

---

[6] R. H. Chilton.

which the Northerners have devastated the country and wreaked their wrath on women and children in the South wherever they had an opportunity.

They are as cheerful and good-natured a set of fellows as ever I saw—seem to be full of fun, and are always ready to talk and joke, and "chaff," but are never pushing or insolent.

We also met General Early, a gruff-looking man, but with a high reputation as a soldier.

On returning to the hill where we had left the generals in command, we found them still there. They had been joined by Generals A. P. Hill and Heth, the latter of whom was wounded in the head yesterday, and several others.

General Hill sent for water, and they brought him some dirty stuff in a pail, with an apology that no good water was to be had within a mile, and an inquiry whether he would wait. "Oh no, that will do very well," said the General, and I began to realise that we were actually campaigning.

Wherever an army is stationary for a few days, the wells and pumps are soon drunk dry; and in fact, before we left this neigbourhood, most of the wells had a guard on them, who only permitted water to be fetched for the wounded. For men in health, water brought from the nearest brook or creek is good enough, and sometimes details of men have to be sent a considerable distance for it.

On riding to the rear of our present position on the Fairfield road, we met with Colonel Walton,[7] chief of artillery to General Longstreet, and his adjutant, Captain

---

[7] J. B. Walton.

Owens,[8] and for some time we lay in a meadow under a hedge awaiting events.

Colonel Walton is a New Orleans man, who in the beginning of the war was in command of "The Washington Artillery," a picked corps raised in that city, which boasts that every member of it is a gentleman of property and position. Of course their commander was a man of mark in his native city, where he was, I believe, a wealthy merchant.

Like many others, Colonel Walton, though not a young man, had cheerfully sacrificed all his worldly advantages to his principles, preferring the hardships of camp life and "the cause," to luxury and ease at home under Yankee tyranny. But such instances are the rule and not the exception in the South. There are thousands of men now carrying a musket in the ranks, who before the war were gentlemen of wealth and property, which they are now deprived of—"it may be for years, or it may be for ever," [9] as one of them said to me; but not one seems to regret it, or would for an instant dream of submission to the North in order to regain what he has lost.

Almost all the young men from Louisiana, Arkansas, Tennessee, the overrun portions of the Carolinas, Virginia, and Florida, many too from Missouri, Kentucky, and Maryland, are in this position; but they seem to be none the worse soldiers for having been brought up in luxury and comparative idleness.

At about three o'clock in the afternoon we rejoined General Longstreet, who, after a long consultation with the Commander-in-Chief, was at this moment riding

---

[8] William M. Owens.

[9] A quotation from the popular song "Lorena."

down with his Staff towards the front. We found his corps already forming for the attack in a wood.

Longstreet rode up the line and down again, occasionally dismounting, and going forward to get a better view of the enemy's position.

The ground just before us was plain and open, but beyond were those hills, since so celebrated, covered with Federal breastworks and rifle-pits, and bristling with cannon. The Federals had also possession of the open ground below in front of their works, and their foremost guns were about a quarter of a mile from the wood we were in.

I especially remarked a battery in a peach orchard, which was blazing away at one of ours not far off.

As we passed Barksdale's Mississippi Brigade the General came up eagerly to Longstreet; "I wish you would let me go in, General; I would take that battery in five minutes." "Wait a little," said Longstreet, "we are all going in presently."

The men were as eager as their leader, and those in the front line began to pull down the fence behind which they were crouching.

"Don't do that, or you will draw the enemy's fire," said Longstreet, who sees and observes everything.

We passed on, and very soon afterwards the General called for his horse, mounted, dashed to the front of the line, gave the word, and led them on himself. We all followed him.[10]

It was a glorious sight. The men who had been lying

---

[10] "Every one deplores that Longstreet *will* expose himself in such a reckless manner. To-day he led a Georgian regiment in a charge against a battery, hat in hand, and in front of everybody." Fremantle, p. 267.

down sprang to their feet, and went in with a will. There was no lagging behind, no spraining of ankles on the uneven ground, no stopping to help a wounded comrade. Not one fell out of the line unless he was really hurt. On swept the line, breaking out with an occasional yell when they came face to face with the foe, but on the whole silently. The guns in the peach orchard were pounced upon, and half of them taken in a trice, whilst the others limbered up and made off. Hundreds of prisoners were captured, and everything was going so satisfactorily that for a time we hardly doubted that the enemy would be driven from his very strong position on the hills in front.

But at a critical moment General Hood was severely wounded, General Barksdale killed, and their men, at the very moment of apparent victory, when they had overcome almost all the difficulties that lay between them and entire success, hesitated, halted, and at length fell back, losing thereby far more men than they would have done if they had continued their advance.

But still we gained decided advantages, taking prisoners and guns, and getting possession of the ground up to the foot of the hill.

General Lee, in his report to the Government, describes this day's fight as follows:—

"The preparations for attack were not completed until the afternoon of the 2d of July. The enemy held a high and commanding ridge, along which he had massed a large amount of artillery. General Ewell occupied the left of our line, General Hill the centre, and General Longstreet the right. In front of General Longstreet the enemy held a position, from which, if he could be driven, it was thought that our army could be used to advantage in assailing the more elevated ground beyond, and thus enable us to reach the crest of the ridge. That officer was directed to endeavour to carry this position, while General Ewell attacked directly the high ground on the enemy's right, which had already been partially fortified. General Hill was instructed to threaten the centre of the Federal line, in order to prevent reinforcements being sent to either wing, and to avail himself of any opportunity that might present itself to attack.

"After a severe struggle, Longstreet succeeded in getting possession of and holding the desired ground. Ewell also carried some of the strong positions which he assailed, and the result was such as to lead to the belief that he would ultimately be able to dislodge the enemy." [11]

---

[11] Ross excerpted this passage from General Lee's report of July 31, 1863, to Confederate Adjutant and Inspector General Samuel Cooper. The report appears in its entirety in the *Official Records,* XXVII, pt. 2, 305–11.

CHAPTER IV

The battle ceased at dark. As we rode back from the field, General Longstreet spoke with me about the failure to take the position on the hill, saying, "We have not been so successful as we wished;" and attributed it chiefly to the causes before mentioned—Hood's wound and Barksdale's death.[1] Perhaps if the attack had been made a little earlier in the day it might have been more successful; for Sedgwick with the 6th Federal corps reached Meade just in time to assist in repelling the assault, and without this reinforcement the Northerners would probably have been defeated. The men might have been put in position a good deal

---

[1] "General Barksdale was killed and Semmes mortally wounded; but the most serious loss was General Hood, who was badly wounded in the arm early in the day. I heard that his Texans are in despair." Fremantle, p. 267.

sooner; and in fact one of the commanders of division, Major-General M'Laws, was blamed by some people for having been too slow.

We did not return to the camp, but lay down in a meadow near the battle-field, tying up our horses to a fence, and using our saddles as pillows. Some of the officers had blankets, but, as I had none, Major Latrobe [2] shared his with me, and we slept soundly after the fatigues of the day.

At early dawn on Friday, again the sound of cannon awoke us, and told of the bloody fight that was to be renewed that day. The morning was spent in riding over the battle-field of yesterday, the Generals holding a long consultation, and reconnoitring the position to be attacked to-day. I was standing in the road with Dr Cullen and some officers, when Pickett's division of three brigades, which had been left at Chambersburg, and was to take a prominent part in the fight, passed us. They halted and rested for about half an hour, and I conversed with several of the officers; among others with Colonel Allen and Major Wilson,[3] whom I had met at Chambersburg. They were both killed a few hours later; and indeed but few of those I met that morning came unhurt out of the terrible charge made by Pickett's division that afternoon.

One hundred and forty-five guns, I was subsequently informed by Colonel Walton, were on this day placed in position, to open fire simultaneously on the enemy, preparatory to the assault which was to be made on their works. Whilst the preliminary arrangements were being completed, General Longstreet rode with his Staff to the

---

[2] Osman Latrobe.

[3] Not identified.

rear of the guns, where his men were lying down in line in the woods. Here it would have been impossible to have a view of the battle; and we were recommended to ride into Gettysburg, and take our station on the top of a certain church-tower, whence we should have a very good view. Accordingly Colonel F. and I started in that direction. We had just reached the top of a hill from whence we could overlook both positions, when in one instant, at a given signal, the whole hundred and forty-five Confederate guns burst into a roar of cannonading. They were quickly answered by the enemy, and the effect was grander than words can express. We could see but few of the guns on either side, as both they and the men were hidden from our view by the woods; but the smoke rising above the trees presently formed a dense cloud above them, and showed us where the work was going on. We left the hill and rode on towards Gettysburg; but as we approached the town we found that we could not reach it without passing through a sharp fire from both sides, as Ewell on our side and the Yankees on the Cemetery Hill were pounding away at each other across the road. A shell or two bursting not far from us, warned us to proceed no further. Colonel F. rode back to rejoin Longstreet, and I, who was feeling quite faint with hunger, fortunately fell in with General Heth, who gave me and my horse a feed, after which I returned to the hill where we had witnessed the grand spectacle of the commencement of the battle, and where I now found a good many officers assembled watching the fight.[4]

[4] "The Austrian officer and I now rode off to get, if possible, into some commanding position from whence we could see the whole thing without being exposed to the tremendous fire which was about to commence. After riding for half an hour without

The assault by Pickett's division had just been repulsed. They had gone in splendidly, led in gallant style by their daring chief, had stormed the breastworks, and taken the enemy's cannon. Heth's division, commanded by the senior Brigadier Pettigrew, was to have supported them, and they went in for that purpose, steadily at first, but soon got shaken by the storm of shot and shell that met them. Presently a small column of the enemy, emerging from a wood, began to form on their flank; the men saw it, wavered, stopped, and then fell back in a panic, getting terribly punished as they did so. In vain were all efforts to stop them. Longstreet, who had seen the threatening move, sent off Latrobe to warn General Pettigrew, but the rout had commenced before he could meet him. Pickett, whose men were now well in, and in the full flush of the victory they deserved and would have gained if they had been supported, galloped down and implored the men to rally. Many other officers did the same, but it

---

being able to discover so desirable a situation, we determined to make for the cupola, near Gettysburg, Ewell's headquarters. Just before we reached the entrance to the town, the cannonade opened with a fury which surpassed even that of yesterday.

"Soon after passing through the toll-gate at the entrance of Gettysburg, we found that we had got into a heavy cross-fire; shells both Federal and Confederate passing over our heads with great frequency. At length two shrapnel shells burst quite close to us, and a ball from one of them hit the officer who was conducting us. We then turned round and changed our views with regard to the cupola—the fire of one side being bad enough, but preferable to that of both sides. . . . We then returned to the hill I was on yesterday. But finding that, to see the actual fighting, it was absolutely necessary to go into the thick of the thing, I determined to make my way to General Longstreet." Fremantle, pp. 270–71.

was all in vain; it was a panic such as will strike the bravest troops sometimes, and no efforts could induce them to form anew whilst under that terrific storm of fire. The division lost frightfully, but the worst effect was that Pickett's men, who had behaved gloriously, were now left to fight alone against overwhelming odds. Encouraged by their success, the enemy, freshly reinforced, now turned upon them with redoubled energy and courage, and soon their fate was sealed. Some surrendered at once, the rest retreated; nearly half the men of the division were killed, wounded or captured. But they had won undying fame by their glorious onslaught, and as long as the war is remembered, so long will the charge of Pickett and his Virginians be spoken of by their countrymen with the same proud and yet regretful satisfaction with which Englishmen tell of the charge of the Six Hundred at Balaklava.

Another assault was made, I think, under Trimble, but it was unsuccessful; nor, indeed, had it much chance of success, and would, perhaps, not have been made but for the confusion inseparable from the state of affairs in the battle-field. The grand assault had already miscarried, and Colonel G.,[5] an Englishman, who was wounded in the charge, told me afterwards that before they made it he had seen and spoken to Pickett, and said that as he had been repulsed, he did not think that they were going to succeed. However, they went in very gallantly, but had to retire, losing a good many men.

The enemy made no attempt to follow up their advantage, and it was well for them they did not. I see that a General Butterfield, in evidence given before some Fed-

[5] George Gordon.

eral committee, blames General Meade for not attacking Lee's right after the repulse, imagining that enormous captures of guns and other great successes would have been the result. It was, however, well for the Federals that General Meade did not do so, for he would have found M'Laws's and Hood's divisions there perfectly ready and willing to give him a much hotter reception than he would have liked. But in fact the Yankees were a great deal too much cut up themselves to think of anything more than holding their own. They had been huddled up in masses in their contracted position (which was not half so extended as that of the Confederates) in order to repel the expected assault, and the artillery had done tremendous execution among them. Then, though partially protected by breastworks, they had lost very heavily by musketry fire during the assaults, for the Southerners possess a great superiority in this weapon. Almost every individual Southerner has been accustomed to use the rifle from his earliest youth, and has thus acquired a skill in handling the weapon which no amount of drilling can supply, and which the Irish, Dutch, and city Yankees, who form the mass of the Federal army, can never hope to attain. Altogether, I am perfectly convinced that in the three days' fighting the Federal loss was far heavier than the Confederate in killed and wounded; and it is only the fact of about 6000 Confederate wounded having been left behind in the hospitals around Gettysburg that gave the Northerners even a nominal preponderance in the number of prisoners taken. Longstreet's corps, which was the most heavily engaged, lost 6920 men. Pickett's loss was 3500, M'Laws's 1660, and Hood's 1760. I do not know the numbers lost in A. P. Hill's nor in Ewell's corps.

We returned to the camp after the battle, and spent the

evening rather gloomily. In the night it began to rain heavily; and whilst we were asleep a thief came into our encampment and stole two trunks out of the tents in which we were lying—one from Major Moses,[6] which had 5000 dollars of public money in it, and one from Dr Barksdale containing personal effects. Both were, naturally, much provoked; and Dr Barksdale's disgust seemed only increased when his trunk was found in the course of the morning in a neighbouring field, open, robbed of its most valuable contents, and the rest saturated with rain. Major Moses' trunk was also found in the same state.[7]

Colonel F. and I had returned our horses to their owners, but L. still had his (a very seedy animal); and the officers of the Staff and the medical department being occupied with their respective duties, we sallied forth together after breakfast, two on foot and one riding alternately, and in this way we wandered about the lines.

We met General Longstreet, who had been much amused by hearing, through a flag of truce, that he was severely wounded and in the enemy's hands, but would be well taken care of.[8] We also met the Rev. General

[6] R. J. Moses.

[7] "I was awoke at daylight [July 4] by Moses complaining that his valuable trunk, containing much public money, had been stolen from our tent whilst we slept. After a search it was found in a wood hard by, broken open and minus the money. Dr. Barksdale had been robbed in the same manner exactly. This is evidently the work of those rascally stragglers, who shirk going under fire, plunder the natives, and will hereafter swagger as the heroes of Gettysburg." Fremantle, pp. 278–79.

[8] "Lawley, the Austrian, and I, walked up to the front about eight o'clock, and on our way we met General Longstreet, who was in a high state of amusement and good-humour. A flag of truce had just come over from the enemy, and its bearer an-

Pendleton, Chief of Artillery to the army, and remained some time in conversation with him.

---

nounced among other things that 'General Longstreet was wounded, and a prisoner, but would be taken care of.' General Longstreet sent back word that he was extremely grateful, but that, being neither wounded nor a prisoner, he was quite able to take care of himself." Fremantle, p. 279.

CHAPTER V

L. presently rode off to see General Lee, and when he returned, told us that a retreat had been decided on. We were kept a long time at the cottage of a silly old Dutchman, by a heavy downfall of rain, and then went to Bream's tavern on the road to Fairfield, which lay in the direction of our retreat. The road was crowded with waggons, as the whole train had but two roads to move on—the Fairfield and the Cashtown one. When Lee's army entered Maryland, the waggon-train alone, without the artillery, was forty-two miles long, and it was now larger than ever, though most of the waggons and teams procured in Pennsylvania had been already sent to the rear.

Bream's tavern, house, stables, barn, and every out-building, were full of wounded men, some of whom were being moved into the ambulances, and others more badly wounded were being removed to the better accommodation left thereby vacant.

It was a grievous sight to see these fine young fellows, many of them probably crippled for life, and yet all were cheerful and smiling. Looks of deep sympathy greeted them on every side as they were borne past on stretchers. And sometimes the wounded men would address a few encouraging words to some friend who stood near, himself too sad to speak.

Many were to be left behind, too severely wounded to bear removal; and it struck me very much that it should be they who would speak words of comfort to their more fortunate friends who had escaped the dangers of the battle.

Not one complained. All bore themselves in the same proud manly way.

For a time the yard in front of Bream's tavern seemed a regular rendezvous for generals and their staff-officers, and all who passed stopped on their way and entered into conversation.

Here I met General J. E. B. Stuart for the first time, and was introduced to him, and to many others too numerous to name.

When it was dusk we went on a mile or two farther on the Fairfield road, and presently came upon a blazing fire, around which were Generals Lee and Longstreet, with all their Staff.

We were to remain here till the train had passed, when the main body of the army would be withdrawn from its position and join the retreat.

It soon grew pitch dark, and then the rain began again. Oh, how it did pour! I never saw anything like it. Now and then it would relax a little, and then again and again would rush down in torrents. "This is too heavy to last," I thought to myself many a time, but it did last.

Fortunately for me I was tolerably weatherproof, as Colonel F. had very kindly lent me his india-rubber overcoat,[1] he and L. having gone off in an *ambulance,* as a covered four-seated "buggy," specially belonging to the headquarters of the medical department, was called.

It was certainly a dismal night. The fire was kept up and protected from the rain by continually piling on fresh wood, and it was a roaring one, yet I wondered that it was not extinguished. It lighted up the scene with a strange glare.

Lee and Longstreet stood apart engaged in earnest conversation, and around the fire in various groups lay the officers of their Staffs. Tired to death, many were sleeping in spite of the mud and drenching rain; and I well remember one long log of wood, a fence rail, which was much coveted as a pillow. Once Major Moses, unable to sleep, got up and politely offered me his share of it.

I accepted and lay down, but the edges were very sharp, and each time I fell off into a doze, I began to dream so vividly that my head was being cut off, that at last I could stand it no longer, and returned the Major his part of the bolster with thanks. Again and again during the night reports came in from Law, M'Laws, Ewell, &c., stating that the enemy had retreated, and that they had nothing but cavalry in front of them.

General Lee said, a few days afterwards, that he had hesitated whether he should not countermand his own retreat, which he certainly would not have commenced if he had anticipated such dreadfully bad weather. But the

---

[1] For further history of this raincoat, see p. 185.

waggon-trains were now well on their road to the rear, and their safety might have been compromised if the army had not followed them. By eight o'clock next morning the whole waggon-train had got past us, and the troops began to move. It had ceased raining, but the road was a sea of slush and mud, and we got along very slowly. I was on horseback this day, but the next I travelled with L,. in an ambulance,[2] a most tedious way of proceeding on a march, as one has to stick to the line of mud called the road, and keep time with the train, which comes to a stop every now and then by a waggon getting "stalled" in some hole or rut. Once well stuck, it takes a good deal of hard pulling by the mules, and almost as much hard swearing, I am sorry to say, by their drivers, to get a waggon afloat again; and so we moved along, but very slowly, and it was dark before we reached Hagerstown.

Some smart skirmishing had been going on near here before we arrived, as some of the enemy's cavalry had attacked the trains. They succeeded in capturing about forty of Ewell's waggons and ambulances, and twenty of Stuart's, but were driven off before they could do further damage. On this occasion the teamsters were said to have behaved very well, and to have repelled an attack of the enemy by themselves after their own cavalry guard had "skedaddled." We managed to get on a couple of miles beyond the town; but L.; Colonel F., and myself returned next day, and took up our quarters together in

---

[2] "[Ross] was forced at last to give up wearing even his Austrian forage-cap; for the last two days soldiers on the line of march had been visiting his ambulance in great numbers, under the impression (encouraged by the driver) that he was a Yankee general." Fremantle, p. 292.

Hagerstown, at the Washington Hotel.[3] We were anxious to get some supplies here, but the shops were all shut, so we made interest with the landlord of our hotel; and as we engaged to pay in "greenbacks," he promised to introduce us to a "store" keeper of the place. "You'll find him a very fine gentleman, sir, and quite honest," he said. Next morning we were turned out early, our black waiter announcing that the "lady" wished to make the beds, so we had to make room for the chamber-maid, and went down-stairs, and were introduced to the "fine gentleman." I very nearly forgot to shake hands when this ceremony was performed, which would have been a terrible breach of etiquette. However, all went on smoothly; we got into his store through the back-door, and invested a large amount of greenbacks in the purchase of coffee, white sugar, stearine candles, &c. &c., all which luxuries are at present almost unprocurable in the Confederate States.

In the afternoon I rode out to the camp, and stayed there till the evening, talking over the late battles. It seemed undecided whether we should advance again; but in summing up the advantages already obtained by this forward movement of Lee's, it is obvious that the campaign has not been a fruitless one. The war has not only been carried on in the enemy's country, but enormous supplies have been obtained, which will maintain the army for several months to come. Waggons and horses, which were very necessary, have also been secured in incalculable numbers. The men, whose meat-ration for several months past has been a quarter of a pound of bacon, now get a pound and a half of beef. Fifteen thousand cat-

---

[3] "We got an excellent room in the Washington Hotel on producing greenbacks." Fremantle, p. 292.

tle have been driven to the rear for the use of the army, which at present requires about three hundred head a-day. Then the enemy has had to evacuate a large portion of Southern territory, upon which they were pressing heavily, and that, too, just in time for the harvest to be secured to the Confederacy. There is no doubt, however, that the North will claim Gettysburg as a glorious victory; and there will, of course, be great rejoicings over it in "Yankee-doodledom," as my friends say.[4]

---

[4] The decisiveness of Federal victory at Gettysburg was not immediately realized. Both sides claimed success.

On July 7, Kean recorded in his Richmond diary: "General Lee has delivered a great battle at Gettysburg, Pennsylvania with Meade's army, lately Hooker's. It began on Thursday, July 2. We have only Yankee accounts, but these inspire hope of victory. The battle has evidently lasted several days, the last struggle probably taking place on Sunday, July 5. A telegram from the operator at Martinsburg states on the 6th that General Lee has captured 40,000 of the enemy; that Hill in the center fell back as if borne by the enemy who fell into the trap, while Longstreet and Ewell closed in on the flanks and made this capture; and that the prisoners were under escort of Pickett's division, having refused to be paroled. This I do not yet believe. We have no official news from this great battle." By the end of the week accurate reports had reached the Confederate capital. "It turns out that the battle of Gettysburg was a virtual if not an actual defeat." Kean, pp. 78–79. Diarist Jones, too, at first assumed a victory for Lee. More alarmist than Kean, however, (or more realist) he wrote on July 9: "The news from Lee's army is appalling." Jones, I, 374.

Richmond's *The Southern Illustrated News* summarized the official Confederate attitude in its issue for July 25, 1863: ". . . the truth with regard to Lee began to come out. He had gained a great victory, and captured thousands of prisoners. He had fallen back to Hagerstown at his leisure, and in the most perfect order. The Yankees had not dared to pursue him, and he held at

At the Dutchman's cottage I met two officers who had been prisoners of war in the North, and confined in Fort Delaware, near Baltimore. They described the horrors of their existence there; and it seems, indeed, by all accounts that I have heard before and since, to be a very filthy and unwholesome place, utterly unfit for the confinement of prisoners of war.[5] The fact that both sides speak the same language makes it extremely difficult to recapture a man when he has once escaped, and renders it perhaps

---

the last dates a strong position, with an army in fine condition and eager to renew the trial of strength."

In London the Confederate conducted *The Index* summarized in its issue for July 30: ". . . looking only to the conduct and the results of the expedition, the inevitable verdict given on such *data* must be to pronounce it substantially a success." III (1863), 209.

Pyrrhic victory is not enough. Lee failed to win when he had to win. If Meade failed to grasp his advantage, he at least did not lose.

[5] Confederate newspapers were full of excoriation of the treatment of Southerners imprisoned at the North. Typical is this account which *The Index* (IV (1864), 53) reprinted from the Richmond *Examiner:* "From the notebooks of several Confederate prisoners who recently purchased their freedom from Point Lookout we extract at random a few of the instances of barbarous treatment there chronicled; and the truth of the statements can be vouched for by the 500 returned prisoners. Whoever can read them without feeling his nerves tighten the gripe of his sword hand, and clench his teeth with indignation, lacks one of the essential principles of human nature. Murder was not only scrupled at, but opportunities sought for its commission, by the guard, who are known to have been offered by the officer of the day, as much as ten and fifteen dollars apiece for every prisoner they could shoot 'consistently' in the discharge of their duty. Of course, if opportunities did not present themselves by the slightest infraction of the rules by the prisoners these opportunities were sought."

necessary to resort to restrictions far more stringent than usual in Europe; and if only close confinement and want of exercise were complained of, there might be some excuse: but there is none for choosing a place notoriously unwholesome, denying the unfortunate captives the means of keeping their prison and themselves clean, and supplying them at the same time with scanty food, which is sometimes so bad as to be almost poisonous. I visited the Libby Prison at Richmond some time afterwards, and found it kept scrupulously clean and well ventilated; there was not a bad smell about the place; and, to attend upon the 900 to 1000 officers confined there, forty negro servants were kept.[6]

---

[6] Visits to the Yankee prisons at Richmond were later made by John R. Thompson, Confederate literary figure who was then the Richmond correspondent for *The Index,* and Vizetelly. Reports of the prisons have been left by both of them as well as by Ross.

"The exchange of prisoners," wrote Thompson in *The Index* (IV (1864), 28), "has not yet been resumed; and the howl of the Yankees over the alleged inhumanity practised upon their prisoners grows louder and deeper. In company with the correspondent of the London *Times* I visited the Libby Prison and the encampment on Belle Isle a few days ago, to ascertain from personal observation what amount of truth there might be in the statements of the Northern press as to the starving condition of the prisoners. We did not see one emaciated man. Without exception, officers and men were in fine bodily health, and showed no symptoms of wasting from want of food. But the kitchens into which we were ushered, emitting a steam of soup, and the bakeries, where the opened ovens displayed hundreds of large loaves of excellent bread browning under the heat, afforded the most satisfactory refutation of the lies of the enemy. The temperature of Libby Prison was as comfortable as could have been desired, and on Belle Isle every tent was provided with a brick chimney, from which the smoke was curling up into the blue frosty air. The condition of the prisoners was far better, having reference only

At Belle Isle, in the James river, close to Richmond, there were about 8000 prisoners living in tents, in a regular encampment, with plenty of room for exercise, any

---

to the supplies furnished them in food and fuel, than that of our own armies in the field; but when the supplies sent to them from the United States were taken into account it was positively luxurious. As we entered the Libby we found the passageway obstructed with great piles of boxes just received from Fortress Monroe, while several wagons laden with other boxes were standing before the door. On entering the lofts occupied by the prisoners a picture of profusion met the eye. The rafters were thickly hung with hams of bacon and venison, beef tongues, Bologna sausages, dried fish, and other substantials; and around the walls, upon convenient shelving, were disposed cans of potted meats, sardines, green peas, jars of jam, currant jelly, and assorted pickles, bottles of Worcester sauce, and such appetizing *et cetera.* The prisoners, to the number of 1,000, all commissioned officers, from the rank of brigadier-general down to that of second lieutenant, were confined on six different floors of lofts. 75 per cent of them were beguiling the tedium of their imprisonment with the ingenious stories of Miss Braddon and Anthony Trollope, or the last number of the *Atlantic Monthly* or *Harpers Magazine.* Great packages of books from the New York publishers were opening as we passed along. Of the remaining 25 per cent some were playing whist and euker [euchre], and some pondering the gambits on the chess-board. One man, a colonel, was reading the Bible. From the prison we went to the hospitals, which we found in the best possible order, cleanly, well-ventilated, lighted and warmed. Out of the whole number of officers confined in the city but thirty were in the hospital—only 3 per cent. of sick men as the result of the starvation and cruelty to which the Yankees say they have been subjected. On the subject of cleanliness I must not omit to mention that a corps of eighteen negroes are kept constantly employed in washing and sweeping up the floors of the Libby; wherein our inhuman practice differs from the régime of the Yankee prisons, it being the boast of the Northern papers that the Southerners have had their pride humbled in being compelled to do all the menial work in those model establishments."

amount of water, bathing allowed in the season, and better rations than the Confederate soldiers get in the field, though nominally the same. They had been on Belle Isle six months when I went there, and I counted seventy-six graves in the island. As many have died in one day at Fort Delaware—so Captain Boissieux,[7] the Commandant of Belle Isle, informed me. During the first three months only one had died; but latterly, since the exchange of prisoners had been stopped, the men easily fell ill, grew despondent, and died.[8]

---

[7] Lieutenant Boissieux is verified as "commandant" at Belle Isle in William B. Hesseltine's *Civil War Prisons* (Columbus, Ohio, 1930), p. 124, but his full name is not given.

[8] Vizetelly's account of his visit to the prisons was published in *The Illustrated London News* April 9, 1864 (XLIV (1864), 354) to explain his drawing "Camp of Federal Prisoners on Belle Isle, Richmond, Virgina" printed in the same issue. Here is his description of his sketch:

"For some time the cartel regulating the exchange of prisoners between the North and South has been in abeyance, the Federal and Confederate commissioners being at issue on a point of objection raised by the Lincoln Administration. The result of this misunderstanding has been a large increase of the captives on each side, and in Richmond especially the prisons are full to overflowing. In fact, those buildings originally set aside for the accommodation of prisoners of war in the Confederate capital have been found insufficient for that purpose, and the authorities, to provide a remedy, have established a camp of détenus on Belle Isle. . . . When I visited Belle Isle, at the latter end of January, there were more than 7000 prisoners in the camp, all of whom were rank and file from the Federal armies of Virginia and Tennessee. The officers are confined in the 'Libby,' a large and well-ventilated building formerly used as a tobacco warehouse—since it has been found politic to separate the private soldier from his commissioned superior. At the time I mention, the Northern journals were filled with accounts of barbarities practised by the

The Yankees have tried very hard to get up a sensation in the North, about the alleged ill-treatment of Federal prisoners in the South. For this purpose they have had photographs taken of some poor fellows who had been for a long time ill in the hospitals at Richmond, and had been sent home to their friends to save their lives. Of course, these poor wretches looked in the most miserable condition, although it was through illness and not from starvation: but the Yankees did not scruple to scat-

---

Confederates upon those whom the fate of war had placed in their hands, and I was anxious to judge for myself of the correctness of these statements. Let your readers determine from my statement whether the charge of cruelty can be established:—The rations which I saw distributed to the prisoners were in every respect the same as those issued to the Southern soldier; possibly the former may get more fresh meat, and that, I apprehend is scarcely a ground for objection. They certainly do not get such luxuries as coffee or sugar, but then the Confederates themselves are no better off with respect to these condiments, which, indeed, are only to be procured in the Southern States at such ruinous blockade prices as to prevent their finding their way into the commissariat of the Southern army. The doctor's report, on the day I visited the island, will also serve to indicate that the treatment to which the prisoners are subjected is not such as to affect their health. I am convinced your readers will be astonished when I tell them that, out of 7000 of these *cruelly*-used captives, the sick-list only gave thirteen in hospital. Why, I have known, in one morning's report, as many as seventy-five or a hundred to be returned as unfit for duty out of a skeleton brigade of fifteen hundred, in Bragg's army. After six months' confinement of these Federal prisoners at Belle Isle, there were only seventy-five graves to indicate the number of those who had died under the privations to which they are said to have been subjected! Any Adjutant-General of a division of 5000 men in Lee's army could show a very different bill of mortality from sickness and hardship embracing a corresponding period."

ter portraits of them about by the million, as samples of the state of all the prisoners held in the South. It was a *jeu d'esprit* very laudable, "as it might injure the South," like Mr Seward's forged despatches; but, after what I had seen with my own eyes at Belle Isle and the Libby Prison, and what I heard with my own ears from Southerners of their treatment as prisoners in the North, I could not help being reminded of the old Scotch proverb, "Ill doers are ill deemers." [9]

---

[9] Ross, when he was in the North in 1864, doubtless saw the propaganda pamphlet issued for the Loyal Publication Society, *Narrative of Privations and Sufferings of United States Officers & Soldiers While Prisoners of War . . . Being a Report of a Commission of Inquiry, Appointed by the United States Sanitary Commission* (Boston, [1864]).

CHAPTER VI

Two days after our return to Hagerstown, Colonel F. left us, being obliged to return to England without delay, and made straight for the Federal lines, determined to take his chance of getting through them. Most of his friends were rather anxious about him, but Longstreet, with whom he was a great favourite, was confident he would succeed. "A man who has travelled all through Texas as successfully as the Colonel, is safe to get through the Yankee lines all right," he said.[1]

---

[1] "I rode to General Longstreet's camp . . . and consulted him about my difficulties with regard to my leave. He was most good-natured about it, and advised me under the circumstances to drive in the direction of Hancock; and, in the event of being ill-treated on my way, to insist upon being taken before the nearest U. S. officer of the highest rank, who would probably protect me. I determined to take his advice at once; so I

L. and I visited General Lee in the afternoon, and he spoke very openly on the subject of the late campaign.

Had he been aware that Meade had been able to concentrate his whole army—for which he deserved great credit —he certainly should not have attacked him: indeed, it had not been his interest nor his intention to bring on a great battle at all; but, led away, partly by the success of the first day, believing that Meade had only a portion of his army in front of him, and seeing the enthusiasm of his own troops, he had thought that a successful battle would cut the knot so easily and satisfactorily, that he had determined to risk it. His want of knowledge of the enemy's movements he attributed to Stuart having got too far away from him with his cavalry.

Stuart, who had gone to within sight of Washington and captured a large train of waggons close to Georgetown, a suburb of that city, had expected to rendezvous with the main army on the Susquehanna, but when he reached York he found that General Lee had not advanced as far as he expected, and that the whole Federal force was between him and General Lee. Consequently he had to make a long detour, coming round by Carlisle, to rejoin the army, and did not arrive till the evening of the second day's battle.

General Lee, when he had commenced his forward

---

took leave of him and his officers. Longstreet is generally a very taciturn and undemonstrative man, but he was quite affectionate in his farewell. His last words were a hearty hope for the speedy termination of the war. All his officers were equally kind in their expressions on my taking leave, though the last sentence uttered by Latrobe was not entirely reassuring—viz., 'You may take your oath he'll be caught for a spy.'" Fremantle, p. 294. This was written on July 7. Two days later Fremantle set out on his return to England.

movement, had gained several days' march upon General Hooker, who was at that time opposed to him; but at Chambersburg he had been obliged to halt with his main force for three days, as there had been some delay in forwarding his supply-trains. This gave Meade, who had now superseded Hooker, time to concentrate his forces in the right direction. Otherwise, and if Lee had been able to follow closely upon Ewell's corps, which had advanced as far as Carlisle, he would have crossed the mountainous region of Pennsylvania, and got into the rich and fertile valley of the Susquehanna without any opposition.

Here his army would have found plentiful means of subsistence. Philadelphia would have been threatened, and Washington, Baltimore, and the army of the Potomac would have been cut off from their supplies, and from all communication with the North except by sea. The communications of General Lee could not have been *seriously* interfered with without the Federal army entirely uncovering Washington and Baltimore. He might have taken up a position where it would have been very difficult for Meade to attack him; and without further fighting, by merely maintaining his army at or near Harrisburg or some other central point, incalculable results might have been secured. But it was not so ordained.

If the campaign had such an object in view as I have supposed, it was already defeated, when Meade was able to concentrate his whole army and place it in Lee's way before he had got through the mountains.

Far from his base of supplies, with an enormous waggon-train. Lee could not hope by manœuvring to dislodge Meade from before him; and in that difficult mountainous region, where strong defensive positions are to be found at every few miles' interval, it would have been very unreasonable to expect to inflict such a crushing defeat upon Meade's army as would prevent him from making any further resistance.

Had the strong positions at Gettysburg been stormed, no doubt cannon and colours and prisoners would have been taken, but at a great sacrifice of life. The Federals would have fallen back, and probably taken up a still stronger position a few miles to the rear. Lee would have had to retreat all the same, especially as, after the third day's fight, ammunition—particularly small-arms ammunition—was getting short.[2] Had there been only a portion of Meade's army at Gettysburg, and that portion had been overwhelmed, of course it would have been a different thing; and, as General Lee said himself, it was under the impression that he had only a part of Meade's army to deal with that he fought the battle.

As we were riding back to Hagerstown we fell in with Colonel Wickham, who commands a brigade of Stuart's cavalry, in connection with whom the following story was told me.

It will be remembered that Virginia was one of the last States to secede, and did not do so until she had exhausted every effort to effect a compromise; and when she did so, the few Southern States that were still hesitating followed her example, and the war became inevitable.

---

[2] Commenting on the Confederate retreat when Lawley brought the news of it from Lee's headquarters, Fremantle declared, "This step is imperative from want of ammunition." Fremantle, p. 280. Before the battle, he had noted (p. 246), ". . . the Staff officers say, 'In every battle we fight we must capture as much ammunition as we use.' This necessity, however, does not seem to disturb them, as it has hitherto been their regular style of doing business."

Matters were coming to a crisis when the leading men of Virginia sent a deputation of three of their number * to wait on the President, Mr Lincoln.

They tried to impress him with a sense of the gravity of the situation, and urgently entreated that he would do something to calm the excitement amongst the people, whose irritation at the threats of the Administration and of the Northern States was getting beyond control.

It was just after the taking of Fort Sumter, and Lincoln's having called out 75,000 men to coerce the South.

"But what would you have me do?" said Mr Lincoln.

"Mr President," replied one of the deputation, "I would beg you to lend me your finger and thumb for five minutes"—meaning, of course, that he wished him to write something that should allay the prevailing excitement.

But Mr Lincoln did not choose to understand him. "My finger and thumb!" he repeated—"my finger and thumb! What would you do with them? Blow your nose?"

The deputation retired in disgust, and Virginia seceded.[3]

---

*I have since heard that Colonel Wickham, although a very prominent man in the councils of his State, was not one of this deputation, which consisted of Messrs W. B. Preston, G. W. Randolph, and A. N. H. Stuart [A. H. H. Stuart.]

[3] In commenting on the first installment of Ross's narrative *The Index* quoted this passage and remarked: "We shall conclude with an anecdote about Mr. Lincoln, which we might forbear to tell were it not that Mr. Edward Everett, who has been in London drawing-rooms, has ventured to affirm that Mr. Lincoln will in point of manners compare favourably with the most refined members of the diplomatic corps." *The Index,* IV (1864), 778–79.

We remained about a week at Hagerstown, being all the time, as we discovered afterwards from the Yankee newspapers, in the most frightful danger of being captured by Meade's victorious and pursuing army. Lee's army, upon which we relied for security, was, it is true, only a mile off, Hagerstown and ourselves lying between them and the Yankees, but it was a demoralised horde of fugitives; and Meade lost all the credit he had gained at Gettysburg, because he did not capture the whole "crowd," or drive them into the Potomac. Fortunately we were in happy ignorance of the peril in which we were placed, or it might have disturbed our peaceful slumbers at the Washington Hotel.

Whilst we were at Hagerstown, the news arrived of the fall of Vicksburg, and this may perhaps have had some influence in deciding General Lee to recross the Potomac. Many were disappointed at this decision, as it had been the general opinion that the army was only waiting for fresh supplies to recommence offensive operations.

Again the rain came down in torrents, and the generals must have had an anxious time of it, as the Potomac was much swollen already, and there was but one pontoon bridge at the point where we crossed. However, all got over safely, and Meade did *not* capture a rearguard of two brigades, as he afterwards boasted he had done. There was, however, a furious attack made by some forty tipsy cavalrymen upon the rearguard; and though they were entirely cut to pieces themselves, they killed General Pettigrew and several soldiers. General Pettigrew, as they came tearing along with a Yankee battle-flag flying, had forbidden his men to fire at them, thinking it was a party of Confederates who had captured a Yankee flag;

he could not conceive it possible that a squad of cavalry should attack his strong force.

The Yankee cavalry has not the credit of doing very dashing things, and at present the Confederate cavalry is also a little under a cloud. The cavalry have always artillery with them, and Longstreet says it is this which demoralises them. When two cavalry parties meet they do not fight themselves, but set their artillery to work at a game of long bowls.

I think the fact of the men owning their own horses is likely to make them more careful than they should be. If a man loses his horse and cannot buy another, he is transferred to the infantry, which of course he does not like. Besides, the perpetual raiding, and pouncing upon supply-trains and sutlers' stores, though capital fun, does not conduce to make good soldiers.

We pitched our tents a mile or two south of where we had crossed the river, and made ourselves comfortable. The army is in good spirits in spite of our own retreat and the bad news from the west. As for despondency, or being weary of resistance and of the war, which kind of feeling I see the Northerners are fond of attributing to the South, there are certainly no symptoms of it in this army. "We will fight them, sir, till h—— freezes, and then, sir, we'll fight them on the ice," said an energetic officer to me; and the same sentiment seems to animate every one, though they do not all express themselves in such strong language.[4]

---

[4] Ross quoted a cliché of the period. But cliché or not, it was representative of Southern statements from James Chesnut's confident "The man most averse to Southern blood might safely drink every drop shed in establishing a Southern Confederacy" (quoted in W. A. Swanberg, *First Blood* (New York, 1958), p.

The Southerners are of course not nearly so commercial a race as the Yankees, but still they are much given to "trading" amongst each other; and the other day at an hospital in Gettysburg, an artilleryman whose leg was to be taken off, no sooner knew that the amputation was decided upon by the doctors, than he turned to another wounded man in the next bed, and before the operation was performed had "traded" the boot which was henceforth to be of no use to him.

The negroes in camp are a great study. Of course they are all slaves. They have a great horror of the Yankees, and when in Pennsylvania could not be got to move a hundred yards from the camp for fear of being kidnapped, whilst here they delight in roaming about the country in search of poultry, eggs, fruit, and suchlike delicacies, for which they are excellent caterers. I heard of only a single instance of a servant being lost during the campaign, and his master was convinced that he had been stolen, and that he had not run off of his own free-will. Our excellent cook Jeff is a great character, and has arrived at the dignity of being an "uncle" on account of his

---

16) to the unreconstructed defiance of Innes Randolph's "The Lay of the Last Rebel."

Robert Toombs, later the apotheosis of the Unreconstructed Southerner, stated the determination of the South in a letter quoted in the Sumter, Georgia, *Republican* some time after the battle at Gettysburg. "I can conceive," he wrote, "of no extremity to which my country could be reduced in which I would, for a single moment, entertain any proposition for any union with the North on any terms whatever. When all else is lost, I prefer to unite with the thousands of our own countrymen who have found honorable deaths, if not graves, upon the battle-field." *The Index,* III (1863), 391.

mature age; whilst Andrew, a handsome lad of about twenty, who cleans my boots now and then in fine weather, is a "boy," and will remain one till he is forty.[5]

Jeff is a preacher, and holds religious meetings with his fellow-darkies. They are very shy of white people coming to these meetings, and of course their masters let them alone, and do not intrude upon them. Lying in my tent one morning, I overheard Jeff lecturing Andrew for using profane language: "Andrew, I hear you say 'by ——.' Now, Andrew, you know you've not money enough in your pocket to buy a bit of biscuit, and yet you say, by ——. Andrew, you'll never go to heaven," &c. &c. And Andrew hung his head, and was ashamed of himself. They always call their masters and mistresses by their Christian names, whatever may be their rank and titles. General Lee, for instance, will never be anything but Master Robert to any of his servants. They have a strong sense of humour, and are always laughing at something or other. Sometimes their repartees are not bad. A few days ago I was in the tent of an officer who had just been promoted. His servant was making up his bed, and the officer told him to be sure and make it long enough. The "boy" looked up and grinned. "S'pose, Master William, you'se now grown taller since you was major," he said. Their teeth are remarkably fine, and they are proud of them, I suppose; at least they mostly wear

[5] "I have often told these planters that I thought the word 'slave' was the most repulsive part of the institution, and I have always observed they invariably shirk using it themselves. They speak of their servant, their boy, or their negroes, but never of their slaves. They address a negro as boy or girl, or uncle or aunty." Fremantle, pp. 120–21.

a toothbrush very prominently stuck into their coat button-hole, as a dandy would carry a flower, or a Frenchman his ribbon of the Legion of Honour! [6]

They are a very affectionate race, and the attachment they have for their masters is very like the clannish feeling which we read of as having existed formerly in the Highlands of Scotland between the lower classes and their chiefs. Whenever they have occasion for a surname, they make use of their master's. They display great contempt towards the poor "free niggers" in the towns, who are generally dirty and ragged. They look up to their masters for protection, which is readily given, not only as a matter of course to their own servants but to any other "darkies" as occasion may require.

If any one in the South wished to make quite sure of getting into trouble, he need only abuse or ill-treat a negro; and though the "boy" might be submissive, he would soon have every white man in the neighbourhood down upon him, and perhaps a revolver or two emptied into his body.[7]

---

[6] Fremantle commented on this same custom as a sartorial mark of the Confederate soldier: "This tooth-brush in the button-hole is a very common custom, and has a most quaint effect." Fremantle, p. 301.

[7] "My fellow-travellers of all classes are much given to talk to me about their 'peculiar institution,' and they are most anxious that I should see as much of it as possible, in order that I may be convinced that it is not so bad as has been represented, and that they are not all 'Legrees,' although they do not attempt to deny that there are many instances of cruelty. But they say a man who is known to illtreat his negroes is hated by all the rest of the community." Fremantle, p. 79.

Ross's book was attacked for its pro-slavery attitude by its reviewer in *The Athenaeum* for May 13, 1865 (number 1959, p.

646). Sarcastically he noted, "Charming is Capt. Ross's picture of the peculiar institution." "Clearly Capt. Ross," he wrote, "thinks that all the sting of slavery is taken away when it is called service. Most Englishmen have seen in this usage of Southern masters a sad consequence rather than a mitigation of slavery. The manual labor of the country being performed for the most part by slaves, all sorts of humble toil were deemed disgraceful, and the more honourable title of 'servant' was conferred on the slave because no free man deigned to work like persons of the poorest class in the free states. To be a servant was to be a slave, and therefore the mean white preferred indigence and any form of social degradation to useful industry. If the word 'servant' had not been used to designate a slave, it would not have been used at all. The substitution of the honest for the vile appellation was an insolent declaration of disdain for all workmen rather than an act of grace to the slaves. Had Capt. Ross reflected on the matter, he would have seen that where slaves are called servants, the 'servant' means *slave,* and carries with it all the indignity and contumely of that loathsome name."

The Athenaeum took every opportunity to set Ross's comments on slavery in a bad light. He received more favorable treatment from his reviewer in *The Saturday Review,* who wrote in part: "Captain Ross, in testifying to the mutual good will of the two races, and in telling anecdotes of white patience and black fidelity, only confirms the evidence of all who have gone over the same ground. And, allowing for the obvious truth that travellers do not see everything, we cannot doubt that their testimony is in the main correct. The notion that the life of the slave is one of systematic wretchedness and ill-usage is in the highest degree improbable. It is not likely that men should be habitually cruel to valuable chattels, to affectionate dependents, to labourers on whose work their fortunes depend, to attendants who at every hour of the day and night hold their master's life, and his children's lives, at their mercy. . . . What we must add to this is, that wherever there is power, there will be those who will abuse it; that, as here we have men who ill-treat their wives, and women who maltreat their servants, so in the South there will be men and women who will ill-use their negroes; that, as authority cannot be upheld without coercion of some kind, and as dismissal is inapplicable to a slave, the whip must now and then be employed; and that strangers will hear and see nothing of these unpleasant incidents that can be kept from them. When we brush aside the unauthenticated reports or absolute fictions of Abolitionist writers, this is about the amount of truth that is left at the bottom of their invectives. . . . Such, in its vices and its merits, was the system whose overthrow, in the opinion of a large number of our countrymen, is cheaply purchased by the sacrifice of half a million of lives, of five hundred millions of money, the conflagration of half a score of cities, the destruction of a gallant nation, and the conversion of an Eden into a desert. How much suffering and sacrifice may yet remain for victor and vanquished, for slave and master, before the new relations of the races can be placed on a satisfactory footing, is beyond the reach of human conjecture." *The Saturday Review,* XIX (1863), 546.

CHAPTER VII

The Northerners are not very fond of being called Yankees, but they are never called anything else in the South now.

About the commencement of the war, before the behaviour of the Federal armies had entirely put a stop to all intercourse between them and the inhabitants of such portions of the South as they were invading, a Northern regiment marched into some little town in Tennessee. The colonel of the regiment had out his band to perform for the edification of the townspeople, and requested the lady of the house where he was quartered to choose what she would desire them to play. The lady, wishing to gratify her guest, and at the same time careful not to offend, requested that the band might play the "Federal doodle."

I have attempted in my narrative to imitate the delicacy of this Tennessee lady, and have substituted "Federal" and "Northern" as often as I could for the obnoxious term, but I find it impossible to avoid it entirely.

The day after we crossed the Potomac we reached Martinsburg, where I had the pleasure of again meeting Colonel Faulkner, who entertained and lodged a large party at his house—amongst others Major Norris, who had come up in hot haste from Richmond, expecting to march triumphantly with Lee's victorious army into his native city of Baltimore. There had been most extravagant rumours of extraordinary success at Richmond, and the disappointment there at the retreat was proportionate. It is astonishing what people can bring themselves to believe if they try.

According to rumours at Richmond, the whole Federal army had been captured; whilst in the North, the Yankees were persuading themselves that Lee's army had been utterly annihilated!

A few miles south of Martinsburg we made a halt again of several days, and as I had by this time been able to procure a horse of my own, I could move more freely, and visit all the surrounding camps. The waggon-train, which had grown to be excessive during the campaign, was being cut down very strictly, and large numbers of horses and waggons sent to the rear, at which of course many people grumbled. Provisions were plentiful, and the men were in excellent spirits, and much given to exhibit them by chaffing any parties who might ride through their camps. "Look at that man with the Parrot [Parrott] gun on his back," they would cry to one who carried a spy-glass strapped over his shoulders. "And what a fine see-gar that other one's smoking!" "And there's the chap what carries the whisky!" as another rode past with the neck of a bottle suspiciously protruding out of one of his saddlebags. And then the whole "crowd" would burst out into a regular Southern yell.

I was surprised to see how well the men were shod. The weather was fine now, but it had been horribly bad. The mud on the roads had been ankle-deep, and several rivers and streams had been waded and forded. Many a European army would have been half without shoes, but here there were very few barefooted men, and during our halt these few were supplied by stores sent up from the rear. Almost all their boots and shoes are imported from England through the blockade.

We had a charming camp under a grove of trees, with a stream close by where we could bathe, and were rather sorry when it was broken up, and we continued our retreat.

I need hardly say that the camps here are not constructed according to the rules in the books, in long straight parallel lines, with a place for every one, and every one in his place.

On the contrary, the tents are pitched according to the formation of the ground, wherever their owners choose, keeping, of course, within a certain distance of each other; and, grouped together as they are in shady places, they are not only much more picturesque, but also much more pleasant and comfortable, than if rules were strictly adhered to.

On leaving our pleasant camp we marched rapidly for five days consecutively to Culpepper [Culpeper] Courthouse, marching from eighteen to twenty miles a-day.

The Confederates make very long marches, and show small signs of fatigue. I am told that the average distance of a day's march during this war has been about eighteen miles, though sometimes they have marched thirty and more for days together. Stonewall Jackson was especially rapid in his movements, and his men had often nothing to eat on their march but ears of Indian-corn which they gathered and parched. The second day we crossed over the two forks of the Shenandoah at Front Royal. The river was swollen by the late rains, and mounted men had to be employed during the crossing to prevent those who were weak, or who were attacked with giddiness, from being swept from the ford into deep water.

The army got across safely, but a pontoon-bridge had to be made for the artillery and waggon-train, which caused some delay. The pass in the mountains through which we had to march is called Chester Gap.

The Yankees were on the other side of the gap, trying to hold it against us, and when we got to the top of the mountain, about five miles from Front Royal, a smart skirmish was going on.[1] The enemy was driven away; but as we were in advance of the main body of the army, we retraced our steps some half-mile down the mountain again to a house where a Mr Gardner [2] received us very hospitably. As *"we"* on this occasion consisted of General Longstreet, with all his staff and couriers, the house was rather too small to shelter us, and most of our number camped at night on the piazza and in the garden; but we all got plenty to eat, and so did our horses, which was very agreeable, as we had fasted since breakfast.

Next morning, when we reached the top of the mountain again, we found the Yankees had returned, and were go-

[1] Skirmishes at Chester Gap, Virginia, July 21, 22, and 23 are reported in the *Official Records,* Ser. I, XXVII, pt. 3, 741–42.

[2] Not identified.

ing to dispute our passage a mile or two further on than where the skirmish took place yesterday.

They had only a brigade of cavalry, however, and a couple of guns. Longstreet sent a brigade of infantry to drive them off, and the sight which followed was very interesting. We had a magnificent view, and could distinguish every figure in the fight which took place far below us. The Confederate brigade—I think it was Wolford's [Wofford's]—threw out skirmishers first, but presently, as the Yankees, who had dismounted, fell back towards their horses, the whole body advanced in line of battle over a broad open space. The Yankees got to their horses, mounted, and I fully expected would charge and ride down the Confederate brigade: they had a splendid opportunity for doing so, as the open ground sloped towards them, and they could have got close to their opponents, who were in line, before they could have been fired upon. The open ground was skirted, too, by a wood through which a flanking squadron might have been sent without being perceived, and at the same time their two guns might have gone forward and prepared for their charge with grape and canister. But nothing of the kind occurred.

As soon as they were on their horses the guns limbered up, and all trotted off together.

After seeing such an opportunity lost, I was not surprised to hear that mounted cavalry never attacked infantry. We continued our march unmolested. On the road I got into conversation with a sergeant of the signal corps. This signal corps is an institution peculiar to the American armies. On marches and during battles, high and commanding positions are occupied by squadrons of this corps, who communicate with each other by flags, on the old semaphore system, and report all important communications to their generals. The corps was found very useful last year, and has been much increased since. When Jackson was forcing the surrender of Harper's Ferry he was able to communicate from the Virginia heights with M'Laws, who was on the Maryland heights, by means of two posts of the signal corps; whilst, if he had been obliged to send couriers, they would have had to make a detour of twenty-five miles.

This year Lee and Ewell were in constant communication from Culpeper to Winchester, I forget whether by twenty-five or thirty-five posts.

Sometimes they discover each other's alphabet. The Yankees did this just before the battle of Chancellorsville, but the Confederates found it out and changed their signals; so when the Yankees, having got to a Confederate post, telegraphed with the old alphabet to know where Lee and Jackson were, they got a wrong answer. Major Norris is the chief of this corps.

CHAPTER VIII

We reached Culpeper Court-house on the 24th of July; and as it was evident that the army would remain here inactive for some time, I "took the cars" to Richmond, where I spent ten days very agreeably.

Richmond was never intended to hold so many inhabitants as it does now. Its population before the war was, I believe, about 30,000; now, they say, it is 100,000; so that many of the Government employés are hard up for lodging. One gold dollar is now worth about ten paper ones of Confederate currency, *"fundable in stocks or bonds of the Confederate States six months after the ratification of a treaty of peace between the Confederate States and the United States,"* and not "A LEGAL TENDER *for all debts, public and private, except duties on imports and interest on the public debt,"* as the "greenbacks" in the North are. And as Government officials and the army are paid in this currency, at the same rate as if it were worth its nominal value in gold, of course those who have no private means are obliged to be very economical. Planters, and those who have anything to sell, are nearly as well off as before, as they get proportionately high prices for their goods. For those who can command gold or exchange upon England, living is exceedingly cheap. Board and lodging at a first-rate hotel, for instance, is six paper dollars a-day, or about half-a-crown in English money. But as Richmond is crowded with Government officials, most of whom have only their salaries, and with refugees from parts of the country occupied by the Yankees, who have little or nothing at all, the war is much more severely felt here than anywhere else in the Confederacy. Still it is a pleasant place, and pleasant people live here. The houses are cosy and comfortable, especially in the better streets, which are lined with "shade" trees, a great feature of Southern cities. Americans, like the English, always have a house to themselves if they can, so the only very large houses are the hotels.

Captain Scheibert, the Prussian Commissioner, with whom I had associated a great deal during the campaign, was my next-door neighbor at the Ballard House; and as he was soon to leave for Europe, we agreed to go down to Charleston together, where great events were expected to take place. The journey was very disagreeable. It was scorchingly hot, and the cars, always inconvenient, were excessively crowded. They invariably are so, both in the North and South, and the discomforts of travelling are greater than any one can imagine who has not experienced them.

We left Richmond at five o'clock in the morning of Thursday, August 6th, and breakfasted at Petersburg, where we had to stop for four hours, which we spent in wandering about the "city." It is not necessary in this country for a city to have a bishop and a cathedral; a good-sized church is enough, and every town sufficiently large to boast such an ornament is a city here. Petersburg, moreover, is a good-sized place, has several churches, some handsome "stores," and is said to be a delightful residence.

From Petersburg to Wilmington we were constantly travelling through the enormous pine forests for which North Carolina is famous, and from which, in time of peace, they extract rosin enough to supply the world.

It was getting daylight as we crossed the river at Wilmington. We counted twelve blockade-runners lying at the wharves.[1] From thence to Charleston most of the road was through forests, but of a different description from those of the day before. The trees were chiefly live oak, and others of a tropical character, bearded all over with long Spanish moss, on ground which was almost a swamp.

---

[1] On June 16 Fremantle had passed Wilmington on his journey to Richmond. "This river [the Cape Fear]," he commented, "was quite full of blockade-runners. I counted eight large steamers, all handsome leaden-coloured vessels, which ply their trade with the greatest regularity. Half these ships were engaged in carrying goods on Government account; and I was told that the quantity of boots, clothing, saltpetre, lead, and tin, which they bring into the country, is very great. I cannot suppose that in ordinary times there would be anything like such a trade as this, at a little place like Wilmington, which shows the absurdity of calling the blockade an efficient one." Fremantle, pp. 205–206.

The spaces cleared on each side of the road were covered with cane-brake several yards high; and in the ditches, full of black water, which ran parallel with the line, cooters and terrapins and various reptiles were swimming about. At intervals, and always near the stations, there were large clearings, with country houses and negro villages; and I have no doubt, from the look of the soil, that the plantations must be very productive.

We reached Charleston at ten o'clock in the evening, and took up our quarters at the Mill's [Mills] House Hotel, very hot and dusty and rather knocked up. However, after spoiling a good deal of cold water—making it very nearly black—we felt more comfortable before we retired to rest.

Next morning, in spite of the scorching sun, we paid a round of visits to the generals and others, presenting letters of introduction with which we had been furnished at Richmond. We were very kindly and cordially received, and I soon began to feel at home in Charleston.

"Charleston, the metropolis of South Carolina, is picturesquely situated at the confluence of the Ashley and Cooper rivers, which combine to form its harbour," says Appleton's Guide. "It was founded about 1670, and subsequently laid out on a plan furnished from England, which was then considered of very magnificent scale."

There are some fine churches and public buildings, museum, orphan asylum, libraries, &c. No State has so many charitable institutions as South Carolina. Before the war Charleston had nearly 70,000 inhabitants, but now there are less than 20,000, they say.

A terrific fire, in December 1862, destroyed one-third of the city, with the Roman Catholic cathedral, several churches, the theatre, and many of the finest public and private buildings. The centre of Charleston is now a wide waste of ruin and rubbish.[2] There is a fine arsenal here, and a military college.[3] It is a curious fact that several of the Southern States have had for many years military colleges, where the pupils received a complete military education, although they were never intended for soldiers, and, indeed, could not enter the regular army, which was exclusively officered by graduates from Westpoint, the United States military school.

At dinner I met V.,[4] whom I immediately recognised

---

[2] "That portion of the city destroyed by the great fire presents the appearance of a vast wilderness in the very centre of the town, no attempt having been made towards rebuilding it; this desert space looks like the Pompeian ruins, and extends . . . for a mile in length by a half a mile in width. Nearly all the distance between the Mills House hotel and the Charleston hotel is in this desolate state. The fire began quite by accident, but the violent wind which suddenly arose rendered all attempts to stop the flames abortive." Fremantle, p. 181.

[3] The Citadel.

[4] Frank Vizetelly, correspondent for *The Illustrated London News*. Vizetelly would be the companion of Ross during most of his further travels in the Confederacy. His career in the Confederacy has recently been delineated by W. Stanley Hoole in *Vizetelly Covers the Confederacy* (Tuscaloosa, Ala., 1957). His fuller career is covered in Henry Vizetelly's *Glances Back Through Seventy Years* (London, 1890; 2 vols.).

Vizetelly was as successful socially in the South as he was professionally. A charming picture of him in the highest of Richmond social circles is given by one who knew him there in Mrs. Constance Cary Harrison's *Recollections Grave and Gay* (New York, 1911), pp. 132–33: "Frank Vizitelly, correspondent and artist for the *London Illustrated News,* could hardly have been called a 'ladies' man,' but we nevertheless met him several times and were immensely entertained by his varied accomplishments. He was a big, florid, red-bearded Bohemian, of a type totally unfamiliar to us Virginians, who could and would do anything to enter-from having seen his photograph, and we walked out in the evening to the "Battery," a promenade on the bay, whence there is a splendid view of Fort Sumter and the shore on each side of Charleston Bay, now covered with forts and batteries. Fort Sumter is three miles off, Fort Wagner four; so when battles take place it is perfectly safe to look on, and on such occasions the Battery is crowded with ladies and gentlemen. Cannonading is kept up night and day between Sumter and the batteries on James Island on one side, and the Yankees on the other. These last have now a firm footing on Morris Island, and are working their way towards Fort Wagner, which they failed to take by storm the other day. In the evening especially it is very interesting to watch the contest, as all the guns use hollow shot, with time fuzes, which go blazing through the air like meteors. The mortar-shells are the prettiest, going high up into the air, and then slowly descending.

One of my first excursions was to Fort Sumter, whither I went one evening with General Ripley in his barge.[5] It was then almost entirely intact, having been hurt very little indeed by the Monitor attack in April; and when I observed the thickness of its walls, and compared them with what I had seen in other countries, and when I saw that no land-batteries could be brought within much less

---

tain a circle. In our theatricals, tableaux, and charades, he was a treasure-trove. . . . He painted our scenery and our faces, made wigs and armor, and was a mine of suggestion in stage device. He sang songs, told stories, danced *pas seuls,* and was generally most kind and amusing. The men said he was very plucky in the saddle and on the battle-field."

[5] There is a more military and more detailed description of Fort Sumter in Fremantle, pp. 182–85.

than a mile of it, I confess I did not foresee the destruction it was to undergo within a very short time. They were blazing away from a mortar in the yard at the Yankee works on Morris Island; and Colonel Rhett,[6] the commandant at Sumter, told us as a curiosity that this firing from the fort spoils their bread, as it shakes the foundation so that the yeast cannot make the dough rise. From Sumter we rowed over to Battery Gregg, on Morris Island, and thence took horse to Fort Wagner, a very strong little work made entirely of sand, lined or faced with palmetta [palmetto] wood, which does not splinter. Every one knew it was doomed, and must fall in time, but it was intended to hold it as long as possible. The garrison is relieved every five days. The impression of most people then was that the Yankees would work their way up to Fort Wagner and force its evacuation and that of Battery Gregg, and then place their own batteries there and attack Sumter. The bombproofs at Fort Wagner were stiflingly close and hot, but we went outside and lay on the parapet for an hour, chatting. The Yankees were so obliging as not to shell whilst we were there, as they otherwise do pretty nearly all day and all night long, keeping the garrison under-ground, with the exception of those who are working the guns. But the land guns do not trouble them so much as the monitors, and especially the new [New] Ironsides, an iron-clad frigate carrying seven 11-inch Dalgrens [Dahlgrens] on a side, as well as two 200-pounder Parrotts on pivots, which are used as broadside guns. It is surprising how little damage they do to the fortification. A 15-inch shell, weighing 340 pounds, will bury itself in the sand, explode, and create an enormous amount of dust;

---

[6] Alfred Rhett.

but the sand not being heavy enough to be thrown far, it presently subsides, and the damage is repaired by a very little shovelling.

As yet there have not been many casualties on the Confederate side since the siege of Charleston has commenced; and General Jordan tells me he has calculated that it takes the Yankees 70,000 pounds weight of iron to kill or wound a Confederate soldier. Still the incessant, tremendous, deafening, *agaçant* crashing of the enormous guns affects the nerves of the men, and they are thoroughly knocked up at the end of their five days' service; and the worthy missionaries, who hold revival and prayer meetings at the different camps, reap a large harvest of repentant converts each time the garrison is relieved. We did not return from our expedition till near daylight the next morning.

Another day we drove over to see the fortifications on James Island. When the British took Charleston in May 1780, it was through James Island that they made their attack, and General Beauregard is very thankful that the Yankees did not follow their example. It is now, however, covered with strong works. Formerly, it was considered certain death to sleep out one night there during the malaria season, and now thousands of men are quartered on it. They have to be well dosed with quinine, however. Major Lucas,[7] who commanded at the principal work on the island—Fort Pemberton—told me that he made his men take their dose regularly every morning after dress-parade. Last year, when it was left more to the option of the men, there was a great deal of fever; but this year, since the men had no choice in the matter, they are very

---

[7] J. Jonathan Lucas.

healthy. The island used before the war to be covered with cotton-plantations, but it has gone out of cultivation now.

Another excursion was to Ashley Hall, some five or six miles from Charleston, belonging to Colonel Bull, whose grandfather, Sir William Bull, was the last British Governor of South Carolina. The Colonel drove me over in his buggy, and Scheibert, V., Captain Fielden [Feilden],[8] an Englishman on General Beauregard's Staff, and Mr Walker,[9] a Charlestonian, followed in a carriage. We spent a delightful day, roaming over cotton-fields and rice-plantations, woods, and "park-like meadows," studded with the most magnificent live oaks. At lunch, some fruit was brought in, which I began to eat, and said, "What delicious gooseberries!" upon which I was informed that I was not eating gooseberries at all, but grapes—Scuppernong grapes, an indigenous fruit of the country. I found a vine afterwards in the garden with these grapes growing upon it, singly and in bunches of two or three, like cherries. They have a hard skin, rather hairy: a capital wine is made from them. It is remarkable that most attempts to make wine in this country have failed, though of course the grape thrives in perfection; but I am told that they ripen too early, and the juice will not ferment properly in the hot weather which follows the pressing.

One of the most striking features in the forests are the

---

[8] Henry Wemyss Feilden. "A Captain Feilden came to call on me at 9 A.M. He is an Englishman, and formerly served in the 42d Highlanders. He is now in the Confederate army, and is on the staff of General Beauregard's army. I remember his brother quite well at Sandhurst." Fremantle, p. 182.

[9] Probably H. Pinckney Walker, the British vice-consul at Charleston.

enormous wild vines which twine round the larger trees.

The house at Ashley Hall, like many more on the old plantations, was built before the revolutionary war, of bricks brought from England.

We had hardly been a week at Charleston, before the Yankees, having mounted some heavy batteries at a distance of from two and a half to three miles from Sumter, commenced a furious bombardment of that fort, firing over Fort Wagner and Battery Gregg, and at the same time continuing their approaches. It was an entirely novel feature of war; but it soon became evident that they would have the best it, and that the brick walls of Sumter would not be able to stand the pounding of their two and three hundred pound shells, thrown from that extraordinary distance. From Fort Johnson on James Island, which is distant about three-quarters of a mile from Sumter, and where we went now daily to watch the progress of events, we could clearly see the effect of every shot fired.[10]

---

[10] Vizetelly wrote: "The Federal commander, General Gilmore [Gillmore], having succeeded in erecting batteries on Morris Island some time since, commenced the bombardment of Fort Sumter with 200 lb. parrotts at over a range of two miles and a half. The grand old work which did such good service on the 7th of April last was unable to reply, and its brave garrison was compelled to be silent spectators of the gradual demolition of its walls. I have frequently paid visits to the work since the bombardment commenced, and the inclosed Illustration will give you an idea of the severity of the fire concentrated upon it. Every gun is dismounted, and nearly the whole of the parapet is swept away. The gorge-face is one mass of ruins, and the casemates scarcely afford shelter to the garrison. The fort will be held, however, as long as a brick remains; by the bayonet, if necessary. Such is the determination of General Beauregard." *The Illustrated London News,* XLIII (1863), 574.

Day by day more of the wall disappeared, and more guns were knocked from the parapet and the upper casemates into the area behind them. Every now and then the fleet would come in and join in the attack. Thus on Monday morning, August 17th, the New Ironsides, six monitors, and six wooden ships, and all the Yankee batteries, commenced a furious attack of Forts Sumter and Wagner,[11] and Battery Gregg. Fort Moultrie and the batteries on Johnson's Island joined in the affray, and the din was tremendous till half-past ten, when the fleet drew off.

Again, on the 23d, there was a furious combined assault by the fleet and the batteries, which did not, however, last very long, and then there was a lull for a week. Speaking of this last attack, the 'Charleston Mercury' of August 31st says:—"There are few who have known how fortunate for that fort was the inaction of the enemy. When the monitors drew off after their brief assault, in which their fire had been exceedingly accurate, Sumter was in a very precarious condition. If the fleet had then pushed

---

[11] To accompany his sketch "The Fight for the Rifle-Pits in Front of Battery Wagner, Charleston" Vizetelly wrote: "During the last days of August the enemy made a great struggle for the possession of the Confederate rifle-pits in front of their own works. In their attempt they were successfully repulsed; but on their second, the night after, they succeeded, owing to the bad conduct of some North Carolina troops, who were on picket. My sketch illustrates the first effort made to dislodge our troops, in which the Federals were defeated, with great loss. The entire garrison of Wagner, which is only a sandwork, never exceeded 1500, and this brave band defied the combined attacks of the Federal iron-clad navy and an army of twelve thousand men." *The Illustrated London News,* XLIII (1863), 574.

the bombardment with vigour, or if they had renewed it with determination after a brief interval, they would have penetrated the magazine, and, doubtless, have blown up the fort or compelled the garrison to surrender. As it happily turned out, the monitors withdrew before the destruction was complete. In the interval that has elapsed the powder has been taken care of, and the defences of the fort strengthened by sand-bags."

Sumter's chief power of offence lay in its barbette guns on the parapet, and in those of its upper casemates, which could pour a plunging fire upon any vessels approaching; thus giving it an advantage such as in throwing stones a man on a tower would have over an opponent on the ground below him.

Only a short time ago the fort was considered strong enough to defend the entrance of the harbour, and the works on the land were considered of small importance, but they have now been enormously strengthened and increased: indeed the whole shore on each side of the bay is lined with batteries, and the defenders of Charleston believe that no fleet could enter the inner harbour without being certainly destroyed.

Although it took little more than a week to knock Sumter into what is here metaphorically called a "cocked hat," yet as the walls fell and the bricks got pounded into dust, they covered the lower casemates with such a mass of debris as materially increased their strength; and in time, assisted by skilful engineering, the ruins of Sumter became stronger for internal defence than the untouched fort had ever been. The flag never ceased to float defiantly from its dilapidated walls, and the boom of its evening gun never failed at sunset to remind the Yankees that Fort Sumter would not be so easily given up to them as it had been taken from them.[12]

The Charlestonians are fully determined never to give up their city to the Yankees except in ruins, and have all provided themselves with the means of setting fire to their houses if by any mischance the place should become untenable.

I am told by those who have studied the science of arson, that half-a-dozen bottles of spirit of turpentine are sufficient to set the largest house in a blaze. A good many of the houses are what are called "frame houses"—that is, built of wooden planks—and almost all have a wooden piazza all round them, up to the top, which would greatly facilitate operations if extremities have to be resorted to, which I sincerely hope will not be the case.

All this time the weather was oppressively hot in the day-time, although now and then the rain would come down in torrents, for when it rains in this country it does pour! and then the air would be cooler for a few hours. The evenings, however, were delightful, and the sea-breezes on the Battery made it always a very pleasant promenade. Besides, there were "fireworks" in abundance there, but these we were soon to have a little closer than was agreeable.

One night we had retired to rest, and as I was dropping off to sleep a whizzing sound came rushing through

---

[12] In an article "An Inside View of the Siege of Charleston" published in *The Index* October 22, 1863 (III (1863), 411) "Personne" (Felix G. DeFontaine, a Confederate newspaperman) wrote: "Eight times the flagstaff has been shot away and replaced, and there it still floats—a symbol of the heroic determination of Colonel Alfred Rhett, its brave commander."

the air and roused me again; and when it was repeated a few minutes later, I knew that they were shelling the city. Scheibert, who was still reading in the next room, would not believe it at first; but the next shell which burst with a crash not far off, convinced him. We sallied out presently, and found that most of the inmates of the hotel had taken the alarm, and the hall was crowded. There was great excitement, and many were the maledictions on the Yankees.

Soon after V., who was staying at the Charleston Hotel, came in. There the consternation had been considerably greater than with us, as the very first shell had struck a house close by, and a sort of panic had been the result. Some had "stampeded" without waiting to dress, and had been seen with coats flying in one hand and pantaloons in the other, rushing frantically in the direction of the railroad depôt.[13]

I am bound to say that the inmates of our hotel

---

[13] Vizetelly sketched "The Federals Shelling the City of Charleston—Shells Bursting in the Streets" and elucidated his drawing with words: "The Federals as yet . . . have accomplished little or nothing as far as dash is concerned. In fact, General Gillmore, thwarted in his attempts on Battery Wagner and smarting at his frequent repulses, has demanded the surrender of the last-named work or has threatened to shell the city; and, in violation of all rules of warfare, he has turned his guns on unoffending women and children. The shelling commenced at midnight, but, fortunately, did little harm beyond terrifying the ladies left in the city. One house only was set on fire. I send you a sketch of a scene I witnessed in the neighbourhood of my own quarters. A fireman is running through the streets giving the alarm, and a watchman, thoroughly overcome, is taking leave of his senses and his staff in the foreground. Fortunately, the gun [the Swamp Angel] burst after a few discharges. The distance was over four miles." *The Illustrated London News,* XLIII (1863), 574.

behaved with entire dignity, and showed far more wrath and scorn at this cowardly attack of the Yankees, than any apprehensions of danger.

It was expected at first that houses would be set on fire by the exploding shells, as the Yankees had been boasting for some time of their "Greek fire;" [14] and the fire-engines rattling and jingling about the streets added to the excitement of the hour. Altogether it was a scene to be remembered. We walked down to the Battery, where a multitude had assembled. We could hear the whizz of the shells long before they passed over our heads, and I offered V. a thousand to one that a shell we heard coming would not hit either of us. He took the odds—forgetting that if he won he would have had but a small chance of realising his wager—and, of course, I won my dollar.

The shelling lasted scarcely more than an hour, and did little mischief. Next morning we heard of the "fair warning" General Gillmore had given of his intention to shell the city. It seems that at nine o'clock in the evening a note had been sent to the commanding officer at Fort Wagner to forward to General Beauregard, in which it was demanded that Fort Wagner, Fort Sumter, and the other defences of the harbour, should be immediately given up to the Yankees; if not, the city would be shelled. Four hours were graciously given to General Beauregard to make up his mind, and to remove women and children

[14] "Greek Fire" was an incendiary material devised by Leir Short of Buffalo, New York. A highly combustible substance was placed in small cylinders, several of which were then put in one shell and fired together. At the bursting of the shell the cylinders scattered and dropped fire over a large area. See Robert V. Bruce, *Lincoln and the Tools of War* (Indianapolis, 1956), pp. 179–82, 200–201, 241–44, 284.

to a place of safety. This note was entirely anonymous, no one having taken the trouble to sign it. It reached General Beauregard about midnight, and was of course returned for signature and without an answer. At half-past one the shelling commenced. No doubt General Gillmore wished that the effects of the bombardment should have their influence on General Beauregard before it was possible that he should give an answer to the summons. It was a "mean Yankee trick" says everybody.

It is rather an extraordinary proceeding, to say the least of it, to bombard the city because the harbour defences, which are three and four miles distant, cannot be taken; and the attempt to destroy it by Greek fire is very abominable; but the spite of the Yankees against Charleston, "the hotbed of the rebellion," is so intense that they would do anything to gratify it. Fortunately their Greek fire is a complete failure; some of it has been extracted from shells that had burst here, and it has been found difficult to ignite with a match.

Two days afterwards they commenced shelling again in the night, but this time everybody took it with remarkable coolness. They took their aim at the steeple of St. Michael's Church, which is only a few yards from Mills House Hotel, and we therefore regarded it as one of the safest places is Charleston; for to hit us would be making a sort of bull's-eye shot at 9000 yards, which is hardly to be expected. Their gun, which they call a swamp-angel, burst, and there was no more shelling for a long time.[15]

We made several more excursions into the country during our stay at Charleston, and as the planters take

[15] The 1863 campaign against Charleston is detailed in the *Official Records,* XXVIII.

great pleasure in showing and telling us all about their plantations, I had a pretty good opportunity of seeing the working of their system. The "hands," who have each and all a cottage allotted to them, with a "patch" to raise corn and vegetables and poultry, show every external sign of material happiness. They are well fed and well clothed, and sport as much finery on Sundays, and are as fond of doing so, as a millowner's "hands" in England.

When the market is dull, they are not put on half food, or none at all; nor do their masters, who enjoy the fruits of their industry, expect other people to support them in bad times. They are singularly attached to their masters, who invariably treat them with the greatest kindness. No clergyman's wife in England can be more conscientious in visiting the sick and aged amongst her husband's parishioners, reading the Bible to them, and furnishing them with medicine and little comforts, than are the ladies in the South in administering to the wants of the helpless amongst their own people. To exercise charity in this way is taught them as one of their first duties. That there is no disposition on the part of the negroes to rebel against the present system, has been clearly shown in the course of this war. At the commencement, many—wiled away by false representations, and foolishly thinking that the freedom promised them by the Yankees meant a total exemption from labour for all future time—did certainly run away and take refuge with the Yankees; but they have, most of them, bitterly repented of their mistake, and many have returned whenever they could find an opportunity. The Yankees "liberate" a great many, sorely against their will, wherever they penetrate, but that is to make soldiers of them.

There are, at the present time, thousands of plantations

where the only whites are women and children; and if the negroes were as wicked as many good people wish they were, nothing could prevent them from murdering their mistresses and the children, and escaping in bodies wherever and whenever they choose. But not a single instance of this kind has ever occurred. Some persons, especially in Virginia, have told me that they would be happy to be entirely without negroes, and that if the Yankees take it upon themselves to exterminate them—as they seem likely to do, to judge from what has happened in the regions where they have penetrated, where they generally make soldiers of the able-bodied men, and leave the worn-out ones with the women and children to starve—they would have no objection, as far as they themselves are concerned. But they object to be the agents of their destruction; and yet it would be intolerable to live side by side on terms of equality with a black population, almost equal in number, who should be under no control, and who, being utterly averse to labour, would pick up their living like gypsies in Europe. Eventually the negroes who have been raised from barbarism, and educated to work here, may become the means of Christianising and civilising their own race in Africa; and it ought not to be forgotten, that four millions of negroes have become Christians in the Southern States, whilst all the efforts of missionaries in Africa have not perhaps succeeded in converting 4000. To emancipate the negroes now, as the Abolitionists propose, would be an act of the greatest cruelty towards them, and would certainly in the end result in their extermination, just as the Red Indians, a far nobler race, have perished before them. For the fact of their having negroes amongst them, England, they say, and the Yankees are responsible; England for having insisted on their importation in spite of the repeated protestations of the colonies, and the Yankees for having carried on the trade.

It is a fact, that when the traffic in slaves from the coast of Africa to the United States was for ever prohibited by Act of Congress in 1808, this measure was carried by Southern against Northern votes; for the reason, that all the vessels engaged in the trade were fitted out from Yankee seaports, manned by Yankee seamen, and commanded by Yankee captains, so that the abolition of the traffic was in point of fact the destruction of the Yankee maritime interest. New Bedford, New Buryport [Newburyport], and Nantucket, all in Massachusetts, were the principal ports from which these vessels were fitted out.

It is worthy of remark that no act of absolute emancipation ever was adopted by any Northern State. When it became evident that slave labour was no longer profitable in the North, acts were passed at different times by the legislatures of the Northern States, naming a date in the future from and after which all negroes born within the limits of the respective States should be free; but care was taken to place the date at a sufficiently remote period, to enable the masters to dispose of able-bodied and valuable slaves to purchasers in the South, where their labour would be profitable. This was invariably done, and the superannuated and helpless alone remained to enjoy the benefit of this spurious philanthropy.

I doubt whether the country gentlemen in South Carolina would be entirely indifferent to the loss of their "hands," and I am quite sure that their "hands" would very much object to being exterminated if their opinions were asked.

The darkies are all very fond of music, singing, and dancing, and delighted to exhibit before strangers; but the performances of "Ethiopian serenaders" are so well known to everybody, that I need not describe them.

CHAPTER IX

Before we left Charleston the Yankees had succeeded in taking Fort Wagner and Battery Gregg, but not till they had brought up their parallels to within a few yards of Fort Wagner, so that they could almost jump from their own works into it. They then cannonaded it for thirty-six hours consecutively, during which the garrison lost a great many men, and would probably have stormed it earlier in the morning, had it not been evacuated during the night, together with Battery Gregg; Colonel Keitt,[1] who was in command, bringing off all his wounded, as well as the garrison of both places. They were to have been blown up, but by some mischance the trains did not explode the mines that had been laid.

An attempt was then made to storm Sumter, but it failed signally, and the

[1] Lawrence M. Keitt.

attacking party was taken instead of the fort. They had been confident of success, and had brought the identical stars and stripes with them which caused such a commotion at the beginning of the war, when it was first fired at, and which Major Anderson had been permitted to take away with him [2] when he surrendered. They had hoped to plant it again in triumph on the ruins of Sumter, but it was no go, and the celebrated flag fell definitely into the hands of the Confederates.[3]

Whilst we were at Charleston, it became evident that the next great events of the war would take place in the West, where Bragg was opposed to Rosencranz [Rosecrans], but had just been obliged to fall back from Chattanooga into Georgia. Longstreet's corps from Lee's army in Northern Virginia was being sent to reinforce Bragg, and an attempt was to be made to recover the ground that had been lost. Accordingly, on the 14th of September, V., Captain Byrne,[4] an Englishman in the Confederate service, and I, started together in that direction. A day's journey by rail took us to Augusta, a thriving inland city of some fifteen thousand inhabitants, on the Savannah river, which here becomes navigable.

Most of the goods which run the blockade into Charleston and Wilmington are sold by auction here, whence they are dispersed all over the interior.

---

[2] Robert Anderson.

[3] This flag was reflown over Sumter April 14, 1865. See Justus C. French's *The Trip of the Steamer Oceanus to Fort Sumter and Charleston, S. C., Comprising the . . . Programme of Exercises at the Re-raising of the Flag over the Ruins of Fort Sumter, April 14, 1865* (Brooklyn, 1865).

[4] C. H. Byrne.

We found several English friends in Augusta engaged in the blockade-running business, and a capital hotel; and as Longstreet himself, and the greater part of his corps, had not yet passed through on their way to the front, we were induced to remain several days in this pleasant little city. To judge from Augusta, no one would have supposed that two formidable armies were confronting each other within a twenty-four hours' journey. Every one seemed engrossed in business, and the shops were all plenteously filled with stores and customers. Soldiers, it is true, were passing through the place in large bodies, but we saw little of them, as they did not come into the city, but went to the front "right away."

The number of able-bodied civilians we saw here confirmed what I had been told before, that the supply of men for the army is far from being exhausted.

We had spent a few days very pleasantly, when we heard that Longstreet and his Staff had passed through in the night; and seeing that we had now no time to lose, we started early next morning. The cars were crowded inside and out, the roofs being covered with soldiers; but fortunately we met with General Jenkins, who, with his splendid brigade, was "hurrying up" to the front.

The General and his Staff had a small car to themselves, to which they made us welcome; and the journey to Atlanta, one hundred and seventy-one miles, passed off very agreeably.

We had plenty of room to move about, and to sit down —a great novelty in American travelling. We made several excursions into the ladies' car, for one can move from one car into another in this country, and any one does so who chooses, although it is "strictly prohibited;"

and Colonel Geary,[5] one of our party, discovered a Confederate captain in one of the ladies. Her husband was a major in the Confederate army, and she had taken an active part herself in the war, and fairly earned her epaulettes. She was no longer in uniform, having lately retired from the service, was young, good-looking, and lady-like, and told her adventures in a pleasant quiet way.[6] It was Sunday, and at every station crowds were collected to see the soldiers pass; and they cheered us with loud shouts, and waving of handkerchiefs and small Confederate flags by the ladies. The gaily-dressed and widely-grinning negroes were especially enthusiastic. At Atlanta the General found a telegram to hasten his arrival; so after taking supper at one of the hotels in the city, we continued our journey in an extra train; we therefore saw but little of the place which has since become so celebrated.

Atlanta is, or was, a new and thriving city, and had before the war 16,000 inhabitants, though but a few years ago the town and the whole surrounding region was wild unpopulated forest-land. There was a manufactory of small-arms here. Atlanta used to be called the "gate city,"

---

[5] Not identified.

[6] Fremantle too met a Confederate female soldier—on the train from Chattanooga to Atlanta. "A goodish-looking woman," he wrote, "was pointed out to me in the cars as having served as a private soldier in the battles of Perryville and Murfreesborough [Murfeesboro]. Several men in my car had served with her in a Louisianian regiment, and they said she had been turned out a short time since for her bad and immoral conduct. They told me that her sex was notorious to all the regiment, but no notice had been taken of it so long as she conducted herself properly. They also said that she was not the only representative of the female sex in the ranks. When I saw her she wore a soldier's hat and coat, but had resumed her petticoats." Fremantle, p. 174.

because all travellers by railroad from the north-east to the south-west, and from the north-west to the south-east, and *vice versâ,* had to pass through here. Now that all communication between the North and the South has been put an end to, it is of very little real consequence in whose hands the "gate" may temporarily be.

The night was very chilly; and indeed we found the climate here—and later in camp—very different from what we had left in Charleston and Augusta.

At daylight we came to a stop at Greenwood Mills, near Ringold [Ringgold], the railroad farther on having been broken up. The General immediately rode to the front, and we followed in the course of the morning with the brigade.

This brigade is probably now the finest in the Confederate army. Though belonging to Pickett's division, it was not in the Pennsylvania campaign, being at that time stationed at Petersburg, guarding the railroad communications of Richmond with the South, and holding the Yankees at Norfolk and in North Carolina in check. It has not had much fighting since the seven days around Richmond last year, and has been made exceedingly efficient by drill, discipline, and recruiting. General Jenkins has adopted an ingenious method of filling his ranks. He gives a two-months' leave to every soldier who procures him a recruit. Of course the soldiers write to their friends, who keep a sharp look-out in their neighbourhood for any able-bodied man who may be trying to evade the universal conscription, and very soon manage to catch one and send him up to the army; upon which the soldier in whose interest he has been sent, gets his leave. In this thinly-populated country it would require an army of agents to carry out the conscription regularly; but this method of enlisting the sympathy and assistance of the country-people works remarkably well.

On our march towards the front we met with many wounded men, who were getting back to the railway-station and the hospitals in the rear. All were in good spirits, as a splendid victory had been gained.

At Ringgold, an insignificant little town, the market-place was crowded with Yankee prisoners; there must have been thousands of them.

As we got towards the front, the news of yesterday's battle became more and more favourable. A courier we met gave us the information, which turned out to be incorrect, that the enemy had evacuated Chattanooga. Forrest had dashed in after them with his *calvary,* and captured a whole train of *avalanches.* In this part of the world all army-waggons are called *avalanches* (ambulances), and every mounted soldier is a *calvary*-man.

We reached Longstreet's headquarters, but the General was not there. The negro servants, however, were delighted to see us, and came up and shook hands, and were full of stories of the great success. We had walked a dozen miles, and, not knowing where to find our friends, we "concluded" to stay where we were all night. A tent was pitched for us, and we made ourselves very comfortable, and got plenty to eat.

I had been told a few days before that my horse, which I had left in Virginia with these headquarters, had been stolen; and I was very glad to hear that, though that had been the case, it had escaped from the thieves after twenty-four hours' *mancipation,* and would be at headquarters in a few days.

Next morning Captain Byrne, who is on Cleburne's Staff, left us in search of his General, whilst V. and I trudged off in the hope of finding General Longstreet's whereabouts.

We crossed the field of battle, which had been chiefly fought in dense woods; and the trees were barked to a degree which showed that the musketry-fire must have been intensely severe. Countless dead bodies still covered the ground, and parties were engaged in burying them. Small-arms were lying scattered about in all directions, though many had been collected, and we passed one place where there were large stacks of them; and we counted, besides, thirty-three cannon. The most horrible sight was outside some hospital tents, where amputations had been performed, and great piles of legs and arms were lying in heaps outside.

We had been very much disappointed at being too late for the battle; but I think what we saw to-day rather moderated our regret. We should have been able to see very little amongst the trees, and from the way in which the bullets had evidently been flying about, our own legs and arms would have stood a very good chance of adorning the outside of an hospital tent. Coming the day after, we were sure to see and hear and know quite as much about it as if we had been there. It was midnight before we reached Watkin's [Watkins'] House, where, after wandering about in many wrong directions, we at last discovered that we should find General Longstreet.

All were asleep except Captain Goree,[7] who welcomed us, and found us a couple of saddles for pillows.

We were very tired, and slept soundly till daylight, when we were roused by a furious shelling. For a quarter of an hour the shells flew about us fast and thick, but only two

[7] T. J. Goree.

men of the cavalry escort were hurt by them. One burst in General M'Laws's bed just after the General had left it.

All the negroes, who had built a large fire, and were cooking breakfast, "skedaddled," excepting General M'Laws's boy, who continued to prepare his master's morning meal, and afterwards made a cup of coffee for us all, which we found exceedingly refreshing. The boy was very proud of his performance, and spoke contemptuously of "dose d—— niggers running away." Nobody ever calls the negroes here niggers, except themselves; nor are they ever called slaves, but servants, or boys.

In the course of the morning a gigantic Texan brought in twenty-two Yankee prisoners. He had been down scouting with four other men in the woods by the side of the river, when they discovered a boat full of Yankees. They fired into them, and killed several, when the captain in command of the lot, with half-a-dozen others, jumped overboard, and the rest surrendered. The captain reached the opposite shore, but those who had jumped overboard with him were drowned.

The prisoners were halted for a short time at these quarters, and a ring of spectators soon formed round them. Amongst them was a negro lad of about fifteen, who, as soon as he saw himself amongst friends, got away from the other prisoners, and, standing apart, looked at them with the most superb disdain.

"I have nothing whatever to do with these Yankees," he said; "I have no use at all for them." On being questioned, he told us he belonged to Billy Buckner, over in Tennessee, and had been kidnapped by the captain who had escaped, and who had made him his servant.

"And what did he give you?"

"Never a cent! Oh the mean rascal!—just like a Yankee," &c. &c.

And here I may remark that Southerners are always exceedingly liberal in their largesses to servants, whilst the Yankees have the reputation of being the contrary.

The captured colours of the Yankees are to be sent to Richmond, and men from each corps are being elected to carry them there.

One sergeant, a handsome Mississippian from Vicksburg, had captured no less than three. "I don't take any credit for it, though," he said; "if they had been fifty yards off I should have run like a turkey." With a small party emerging from a thicket of wood he had come close upon a large body of Yankees. "Shall we surrender?" suggested one or two of the party. "By no means," said their gallant leader; and he called on the Yankees to do so, saying there was a brigade in the wood behind him, towards which he beckoned with his hand, calling out, "Don't fire, don't fire, they are going to surrender:" and, sure enough, they did so. The fine young fellow told his story in a modest, straightforward, manly way, and got more credit for his exploit than he claimed.

We had, I am happy to say, found all our old friends safe, except Colonel Manning,[8] who had been badly, but not dangerously, hurt. All attributed the grand success on Sunday to Longstreet. There had been some sharp fighting on Friday, and a pitched battle on Saturday, in which only Hood with five brigades had been engaged. The action had not been decisive, but on Saturday night Longstreet came up with part of M'Laws's division. He took command of the left wing of Bragg's army, worked all

[8] P. T. Manning.

night, and, in spite of the hard fighting of the day before in the woods, where naturally brigades and regiments had become excessively entangled, by the morning of Saturday his command was in perfect order, and when the fight began had it all their own way. Polk and Hardie [Hardee] were repulsed in the morning, and for some hours the right wing of the army was entirely inactive, which enabled the enemy to send reinforcements against Longstreet; but these, too, were caught and scattered almost before they reached those they were to support, and by nightfall—Polk and Hardee advancing again—the whole Yankee army was completely routed. *"They have fought their last man, and he's running,"* said Longstreet.

He was much disappointed that they were not more hotly pursued. Wheeler's cavalry, which Longstreet had sent off for that purpose, were recalled and ordered to pick up the small-arms scattered on the battle-field. Longstreet says that the Yankees were never before so completely routed, not even at the first battle of Manassas (Bull's Run). There was a prevalent idea before this battle that the Yankee Western army fought better than the army of the Potomac; but Longstreet says that such is decidedly not the case: at any rate, his men made as short work of them as ever they did in Virginia. He has not as high an opinion of Rosecrans as General Bragg has, and says he is about equal to Pope, of boasting memory.

General Buckner came over in the course of the morning, and he too attributed the victory entirely to Longstreet. His own corps behaved splendidly, and one regiment belonging to it in General Gracie's brigade, of General Preston's division, the second battalion of the Alabama Legion, had its battle-flag shot through eighty-three times. The same man bore it through the whole fight, and was wounded three times. I saw it a few days afterwards and counted the holes. The flag was shown to the President when he visited the army a short time afterwards, and the bearer was promoted.

With General Buckner came his chief engineer, a wicked Frenchman called Noquet [Nocquet],[9] who some time afterwards, just before the battle of Missionary Ridge, absconded to the Yankees at Chattanooga, after robbing the army-chest of 150,000 dollars; and made himself agreeable there by giving valuable information as to Bragg's position and works. He was very loquacious, and abused General Bragg considerably.

In the afternoon Longstreet's headquarters baggage arrived, and his camp was pitched in a clump of trees by the side of Chattanooga Creek, half a mile to the rear of Watkins' House; it was a charming spot as long as the weather remained fine. In the evening General Wheeler came in and had a long consultation with Longstreet. There was a great deal of shelling at night, but we were now out of range. A report came in that the Yankees were evacuating Chattanooga, but it turned out to be untrue. "No matter, it is not like your Charleston," Longstreet said to me, "which there is only one way of getting at. We can go where we want to go without touching Chattanooga." But General Bragg, as it turned out, thought differently. In the mean time the Yankees were strengthening it, and very soon made it impregnable. There was no doubt, too, that they would be reinforced before very long, so that many people were impatient that something should be done. Last year, after a decided victory at Murfreesboro', where many prisoners and guns had been captured,

---

[9] James Nocquet.

Bragg tried to follow up his advantage, but Rosecrans held on, and he did not succeed, but lost very heavily in the attempt. It was on this occasion that Rosecrans is said to have repeated the proverb, "Brag is a good dog, but Holdfast is a better." [10] The recollection of Murfreesboro', no doubt, had great influence upon General Bragg, and induced him to be more cautious after Chicamauga than the army expected. Immediately after the battle it had been determined, at a council of war, to march straight upon Knoxville, which would undoubtedly have obliged the Yankees to fall back. Polk's corps had already marched ten miles in that direction, and the rest of the army was following, when General Bragg changed his mind and countermanded the order. The army was to march directly upon Chattanooga. Longstreet sent M'Laws on with his division, with orders to march straight into the place. M'Laws marched, looked at it, didn't like it, skirmished, and sent back to say the place was too strong; he could not take it; he had already lost a few men wounded. "I wish he had lost a thousand," said Longstreet, impatiently; and, indeed, subsequent events proved that the capture of Chattanooga would have been well worth such a sacrifice. The place could undoubtedly have been taken immediately after the battle, with small loss: the Yankees were then in no humour for fighting, and they would certainly not have made any stand again before they

---

[10] Mrs. James Chesnut, the diarist of Confederate high life in South Carolina and Richmond, referred to the same proverb in her inimitable record of the war. "There," she quipped, "sat Bragg like a good dog, howling on his hind legs before Chattanooga, and some Yankee Holdfast grinning at him from his impregnable heights." Mary Boykin Chesnut, *A Diary from Dixie* (Boston, 1949), p. 307.

reached Nashville. As it was, a few days sufficed for them to regain their spirits, and make an impregnable stronghold of what had been an almost open place.

A week after the battle of Chicamauga, Longstreet still thought it was not too late to make some profit out of the hitherto barren victory by a flank movement; but as the time wore away it became evident that nothing would be done, and that the army had fought and bled in vain. "The battle of Chicamauga," says General P.,[11] "was badly planned, splendidly executed, and fruitless in its results." Longstreet, like all favourite generals, is familiarly spoken of by his men by several names with which his godfathers and godmothers at his baptism had nothing to do. He is generally called "Old Peter," sometimes the "Old Warhorse." Since the battle of Chicamauga, which was fought in a dense forest, the men out here have christened him "Bull of the Woods."

Our camp lies at the foot of Lookout Mountain, so called from the magnificent and extensive view one has from the top of it. My horse had not arrived, but General Buckner was so good as to send horses both for myself and V., and we rode half-way up the mountain to a farmhouse, and thence scrambled up to the top of a rock called the Pulpit, where a party of the signal corps were stationed. From thence we had a most splendid panoramic view of the plain and lesser hills beneath us. We could see Chattanooga and the Yankee camps, and with a good glass were able clearly to distinguish every individual soldier. We could trace the position of the Confederate camps, though the army was now hidden from our view by trees, which,

---

[11] This could be General Leonidas Polk, General John Pegram, or, more likely, General William Preston.

however, were afterwards pretty well cleared away for firewood.

Riding back, we visited General Jenkins at his quarters. His brigade had been employed to clear Lookout Mountain of the Yankees, and the General had been struck by a piece of shell just on the bridge of the nose, and had consequently two rather black eyes; but it was providential that it was no worse. The piece of shell had struck with the round smooth part, and so did not penetrate; if a jagged end had hit him it might have been fatal, instead of which, though dreadfully stunned, he got off with a few days' headache.

We rode on to General Buckner's quarters, where we dined. I met here Colonel von Scheliha,[12] the General's Chief of Staff, many of whose relations I had known in Europe, and we had a long chat together. General Buckner is a Kentuckian, and so are most of his Staff: they are all splendidly mounted on Kentuckian horses—a very fine breed. On the whole, the horses here are much finer and larger than those I saw in Virginia, which are nevertheless excellent. Their docility is extraordinary—I never saw a vicious horse the whole time I was in the South. Every officer or courier coming to a camp will tie his horse's reins to a branch or twig of a tree, and the animal will stand quietly for hours without even attempting to get away. Dr Morton,[13] of Buckner's Staff, was with the Russians in Sebastopol, and related many interesting incidents of the siege. Among other things he told me that the engineer in charge of building the Malakoff, in spite of Todleben's plan being to the contrary, made it difficult

[12] Victor von Scheliha.

[13] Not identified.

of access behind, to which the Russians attributed their not having been able to retake it as they did the Redan. As it was very dark, we remained the night at General Buckner's quarters. There were no tents, so we all had to camp out. The weather is getting very cold, but we had a roaring fire and plenty of blankets. Next morning we rode with Major Johnstone [Johnston] [14] and Dr Morton, of General Buckner's Staff, to General Bragg's head-quarters, and were presented to the Commander-in-Chief. He told us that the reason he had fallen back from Chattanooga a short time ago was, that he had hoped to capture a Yankee corps of 25,000 men that was trying to flank him, and said that we should advance as soon as his preparations were completed. In the course of the afternoon we met and were introduced to a good many of the Generals of this Western army; Breckenridge [Breckinridge], Walker, Preston, Gracie, Mackall, Lidell [Liddell, Cleburne, &c. &c. General Cleburne—Pat Cleburne his soldiers call him—is an Irishman, and was formerly in the British army. He is in high repute as a "fine fighter." Breckinridge, although not a soldier by profession, has established a very good reputation as a general during this war, before which he took a prominent part in politics, and was the Southern candidate for the Presidency of the United States in opposition to Lincoln. He is a Kentuckian, and so is General Preston, formerly United States Minister to Spain. General Preston, whose camp is on Missionary Ridge, just above Buckner's, and from whence there is a commanding view of Chattanooga and the Yankee camps opposite, pointed out the different positions to us, and explained the conformation of the country beyond. The Yan-

---

[14] William Y. Johnston.

kees were working away at their intrenchments like beavers, and all say their works are getting too strong to be stormed. General Preston's division, though some of his troops were under heavy fire for the first time, distinguished itself very much indeed in the late battle.

We were very fortunate in having tents at our headquarters, though some of them were rather crowded. I am, for instance, in the same tent with Majors Fairfax [15] and Latrobe, and Captain Dunne,[16] each of whom is at least six feet high, and broad in proportion; and as the tent is only intended for two, we have to squeeze. It is universal here to mess in small parties, not more numerous than one servant can cook for, so our headquarters are divided into two messes. The General and my tentmates form one; and Colonel Sorrel, Major Walton, Captains Goree and Dawson,[17] with V., the other. Captain Dawson

---

[15] John W. Fairfax.

[16] Not identified.

[17] Francis Warrington Dawson. Dawson published his own memoirs in 1882. Of the visit to Chicamauga by Vizetelly and Ross he wrote:

"Frank Vizetelly, the artist and correspondent of the *Illustrated London Times* [*News*], joined us here; and with him was Captain Ross, of the Austrian service. Ross was of Scotch descent, but was born in Austria [wrong], and belonged to one of the crack light cavalry regiments. There was a good deal of merry-making, and it was no uncommon thing to see a half dozen officers, late at night, dancing the "The Perfect Cure," which was one of the favorite songs of the day in the London music halls, and was introduced to our notice by Vizetelly.

"There was sharp discussion occasionally as to what should take place when the war should be over and the independence of the Confederate States was assured. Major Walton I had always disliked heartily, and in one of our conversations he said that, when the Confederate States enjoyed their own government, they

is an Englishman, and acts as Chief of Ordnance in the place of Colonel Manning, who was wounded the other day. With his assistance I made the following note about the artillery in the Confederate armies. The field-piece most generally employed is the smooth-bored 12-pound "Napoleon" (*canon obusier*), which fires solid shot, shell, case, and canister: it is much lighter than the ordinary 12-pounder, and they can give it an elevation of nine to ten degrees. Then there are 10 and 20 pound Parrotts, named after their inventor, or rather manufacturer, Parrott of New York; they are rifled guns, with a wrought-iron band at the breach; their bore is 2.90. Those in this army are chiefly captured from the Yankees, but some are made at the Tredegar Works at Richmond; they throw solid bolts, shell, case, and canister. The 3-inch rifled gun is very similiar; and the best of these, too, are taken from the enemy.

---

did not intend to have any 'd——d foreigners' in the country. I asked him what he expected to become of men like myself, who had given up their own country in order to render aid to the Confederacy. He made a flippant reply, which I answered rather warmly, and he struck at me. I warded off the blow, and slapped his face. The next morning I sent him a challenge by Captain Ross. Walton, however, did not want a fight at this time, and offered to make an apology in writing. A day or two passed, and as no apology came I sent Ross to him again. Walton now took the position that he had been hasty in his action, and that if he had not promised to do it he would not make an apology at all. Ross told him quietly, in his quaint way, that he must please consider everything blotted out that had taken place since he had borne the challenge, and that we would begin it again at that point and settle the affair in any way that Walton preferred. This brought Walton to terms, and he made the apology I required." F. W. Dawson, *Reminiscences of Confederate Service, 1861–1865* (Charleston, S. C., 1882), pp. 102–103.

In Northern Virginia 12-pound howitzers and 6-pounder guns are discarded, and Napoleons have been cast from their metal; here there are still a large number, and a few 24-pounder howitzers. Colonel Alexander [18] thinks highly of these last. Opinions are divided as to the merits of Napoleon's [Napoleons,] Parrotts, and 3-inch rifled guns; but for general use, almost all consider the Napoleon most serviceable. There are a few Whitworth guns, which are very accurate and of great range, but require much care. The breech has sometimes been blown off or disabled through carelessness in loading. This was especially the case with breech-loading guns. I understand that the Whitworth guns which are now sent out are muzzle-loading guns. Their field-ammunition the Confederates consider to be far superior to that of the Yankees. Spherical case (shell filled with musket-balls) is the most successful projectile they use.

In the Pennsylvania campaign, General Longstreet had with him

Napoleons, ...	40
10-lb. Parrotts, ...	15
3-inch rifled, ...	15
20-lb. Parrotts, ...	4
12-lb. howitzers, ...	5
20-lb. do.	4
	83 guns.

Considered as good an armament as could be wished for, excepting the 12-pound howitzers, which ought to have been replaced by Napoleons.

[18] E. Porter Alexander.

The artillery is organised into battalions; five battalions in a corps of three divisions, one to each division, and two in reserve. They always mass the artillery now, and commanders of battalions say that they lose no more men in a battalion than they formerly did in a single battery. Each battalion is complete in itself, with quartermaster, adjutant, ordnance officer, surgeon, &c. The whole is under the control of the chief of artillery of the army, but assigned at convenience to the corps commanders, one of whose staff-officers is chief of artillery to the corps, and another chief of ordnance.

The duty of the chief of ordnance is to supply the guns and everything for their equipment, with ammunition and stores of every description, excepting horses and provisions.

The chief of artillery places them in action, and commands them there.

Colonel Walton is chief of artillery to General Longstreet's corps; but as he is now at Petersburg with the reserve, his place is occupied by Colonel Alexander.

Colonel Manning is chief of ordnance; and as he is wounded, Captain Dawson supplies his place. The chief of artillery to an army is a brigadier-general; to a corps, a colonel; and to a division, a major.

The chief of ordnance to an army is usually a lieutenant-colonel, and has two captains as assistants; to a corps, a major, with a lieutenant as assistant; and the divisional ordnance officer is a captain. The ordnance officers of brigades and artillery battalions are generally majors, but some are lieutenant-colonels.

The principal small-arms in use are the smooth-bore musket, 0.69; the Enfield rifle, bore 0.57; the Springfield (Illinois) [*sic*] rifle, 0.58—the same ammunition does for both the last named; the Mississippi rifle (U. S. make), 0.54; Austrian rifle, 0.24; with foresighted bayonet.

In Pennsylvania, Lee's army, with the exception of Hood's division, was armed with Enfield and Springfield rifles. The uniform calibre of 0.57 and 0.58 will be adopted in the whole army as soon as possible. Three-fourths of the arms in the armies of the West are smooth-bore muskets and Austrian rifles; and some think smooth-bored muskets for eight companies out of ten, with rifles for the other two, flanking companies, a very good armament.

The Enfield is the best rifle. The Mississippi and Austrian rifle clog very soon—*i.e.,* after twenty rounds.

I may say here that I never saw a breech-loader in the hands of a Southern soldier, nor were ever any large numbers taken from the Yankees. If they had been, they would certainly have been brought and shown at head-quarters, as was the case with some Spencer rifles and a good lot of revolving six-shooter rifles, and some excellent breech-loading cavalry carbines.

Attached to each corps were some picked sharpshooters, armed with a telescopic Whitworth rifle, with which they did great execution. I never at any arsenal saw machinery or appliances for turning muzzle-loaders into breech-loaders, or heard that such an operation had ever been performed.

Dr Cullen was so good as to furnish me with the following note upon medical matters. The medical department is organised thus:—Medical director of the army; medical director of the army corps; chief surgeon of division; senior surgeon of brigade. Each regiment has a surgeon, an assistant-surgeon, two ambulances, and a medical waggon, belonging to it. Two men from each company are detailed to act as litter-bearers and attendants upon the wounded: these follow the troops on the field of battle, and convey men to the hospitals in the rear. The flap operation is generally performed. Resections of the humerus at the elbow and shoulder joints are done hundreds of times with great success.

By the by, Dr Cullen showed me the returns to his department for the month of August of the year, from which it appears that in the whole of Longstreet's corps in the field there was but one death during that period, and that was a man who had just returned from a Yankee prison, bringing the seeds of disease with him. This month of August was so oppressively hot, that all operations between the opposing armies of Lee and Meade were suspended. This is a very remarkable fact, and shows what good stuff the Confederate soldiers are made of. It must be remembered that the month of August followed immediately after a very severe campaign, where the men had been exposed to many and great hardships from forced marches, bad weather, unequal food, &c.

Thirty-five years ago, the whole country about Chattanooga, down nearly to Atlanta in Georgia, was inhabited by Indians, chiefly Cherokees: and there are a good many still scattered over the mountainous regions of North Carolina, Georgia, and Tennessee, but the majority were induced to emigrate beyond the Mississippi. In the Indian territory set apart for them in the West, the Choctaws, Chickasaws, Creeks, and Cherokees especially have become quite civilised, and are wonderfully thriving. They have some of the best cotton ground in their territory, and are large slave-owners; and many of them are very wealthy. They have churches and public schools, and their native eloquence having been developed by education, some have become famous preachers. Their greatest bane is whisky: and though the Government makes great efforts to prevent it, the traders still succeed in smuggling it in. In this war they have almost all taken the side of the South.

The chief of the Cherokees is John Ross, whose grandfather emigrated hither from Scotland and married an Indian squaw. An old gentleman, whom we met at the top of Lookout Mountain, told us that he had known him well some fifty years since; that he was a very clever man, and had had his children well educated at Nashville in Tennessee. His residence was at Rossville, which is in the centre of our present camp, the Cherokees having in his day inhabited this part of the country. The dignity of chief of that nation has now been hereditary for three generations.

After a few sunshiny days we had some pouring wet ones; it was found that our camp was on too low ground to be comfortable, and we removed some distance to the rear.

By this time Dr Cullen had arrived from Richmond, and with him came L.; and as Dr Cullen had—besides his own tent and those of the other staff doctors who had not yet arrived—a large hospital tent, large enough to accommodate twenty people, I thought I had crowded my friends long enough, and accepted his kind invitation to move over and take up my old quarters again with him.

Old Jeff, the cook, was rather in a grumbling mood. "This is not like old Virginny, sir; I shall find it very hard to keep up my dignity here, sir;" his dignity consisting in providing us good breakfasts and dinners. And, indeed, provisions are scarce and not very good. Beef is tough, bacon is indifferent, and mutton is rarely to be had: chickens and eggs are almost unheard-of delicacies, and we have to ride ten miles to get a pat of butter.

During anything like a long stay in one camp all energies very soon tend to the point of how to improve the diet, and many long rides are taken with that sole object in view, and with very various success.

If any one can boast of a leg of mutton, he considers it quite a company dish, to which friends must be invited. One of the most successful caterers is General Preston, and another is his adjutant-general, Major Owens, an old friend, who in Virginia was aide to Colonel Walton. Owens is believed to have a flock of sheep hidden away somewhere. The General gave us a splendid supper one evening, with a profusion of delicate viands, and more than one bowl of hot punch made of some capital peach-brandy.

Our own little camp was particularly well off, as Cullen came pretty well provided, and L. brought a box of good things with him from Richmond. No schoolboys can hail a hamper of prog with more gratification than a hungry lot of campaigners do, especially if they have been *tee-totalling* rather more than they like.

After a victory in Virginia there had always been a profusion of delicacies in the Confederate camp for a long time, but from these Western people nothing had been captured but guns and empty waggons, at which there was great disappointment; and many were quite indignant, thinking themselves cheated. "Why, these Yankees are not worth killing," said General ——; "they are not a bit better off than ourselves."

L., after having one horse stolen at Richmond, had purchased another at Atlanta,[19] and as mine had arrived with Cullen we had many a ride together. The camp was pretty extensive, and it was a three of four miles' ride to visit many of our friends.

There was grand bombardment of Chattanooga one day, of which we had a splendid view from the top of Lookout Mountain. Not much harm was done, but it was a grand sight to see the guns blazing away far below us. On the top of the mountain is a large hotel, besides several villas and cottages. This used to be a favourite gathering-place in summer, but now every dwelling-place was deserted.

We made our way into the hotel, and purchased half-a-dozen chairs from an old woman, who said they were not hers and that she had nothing to do with them; but she took our money and made our consciences easy. And the chairs were very useful.

About this time the President came to pay a visit to the camp, and there was a general expectation that a change would take place; but none came, except in the weather, which had been dry and sunshiny, with a storm or a shower now and then, but now settled down to be wet and cold and nasty.[20]

---

19 "The Confederate soldier, in spite of his many virtues, is, as a rule, the most incorrigible horse-stealer in the world." Fremantle, p. 239.

20 *The Index* for November 5, 1863 (III (1863), 436) reported —in a dispatch from Richmond, probably written by John R. Thompson, dated October 10: "The President left Richmond three days ago for the seat of war in Tennessee, for the purpose, as some say, of inquiring into the misunderstanding which has arisen between the generals of our army there. . . . It is more likely that the object of the President's journey is to get a look for himself at the situation of affairs before Chattanooga, and to confer with

The President remained two days, and on the second day went with a large suite to Lookout Mountain. Homewards he rode with General Longstreet, a hundred yards in advance of the rest of the party, and they had a long confabulation, and, I believe, not a very satisfactory one. I rode with General Breckinridge, with whom, and General Custis Lee, I dined afterwards at General Gracie's. After dinner we had some capital singing by some young fellows in Gracie's brigade.

Going home, I fell in with a courier who was riding in the same direction. He was a Louisianian, and we had a long chat together. Amongst other things, he told me that if he met a negro in a fight, he should give him no quarter—that they had always treated the negroes well, and if they fought against them now, they deserved no quarter, and he, for one, should give them none. I remonstrated, saying, it was no fault of the negro that he was forced to fight by the Yankees, and that he never would fight if he could help it, &c. To all which my friend assented, with a "That's so," and I thought that I had made a convert; but when I had exhausted my arguments, although he again repeated his "That's so," he added, "For all that, I shan't give them any quarter."

Our black cook, Jeff, confided to me the other day his idea as to how the war should be carried on.

"Why, sir, why don't they do now as they used formerly

---

our military leaders upon the future conduct of the Western campaign."

Serious dissension had arisen in Bragg's staff, opposition to him being headed by General Polk. War Clerk Jones wrote on October 8: "The question now is, who is right? If it be [Polk], Bragg ought certainly to be relieved without delay; and the President cannot arrive in the field a moment too soon." Jones, II, 66.

to do? The generals used to dine together, and take their wine, and then one would say, 'General, I'll fight you to-morrow at such and such a place,' and then they would shake hands, and the next day they would fight their battle. That's what Napoleon used to do," Jeff concluded, "and why don't they do so now?"

A month after the battle of Chicamauga, we rode over the field of battle, which is seven or eight miles to the rear of our camp. The Yankee dead are still unburied, which is a great shame.

Perhaps General Thomas thinks it beneath his dignity to ask permission to bury them; or perhaps he thinks General Bragg will do it for him. This, however, he has no right to expect, as he is little more than a mile further from the battle-field than Bragg, who, if he sent large details of men eight miles to the rear whilst active operations are going on, would just as much have to demand a truce for the purpose as General Thomas, whose business it is. Besides, these poor fellows' friends will be very anxious that they should be identified, that they may know where to find their graves. If there be one good feeling to be found in the North, it is the respect they show to their dead; and doubtless, if these poor fellows had been identified and properly buried, very many of them would have been brought to their homes after the war, and their bones laid amongst their own kindred. Now the pigs are fattening on them—a disgusting sight to behold.

The rains had become continuous now, and the roads were nearly impassable for waggons, and no movements of importance could therefore be anticipated. The army was in a bad way. Insufficiently sheltered, and continually drenched with rain, the men were seldom able to dry their clothes; and a great deal of sickness was the natural consequence. Few constitutions can stand being wet through for a week together; and, moreover, the nights were bitterly cold, and the blankets were almost as scarce as tents. There was a great deal of discontent, which was increased by its being well known that General Bragg was on very bad terms with many of his generals.

The weather made it disagreeable to move about, and L., V., and I resolved to leave the army, and on the 22d of October we bade farewell to our friends, and rode over to Chicamauga station, some eight miles off.

The road, over which the army drew all its supplies, was in a horrible state, and it was five o'clock in the evening before the cart with our small amount of luggage arrived.

The trains were running wild—that is to say, at no fixed hours—and nobody could say when, or whether, any more would start that evening, several having just left, crowded with sick soldiers.

We sat down rather disconsolate by the side of a lot of empty cars, which were guarded by a soldier, who was whistling merrily, with his hands in his pockets. Soon we made friends with him, and he promised us his assistance as soon as his guard should be up.

Accordingly, when he was relieved, he took me with him, leaving L. and V. to guard our traps, promising to introduce me to the stationmaster, and "fix everything straight," which he did. He then insisted on my taking supper with him, which I was very glad to do. He told me that he came from Memphis, and that, at the commencement of the war, his regiment had been reviewed by Lord John Russell, whose stately appearance on horseback had impressed him very favourably. I tried to explain that he might be mistaken, but he was positive, and I only succeeded in so far shaking his belief as to leave him with the idea that the gentleman he had admired was Lord William Russell, a brother to the famous Earl. He was determined not to be balked of his nobleman; but I suppose I need hardly say that the gentleman he alluded to was the well-known William Russell, correspondent of the 'Times.'

He was exceedingly obliging and useful to us; and by eight o'clock we were packed into a luggage-van, and on our way.

It poured with rain, and plenty of water came trickling down through the roof.

One of our fellow-sufferers, a major, had provided himself with a plentiful supper of bread and beef, and offered us some; but L. and V., although they had had no supper, were modest, and declined. After the major had gone to sleep, however, they changed their minds, and picked his pocket, and ate up the last morsel of his provisions.

We travelled a few miles, and reached Cleveland early in the morning. Here the train came to a dead stop, and did not move on till the afternoon. We allayed our hunger during the day with some parched corn and gingerbread, procured from a cottage at hand, and in the evening reached Dalton, where we had supper, and got into the regular train for Atlanta and Augusta.

We were near being stopped by a stupid sentinel, because our passports were signed by Longstreet, and not by Bragg; but Captain Mackall,[21] a nephew and aide of the General of the name, helped us through our difficulty,

---

[21] T. B. Mackall.

and we reached Augusta on the evening the the next day without further trouble. Here we thought ourselves entitled to a good rest, and made ourselves comfortable at the Planters' Hotel.

The largest powder-mills in the South are at Augusta. They, as well as the arsenal, are under the superintendence of Colonel Rains, who is inexhaustible in his ingenious contrivances to overcome the want of hundreds of things necessary to his manufacture, and yet hardly to be procured in the South.

The mills turn out 8400 lb. of powder in thirteen hours. In fifteen hours, over 10,000 lb. have been made. They began to work on April the 27th, 1862, and since then one and a half million of pounds of powder have been sent to Richmond alone. At the present time most of the powder is sent to Charleston, which, with its many heavy guns, consumes an enormous amount.

Percussion-caps used to be imported from the North, and we saw a lot which had been manufactured at some place in Connecticut, but they are already independent of the enemy for this important article. At one time so many were sent from the North that they were absolutely a drug in the market. The charcoal is excellent, being made of cotton-wood, a sort of white poplar, which has no knots like the willow. Of sulphur they had large stores when the war commenced; and saltpetre is imported a good deal through the blockade.

The powder-magazines are under ground, and are, moreover, divided above ground by thick brick traverses. The roofs are of zinc, and very light; so that if one magazine blows up, it cannot set fire to its neighbours.

We were much struck with the powder made for the

enormous Blakely guns at Charleston. A charge of this powder looks more like a bag of coals than anything else, each grain being as big as a hen's egg.

The guard duty at the powder-mills is done by lads of from 16 to 18 years of age, of whom there is a battalion of 500 at Augusta.

Another day, Colonel Rains obligingly lending us his carriage, we visited the old U. S. Arsenal, a couple of miles from the city, where small-arm ammunition, percussion-caps, hand-grenades with sensitive tubes, &c., were being made up under the superintendence of Captain Finny [Finney].[22] Small-arms had been made here, but the workshops were being removed to the city for the convenience of transport. We also went over the Government cannon-foundry, which is under the personal superintendence of Colonel Rains. The Colonel informed us that he could turn out a Napoleon a-day here, but at present it was not necessary. In addition to the cannon captured from the enemy, the Confederates had manufactured and imported above a thousand since the war commenced. They were then making Napoleons of Austrian metal—a composition of copper, tin, wrought-iron, and zinc, very strong and very light, and had already turned out seventy.

Colonel Rains uses a polygonal core of sand and clay in manufacturing his hollow projectiles, which, by weakening the iron in regular lines, causes a round shell to burst into eleven, and a conical shell for rifled guns into nineteen, regular sections.

Colonel Rains told us that Colonel Bunford was the real inventor of the Dahlgren, and Captain Blakeley

---

[22] R. H. Finney.

[Blakely] of the Parrott gun.[23] One of the big Blakely guns at Charleston had been seriously damaged at the first discharge, and the Colonel was one of the committee to inquire into the cause, and made the report on it.[24]

It seems that there was an air-chamber to permit the gas, on explosion, to obtain its full force in the gun—a new invention—and this air-chamber having been stuffed full of powder, the misfortune occurred. The gun has, however, been repaired, and the second one worked satisfactorily from the commencement.[25]

The "stores" at Augusta are excellent, and well supplied; but the bookseller was a queer fellow. I wished to buy one of his books, but he refused to sell it. "Can't let you have that, sir; it's my last copy."

There is a very good theatre here, where they play every night. The Planters' Hotel is an excellent one, everything good except the tea, which was so weak, that V. wondered how it could get out of the spout.

So mild was the weather that, on the 1st of November, we followed the example of other inmates of the hotel, and sat in the balcony with our coats off.

---

[23] The Blakely gun is described in Edward S. Farrow's *Farrow's Military Encyclopedia* (New York, 1895; 3 vols.), I, 186; the Parrott gun, II, 485–86. Charles Bunker Dahlgren discusses the Dahlgren gun in *The Dahlgren Shell-Gun and Its Services During the Late Civil War* (Trenton, N. J., 1887).

[24] Published as *Second Report of the Board of Artillery Officers, Assembled at Augusta, Georgia, by Special Orders No. 278, Headquarters, Dep't S. C., Ga. & Fla., Dated December 19th, 1863 . . . (n.p., 1864).*

[25] A slightly less comprehensive account of Augusta and its powder works appears in Fremantle, pp. 176–78. Rains himself later published a *History of the Confederate Powder Works,* by Col. (General) Geo. W. Rains . . . (Augusta, Ga., 1882).

CHAPTER X

We spent a full week at Augusta, and then L. left us, going straight to Richmond, and V. and I went to Charleston.

We found the city unchanged, except that, since the occupation of the whole of Morris Island by the Yankees, blockade-running had pretty well come to an end, though it recommenced somewhat later.

There had been some intermission in the shelling of the city, and the Yankees had been engaged in turning Fort Wagner and Battery Gregg to their own account, and were now from thence pounding away at Sumter. I made an excursion to this place one night with Major Pringle,[1] the quartermaster, who had to furnish its supplies. It happened that the Yankees were particularly attentive that night, and shelled us considerably. They had got a calcium light on the point of Morris

[1] Motte A. Pringle.

Island nearest the fort, which threw such a brilliant glare all around it that we could not approach in a steamer, but had to take to a row-boat. As we neared the fort and got within the range of the calcium light, where it was as clear as day, they fired at us furiously—being about three-quarters of a mile distant; but we made good haste to reach the fort, and scrambled into it as fast as we could, without any accident.

Here, in the bomb-proof, we were of course perfectly safe; and indeed casualties now seldom occur except through heedlessness on the part of the men. To-day, however, two men were killed and a few wounded. One poor fellow was brought in with half his head shot off; and going out into the area with Major Elliot [Elliott],[2] the commandant, a man met us coming in with his jaw broken.

This night they were firing chiefly with mortar shells, which look magnificent as they soar majestically up in air to a great height, and then slowly descend.

N.B.—If you are anywhere near, and look up, they appear as if they were coming straight towards you, and must inevitably hit the very spot where you are standing.

In the fort there is always plenty of time to get out of way, and whenever one is seen coming the sentinels give warning to "look out." The sentinels themselves generally have a place to dodge into; but on dark nights many have to be posted in insecure places to guard against an assault.

The bomb-proofs at Sumter are lofty, well ventilated, and perfectly secure. The shot from the Parrott guns have brass "fixings," and the men make little fortunes by collecting and selling it for a dollar the pound.

---

[2] Stephen Elliott, Jr.

We made an excursion to Summerville, some twenty miles from Charleston, where there is a large hotel and a number of country residences. Standing in the midst of a magnificent pine-forest, Summerville was always a favourite resort of the Charlestonians during the hot season, and at present it is crowded with refugees. It is said to be remarkably healthy.

From hence we visited Middleton Place, on the Ashley river, a good specimen of a gentleman's country-seat in South Carolina. The residences of the gentry in the South cannot, of course, compare with the "stately homes of England," as property is here usually divided on the death of the owner; and however wealthy a man may be, he cannot reckon upon his grandchildren being able to inhabit a house which may be suitable for his own establishment and style of living. But they are very pleasant abodes, and at Middleton Place the gardens were beautiful. There were tea-trees and coffee-plants, avenues of immense camellias—japonicas, as they insist on calling them here—besides magnificent live oaks in the meadows by the river-side. The owner was not at home, but we were entertained by his servants (slaves), who did the honours remarkably well, brought us luncheon, and showed us all over the place, of which they were as proud as if it belonged to them. Evidently they were much attached to their home, as well as to their master; and, indeed, they are a warmhearted and affectionate race, and deserve to be as happy as they are under the present system, which requires but few alterations to be as beneficial to both parties as any that can be imagined.

The possible division of families and disregard of marital rights, which are repugnant to the feelings of every Southerner, would have been prevented by law long ago but for the irritation caused by the interference of the Abolitionists of the North, and the conviction that cases of the sort were exceedingly rare—much more rare, they maintain, than cases of brutal murder in England—and were already punished by such universal ignominy, that it has been thought better to rely on moral restraint than to enact laws which the Abolitionists would claim the credit of having forced them to make.

The few cases where plantations have been broken up and the negro families sold without regard to marital and human rights, have almost invariably taken place when *Northern creditors,* some of them members of H. W. Beecher's congregation (I could name instances), have insisted upon their *pound of flesh.*

In South Carolina negroes are as well protected by the laws as white men, and in some cases better. In criminal cases, for instance, a negro is tried before a court of three judges, the jury being composed of five white men, who must themselves be owners of negroes, and he can only be convicted by a unanimous verdict of this jury, with which one of the judges at least must agree. Apropos of the laws of South Carolina, I believe it is not generally known that at the settlement of the colony in 1670 the constitution was framed by John Locke, the famous philosopher, after the pattern of that of Plato's model republic.

During our sojourn at Charleston we stayed at the house of Mr Ch.,[3] who is celebrated for his little dinners, and who almost daily invited some friends to meet us; and we had "a good time of it," as they say in this country.

Charleston is celebrated for its madeira, which is al-

---

[3] Not identified.

ways kept in the garrets at the top of the house to ripen, and never in the cellar. It is hardly considered drinkable until it has been twenty years in bottle, but then it is delicious.

At Mr Ch.'s we often met Mr Timrod,[4] a gentleman whose name has not yet spread as widely as it undoubtedly will do; but he writes beautiful poetry, which no one who has read it can fail to admire. I believe a collection of his poems is soon to be published in England.[5]

We had some capital music at this time, as well as when we were here before, at a Mr Walker's, whose musical friends used to assemble at his house every Wednesday.

We left Charleston for Wilmington in the afternoon of November the 12th, and got seats in the "ladies' car." At two o'clock next morning there was a sudden smash, and we found ourselves bumping along on the sleepers. Our car had evidently got off the rails.

Fortunately the engine with the baggage-car broke loose from us, and we stopped; but when we alighted we found we had been in a critical position. The two passenger-cars were piled up against each other in a most extraordinary way, and if we had gone on a few yards farther we must inevitably have toppled over the embankment. No one was damaged; and the only two ladies in the car behaved admirably.

"I am so glad no one is hurt," was all that one of them said: "Yes, I'm so glad," said the other.

And they quietly got out with the rest, and we waited

---

[4] Henry Timrod.

[5] Timrod had galley sheets of a collection of his poems printed in the Confederacy and negotiated for their publication in London. They were never published there, however.

for assistance. Presently the locomotive and baggage-cars came back, and the passengers and traps were picked up and squeezed in amongst the luggage and firewood.

Whilst the transit was taking place, V. facetiously asked the conductor what they intended to charge for the extra performance. "Oh, nothing at all, sir: we make no charge; we break people's bones and bury them for nothing, sir, on this road." And so I believe they do, now and then.

V. had been upset several times before, but it was my first adventure of the kind, and I rather congratulated myself upon the occurrence, as travelling in America would be incomplete without a railroad accident.

We were not far from Wilmington when our mishap occurred, and arrived there early in the morning. We were shown into a very dirty room, with one bed for us both: the hotel was crowded; but happily we were not obliged to remain there, as we found our blockade-running friends, from whom we had parted at Augusta, established at Wilmington in a fine large house, to which they invited us, and made us cordially welcome.

In the morning we paid our respects to General Whiting, who is in command here, and called upon several other gentlemen to whom we had letters of introduction.

Wilmington is at present the most important port of entry in the South, and the custom-house receipts, both here and at Charleston, last year, far exceeded anything they had ever been during a similar period before the war. There were about a dozen blockade-running steamers lying at the wharves, loading cotton, and unloading all manner of stores brought from Bermuda and Nassau. Besides cotton, the chief exports are tobacco and rosin. One great treat we had here was to find English newspapers in abundance, and of dates little more than a month old.

A day of two after our arrival we went down to Fort Fisher, at the mouth of Cape Fear river, the Commandant, Colonel Lamb,[6] taking us down in his boat.[7] Going down we met three steamers coming up the river, having successfully run the blockade, the Hansa, the Lucy, and the Bendigo. We exchanged cheers as they passed us; but the great sight is when they come up to the wharves. They all dress up with flags as if for a victory; and as the ships which belong to the same company do the same, the spectacle is very gay. The cheering, too, is vociferous, and all those who have any interest in the vessel must, no doubt, feel extremely comfortable, as every successful trip brings an enormous profit. The moon is the blockade-runner's greatest enemy; but these vessels to-day had come in, notwithstanding the moon, which did not set till three o'clock in the morning. Fort Fisher consists of

---

[6] William Lamb.

[7] Vizetelly accompanied a sketch of Fort Fisher with the following: "Herewith I send you a sketch of Fort Fisher, commanding the approach to Cape Fear River, the entrance to Wilmington, North Carolina. I was down there one night, and, as it is twenty-five miles from the town, it was impossible to get back that night, so I had to rough it in a casemate till morning. As luck would have it, we discovered a blockade-running steamer, the Hansa, under our guns at dawn, and at the same time the Yankee blockaders also became aware of her presence and opened fire, thinking, as she had already got inside the bar . . . they would destroy her before she made the inlet. To get within range they had to expose themselves to the metal of the fort, which soon drove them off, leaving the Hansa at liberty to make her way safely into the river. . . . Fort Fisher is one of the strongest coast defences I have seen, not excepting any of those at Charleston, that have hitherto held an entire iron-clad fleet at bay." *The Illustrated London News,* XLIV (1864), 76.

a long line of forts and batteries of all sorts and sizes. The most peculiar one is an artificial hill mounted with two guns, in order to give a plunging fire upon any vessel that may attempt to pass. A fleet trying to get into the river would have to run the gauntlet of these batteries for more than a mile, and would most assuredly suffer very severly in the attempt. There are two inlets to Cape Fear river. Fort Fisher is the chief defence of the northern, and Fort Caswell of the southern one. Although very formidable, the fortifications were still being strengthened, and large numbers of negroes were at work.

In the far distance we could see two Federal men-of-war keeping up a nominal blockade. They always remain at a respectful distance, for if they come within three or four miles, Colonel Lamb is apt to make targets of them, and his gun practice is very accurate.* They seldom catch a blockade-runner going in or out, but if on the high seas they can capture a ship laden with a suspicious cargo, they condemn her as a prize without more ado; and as the vessels all sail under the supposed protection of the British flag, the owners never have any redress.

Sometimes a vessel gets "beached," as in a dark night it is very difficult exactly to hit the point for which they are steering. This accident happened to the Ceres, a noble double screw steamer, that was making her first voyage. The Yankees coming up in the morning, the ship had to be set on fire; her mail and a small portion of passengers' luggage were saved, but the cargo was lost.

---

* The U.S. ship Connecticut, 11 guns, can tell of some extraordinarily accurate practice she experienced from a "Whitworth" at the distance of full five miles, much to the astonishment of both captain and crew. I heard this lately through a Northern source.

Some of the passengers had had a narrow escape, the ebbing tide having carried their boat far out to sea, but eventually all got safe to land.

Mr C.,[8] a brother of the head of the firm with whose agents at Wilmington we were staying, after getting to the shore, walked off the wharf again into the sea in the twilight, but being exceedingly tall, the water only reached his neck, and he quietly returned to the dry land.

While we were at Wilmington the news arrived of the disastrous battle of Missionary Ridge. The Yankees had been very heavily reinforced after the battle of Chicamauga, and Bragg had detached Longstreet to lay siege to Knoxville in Eastern Tennessee. The Confederate lines extended to an enormous length; the men were more or less ill and dispirited, having suffered severely from the effects of the inclement weather, and unaccustomed cold climate. Upon the whole, it was a matter of congratulation that affairs turned out no worse than they did.

Bragg gave up the command of the army, and his successor, Joe Johnstone [Johnston], took up a position only a few miles to the rear of the one evacuated, and maintained it during the whole winter. The Yankees turned their victory of Missionary Ridge to no better account than the Confederates had done that of Chicamauga.

The following is a letter I received from an officer who was engaged on the right wing of Bragg's army:—[9]

"Headquarters, Cleburne's Division,
Army of Tennessee,
Tunnel Hill, Ga., 7th Dec. 1863.

". . . I will do my best to relate to you some of the past events since your departure from this army.

---

[8] Collie. The firm was Alexander Collie & Co.

[9] Probably Captain Byrne.

"Shortly after you left, Longstreet, as you may know, received a separate command, and was sent to Eastern Tennessee. There, luck did not altogether favour him before Knoxville, and he has had to beat a retreat into Virginia. Now in regard to our own division: For a long time after you left, the only movements we made were to continually shift our position along the old line of breastworks. However, at last, on the 24th (I think it was), General Cleburne was ordered to assume command of an expedition going to East Tennessee, consisting of Buckner's and his own divisions.

"On the 24th most of Buckner's command managed to get away on the cars from Chicamauga. That evening we received orders to march back at once to Missionary Ridge. The cause for thus suddenly ordering us back to the Ridge was, that the enemy had attacked our pickets and driven them in, and that a general engagement was expected next day.

"Next day, the 25th, we received orders to act as the reserve of the army, and were at once sent over to the extreme right of Missionary Ridge, to defeat a movement of the enemy in that direction. The enemy had been crossing the river on a pontoon, with the aid of two steamers. That day we had no fighting to speak of, only a little skirmishing, which showed the enemy that we were inclined to dispute their advance. On the left, however, the case was different.

"The whole day long, and a great part of the night, a battle had been raging on Lookout Mountain, which ended in the enemy driving Major-General Stevenson, together with his division, from their position, with a loss on their side, as they admit, of 5000 killed and wounded.

"The next day the ball opened pretty briskly on the right. Three times did they charge our position, and three times were they repulsed. General Stevenson was ordered to report to General Cleburne, who made use of one of the regiments of Cumming's brigade. The third charge was the most determined of the lot. They managed to reach the crest of the hill, and there they fought us for about two hours, at a distance varying from twenty to thirty paces;—so close were they that our officers threw stones. Our men fought behind some breastworks, which had been hastily constructed during the night.

"General Cleburne ended this prolonged fight by ordering a charge to be made on the enemy, both in front and in flank: by this gallant movement, we captured about 400 or 500 prisoners, and seven stands of colours.

"General Sherman's corps was the one we fought on the right. It must have numbered about 28,000 muskets. Sherman had promised his men a furlough if they took the Ridge, which, thank God, they never did. During the second charge my horse was shot in the neck, and I was ordered to change my horse, which I was unable to do, so I had to foot it for the rest of the fight. When we took the prisoners, some 400 of them were put in my charge; 333 I turned over to the Provost-Marshal, the rest to the surgery, and returned to my post.

"By this time General Cleburne had heard of the sad catastrophe on the left and centre of our line, and that he was expected to cover our retreat. He ordered me at once to send the prisoners to Chicamauga, which I did, footing it all the way. I shall never forget the sight which I witnessed next morning, when I joined General Cleburne again. He was in Chicamauga with the division in the best spirits possible, and in excellent order, whilst the most of the army resembled more the miserable crowds you would behold gathering around some gallows. Greedy for loot, they were to be seen eagerly ransacking all the burning stores.

"At last we managed to bundle these useless fellows out, and the retreat commenced in a more regular manner. On the 26th the enemy's advance came upon us at Ringgold. General Cleburne ambushed his men, and waited quietly for them to drive our cavalry in. You know the name the cavalry have out here, so you may judge he had not long to wait. The enemy evidently expected to meet some opposition in and on Taylor's Gap and Ridge, for they dismounted their cavalry and sent them forward to feel us. General Cleburne sent me round the skirmishers on our left to tell them not to fire a shot till the enemy should get up close on us, and then to let them have it. They obeyed the order well, and, together with the only two cannon we had, which had been double-shotted with grape, we gave the enemy 'what for.' All the rest of our cannon had been pushed on to the rear. You may readily guess that the enemy's cavalry did not stop long to consider what to do; they just broke and ran. Thus their first line was broken.

"Their infantry, then in heavy masses, tried to dislodge us. Every advance of theirs was boldly met by us, and always ended in their being badly repulsed and roughly handled. I was hit on the right arm by a Minié ball whilst carrying one of the enemy's colours that we had just captured.

"Joe Hooker was the man we had the pleasure of fighting there. We retired from there, carrying with us about fifty prisoners and two stands of colours. You may see my arm was not very badly hurt, as I am writing to you now. The army now is, for the most part, around Dalton, Ga.; and we, the advance-guard, are stationed at Tunnel Hill, Ga.; General Cleburne commands the cavalry in our front as well as his own division. It is generally supposed that he will be made lieutenant-general for having saved the army.

"The enemy's loss on the right at Missionary Ridge must have been very heavy; at Ringgold they left 505 graves, besides carrying off with them two cartloads of dead. Our loss in the two engagements was comparatively small; 600, I think, will cover it all. They burnt the town of Ringgold only for revenge; also the pretty little village of Greenville, and have left the population without food. Grant and Hooker and Casey were the three major-generals before us at Ringgold. At the end of our last fight we got up two more cannons to help us —I remain," &c.

Early in December we proceeded to Richmond, accompanied by Captain Fearn.[10] We had been introduced to the conductor of the train, who secured us comfortable seats, and our hospitable friends at Wilmington had provided us with a large hamper of provisions of all sorts—a very useful precaution before a long railroad journey in the present state of affairs. Thus our travels were not so unpleasant as they might otherwise have been. Thirty hours of railway brought us to our destination, and we took up our old quarters at the Ballard House. Richmond now presented a very different aspect from what it had done in summer. Congress, as well as the State Legislature of Virginia, was in session; the shops were full of stores, and crowded with purchasers; hosts of furloughed officers and soldiers perambulated the streets; hotels, restaurants, and bar-rooms were crowded with guests, and the whole city presented a lively appearance.

There was some outcry, even from the pulpits, against the gaieties that were going on, but General Lee was reported to have said that the young ladies were quite right to afford the officers and soldiers on furlough as much amusement as possible; and balls, tableaux vivants, and all kinds of social gatherings, were the order of the day.

Gambling, however, as an unmitigated vice, has lately been checked by the Virginia Legislature. They debated a little whether to legalise gambling, and by making it a public amusement to check gamblers by public opinion, or whether to put it down by severe measures, and decided for the latter. All gamblers caught in the fact were to be heavily fined, and the banker to be flogged. Corporal punishment is not otherwise generally popular in

---

[10] Walker Fearn.

this country, and has been abolished even in the army, where it is so necessary for the protection of the good soldiers, who under the lockup and imprisonment system are punished by extra duty for the faults of unworthy comrades, to whom a term of imprisonment is generally a matter of indifference, if not of positive satisfaction. Good soldiers are never flogged,[11] and there is no more hardship or disgrace to them in bad ones being thus punished than there is to good people in murderers being hanged. And there is another consideration with regard to flogging, namely, that in time of war many men have to be shot for offences for which otherwise a sound flogging would be an adequate punishment, and, as an example, a sufficient preventive.

Colonel Brien[12] and Major Von Borcke[13] met us at the hotel, and carried us off to the "Oriental Saloon," when we had a capital supper, and sat talking till a late hour.

As the South is supposed just now to be in a starving condition,[14] I will insert here the bill of fare of the Orien-

---

[11] "The Legislature," wrote Jones on October 22, "has broken up the gambling establishments for the time being, and the furniture of their gorgeous saloons is being sold at auction. Some idea of the number of these establishments may be formed from an estimate (in the *Examiner*) of the cost of the entertainment prepared for visitors being not less than $10,000 daily." Jones, II, 79.

[12] L. Tiernan Brien.

[13] Heros von Borcke.

[14] This is evidence of plenty hardly supported by Jones's evidence. "We are," he observed on November 21, "a shabby looking people now—gaunt, and many in rags. . . . A committee of the Grand Jury yesterday submitted a paper to the President, on the subject of provisions—indicating the proximity of famine, and deprecating impressments." Jones, II, 93.

tal Saloon, together with a little bill or two for meals partaken at that establishment:—

ORIENTAL, 8TH JANUARY 1864.

BILL OF FARE.

SOUPS.

	dols. per plate.
Beef,	1.50
Chicken.	
Macaroni.	
Vegetable.	
Clam.	
Oyster.	
Terrapin.	
Turtle.	
Mock turtle.	

FOWLS.

Roast turkey,	3.50
Roast goose.	
Roast ducks.	
Roast chickens,	3.50

FISH.

Rock fish,	5.00
Chub.	
Shad.	
Perch.	
Herrings.	
Crabs and lobsters.	

MEATS.

	plate.
Roast Beef,	3.00
Roast mutton,	3.00
Roast pork,	3.00
Roast lamb.	
Roast veal,	3.00

STEAKS.

	dish.
Beef steaks,	3.50
Pork steaks,	3.50
Mutton chops,	3.50
Veal cutlets,	3.50
Venison steaks,	3.50

SUNDRIES.

Ham and eggs,	3.50
Boiled eggs,	2.00
Poached eggs,	2.00
Scrambled eggs,	3.00
Fried eggs,	3.00
Omelette,	3.00

OYSTERS.

Fried oysters,	5.00
Scolloped oysters,	5.00
Roasted oysters,	5.00
Raw oysters,	3.00

BIRDS.

Partridge,	3.50
Sora.	
Robin.	
Snipe.	
Plover.	
Woodcock.	

VEGETABLES.

Cabbage,	1.00
Tomato.	
Green pease.	
Black-eyed pease.	
Cucumbers.	
Onions,	1.00
Lettuce.	
Squashes.	

Snaps.	
Lima beans.	
Irish potatoes, ...	1.00
Sweet potatoes, . . .	1.00
Salad, ...	2.00
Asparagus.	
Celery, ...	2.00
	cup.
Pure coffee, ...	3.00
Pure tea, ...	2.00
Fresh milk, ...	2.00

WINES.

	bottle.
Champagne, ...	50.00
Madeira, ...	50.00
Port, ...	25.00
Claret, ...	20.00
Chery, ...	35.00

LIQUORS.

	drink.
French brandy, ...	3.00
Apple brandy, ...	2.00
Peach brandy, ...	2.00
Holland gin, ...	2.00
Rye whisky, ...	2.00

MALT LIQUORS.

	bottle.
Porter, ...	12.00
Ale, ...	12.00
Half a bottle, ...	6.00

CIGARS.

Fine havana, ...	1.00

Other brands of a fine quality.

Bread, 50 cents—Butter, 1 dol.—Hot rolls, 1 dol. 50 cents.

GAME OF ALL KINDS IN SEASON.

Terrapins served up in every style.

PETER K. MORGAN, Sen., *Proprietor.*

ORIENTAL SALOON, 15TH JAN. 1864.

	dols.
Soup for nine, ...	13.50
Venison steak, nine, .	31.50
Fried potatoes, ...	9.00
7 birds, ...	24.00
Baked potatoes, ...	9.00
Celery, ...	13.50
Bread and butter, . . .	14.00
Coffee, ...	18.00
Apples, ...	12.00
Dinner, ...	144.50

	dols.
5 bottles of madeira, .	250.00
6 bottles claret, ...	120.00
1 urn cocktail, ...	65.00
Jelly, ...	20.00
Cake, ...	20.00
1 dozen cigars, ...	12.00
Wines and desserts,	487.00
Dinner, ...	144.50
Total, ...	631.50

These, it is true, are most remarkable for the nominal high prices of everything, but it must be remembered that the reason the paper money here is worth so little is that there is such a profusion of it. Indeed, the country has been swamped with bank-notes. For a time, such was the confidence of the people that they would eventually pay their debt, that paper was only at a small discount; but in the spring of this year (1863) Congress passed a measure enabling the Government to issue fifty millions of dollars a-month in paper money, without pledging any material guarantee for its eventual redemption, and since then the currency has naturally become more and more worthless. At present Congress is engaged in passing a measure to correct all this; the whole floating debt is to be funded, and a new currency issued on sounder principles.[15]

But to return to the question of starvation in the Southern States, for it is true that many people here apprehended such a misfortune. I have no opportunity of seeing much of what goes on in the private houses of the poorer people, and can only judge from what I see at hotels, and eating and boarding-houses. Here, not hundreds, but thousands upon thousands of people take their meals, and one may fairly conclude that what is set before them is

[15] In his letter from Richmond dated December 5, 1863, the correspondent of *The Index* wrote: "The question which of all others imperatively demands, and will certainly receive, the earliest action of Congress, is that of the currency. The schemes which have been proposed for the relief of the country in this regard are numberless. All look, of course, to the speedy reduction of the outstanding circulation, to forced loans and heavy taxation. . . . The financial condition of the country is such that holders of Government money might well consent to relinquish three-fourths of what they have to raise the other fourth to the value of gold, and they may reckon themselves fortunate indeed if the *methodus medendi* which is adopted shall secure this most desirable result." *The Index,* IV (1864), 27.

Confederate money at this time was worth in gold about one-eighteenth its face value. Jones, II, 103.

what they are accustomed to expect at their own homes.

I confess I never saw such universal profusion, and, I may say, waste. Hot meats and cold meats, venison pies, fish, oysters (prepared in half-a-dozen different ways), eggs, boiled, poached, "scrambled," and in omelettes, hot rolls and cakes, several kinds of bread, fruit in the season, &c. &c., are served up for breakfast, with "Confederate" (*i. e.,* artificial) coffee and tea, at hotels and boarding-houses, in quantities sufficient to satisfy an army of hungry soldiers.

At three o'clock a proportionate amount of food is served up for dinner, and the supper at eight is little less abundant. And for lodging and this board, a sum about equivalent to two shillings or half-a-crown has to be paid.[16] At the eating-houses on the railroad, where the trains stop for meals, the supply is similar.

Accustomed to this extraordinary plenty, many families may now complain at having to content themselves with less than their former profusion, and yet the country is evidently very far from the starvation which the Yankees so charitably reckon upon as one of their chief auxiliaries in destroying the population of the South.

I never happened to see the official order for rations to soldiers, but the following order shows the ample allowance made to the negro labourers when I was at Mobile:—

---

[16] As evidence of inflation, Jones noted on January 7, 1864, the sale at auction of a dozen cups and saucers for $160. "And yet," he commented in his same diary entry, "an Englishman at the best hotel yesterday remarked that he never lived so cheaply in any country, his board being only three shillings (in specie) per diem, or about $20 Confederate States notes." Jones, II, 125.

"Engineer Office, Department of the Gulf.
Mobile, Ala., *December* 9, 1863.

"General Orders, No. 2.

"I. The rations furnished by the Government to negroes employed on public works, will, in accordance with General Order No. 138, A. & I. G. O., consist of:—

Beef—1 lb. to the ration, daily issue.
Pumpkins—1 lb. to the ration, daily issue.
Meal—1¼ lb. to the ration, daily issue.
Rice—10 lb. per 100 rations, 8 days in 15.
Pease—15 lb. per 100 rations, 7 days in 15.
Vinegar—½ gallon per 100 rations, daily issue.
Soap—4 lb. per 100 rations, daily issue.
Salt—4½ lb. per 100 rations, daily issue.

"II. Yard-masters will see that their Commissaries and Overseers are furnished with the necessary scales, weights, and measures to weigh and measure the issues of rations made for each yard.

"III. The attention of Overseers is again called to Par. I. of General Rules and Regulations, ordered Nov. 11, '63. They will see that the negroes in their charge receive not only full rations, but also that they be properly prepared and justly distributed.

"They will report to the Yard-master any deficiency in the issue of rations, and in all cases in which the Overseer shall have neglected to observe this rule, rations shall be purchased by the Yard-commissary, and their price be deducted from the wages of the delinquent Overseer.

"V. Sheliha [Scheliha], *Lieut.-Colonel.*"

I have alluded before to the visit we now paid to the Libby Prison, where 970 Yankee officers were confined. As I then said, their quarters were remarkably clean and comfortable. At Belle Isle we found 7000 Yankee prisoners in tents. They had only thirteen sick at the time.[17]

Amongst the prisoners General Neil [Neal] Dow, the Maine-liquor-law man, was pointed out to us. He was caught in Louisiana, where he used to be subject to very severe attacks of kleptomania, and it was a matter of surprise and indignation to some that he had not been called to account here for some of his misdoings; but I suppose the authorities thought it better that some good South-

[17] Ross's comments on his visits to Belle Isle and Libby have been noted before. Jones's comments are somewhat at variance with Ross's and Vizetelly's observations.

Jones wrote in mid-October, "Captain Warner took me in his buggy this morning to the military prisons. He did not lead me into the crowded rooms above, where he said I would be in danger of vermin, but exhibited his cooking apparatus, etc.—which was ample and cleanly. Everywhere I saw the captives peeping through the bars; they occupy quite a number of large buildings —warehouses—and some exhibited vengeful countenances. They have half a pound of beef per day, and plenty of good bread and water—besides vegetables and other matters furnished by themselves. Several new furnaces are in process of erection, and most of the laborers are Federal prisoners, who agree to work (for their own convenience) and are paid for it the usual wages. There are baths to the prisons; and the conduits for venting, etc. have cost some $10,000." By November 11, however, the diarist was noting that the Commissary could not supply meat for "the 13,000 prisoners." On November 22 he commuted that there were insufficient tents for the prisoners on Belle Isle. "Our Commissary-General Northrop," he wrote, "has but little meat and bread for them, or for our own soldiers in the field. It must be confessed they have but small fare, and, indeed, all of us who have not been 'picking and stealing,' fare badly." On January 19 (about the time of Vizetelly's visit to Belle Isle), Jones was recording: "The prisoners here have had no meat during the last four days, and fears are felt they will break out of confinement." Jones, II, 73, 94, 102, 131.

erner in captivity should be liberated by an exchange for him, which was soon afterwards done.

For a long time all prisoners taken on either side were immediately paroled and sent home to their own country till an exchange could be effected, which was done by the heads of the Bureaux of Exchange on either side, to whom the written paroles of the prisoners had been forwarded. Now, however, on different pretexts, the Yankees refuse to exchange, as from obvious reasons it is more worth their while to keep 40,000 Southerners in prison than to release an equal number of their own men. That the poor fellows on both sides suffer and die, is not the kind of thing to influence the Washington Administration.

We visited the Tredegar Ironworks, the largest establishment of the kind in the Southern States. Heavy guns, rails, and railroad-car wheels are made here, and every kind of manufacture in iron.

We met several friends who had come on furlough to Richmond from Longstreet's army in Eastern Tennessee. They all said that Knoxville would have been certainly taken if they had had two days more to spare, as the key to the position was already in their hands; but Bragg's defeat at Chattanooga enabled the Yankees to send reinforcements to Burnside, and Longstreet was forced to give it up.

One day, at Major Norris's, I met a gentleman from Maryland who has lately been obliged to take refuge in the South. Colonel Sothern [18] had a large plantation on the Patuxent, in St. Mary's county, Maryland. One day a steamer came up the river and landed some twenty-five

---

[18] Not identified.

or thirty negro soldiers, with two officers, at a wharf near to Colonel Sothern's house. It soon became evident that they were on a recruiting expedition—*i. e.,* bent on kidnapping darkies to serve as substitutes.

One of the officers, Lieutenant Ebenezer White of Massachusetts, with two men, came up to the plantation where the negroes were at work in the fields, and without further ado laid hands upon some forty of them, and was carrying them off to the steamer. Upon this Colonel Sothern, seizing his fowling-piece, which was loaded, and followed by his son, sallied out to protect his servants and his property, and on reaching the party called to his negroes to return to him.

Reassured by the appearance of their master, they immediately did so, and in spite of the threats and menaces of the officer refused to proceed any further with him.

An altercation ensued, and the lieutenant, furious at his disappointment, seized a musket from one of his men, and, pointing it at young Sothern, pulled the trigger. Fortunately the cap exploded without discharging the piece; the lieutenant then rushed at Mr Sothern with fixed bayonet, which was within an inch of his son's breast when Colonel Sothern fired and shot the ruffian dead.

The two soldiers ran off as fast as they could, and the other lieutenant with his party of soldiers immediately got on board the steamer and made off.

Although no homicide could be more justifiable than that committed on this occasion by Colonel Sothern, who acted entirely in defence of his son's life, yet, under the present circumstances, he could not hope for an impartial judgment; so, returning home, he and his son at once saddled their horses and escaped across the lines to the South.

CHAPTER XI

General Stuart had invited L., V., and myself to spend Christmas with him at his headquarters near Orange Court-House. L. was prevented, but V. and I "took the cars" in that direction on December the 24th, a bitterly cold day.

We found an ambulance waiting for us at the station, and Pearson, the driver, took us up and down hill to the camp, over two miles of frozen road, as hard as his mules could scamper. We had a race with a soldier on horseback, and we beat him hollow. All the time we had to hold on tightly, or the jolting of the springless waggon would have pitched us out.

Stuart and the officers of his Staff gave us a hearty welcome, and before long we were seated around a roaring fire in the General's tent. The two Sweenies [Sweeneys] played the banjo and violin; a quartett of young fellows, couriers of the General, sang some capital songs, in the choruses of which we all joined;[1] V., who is a great favourite of the General's, told some of his best stories; and altogether we passed as merry a Christmas eve as we could desire.

One of the songs sung was written by Captain Blackford,[2] one of General Stuart's Staff-officers. Here it is:—

THE CAVALIER'S GLEE.

AIR—*"The Pirate's Glee."*

Spur on! spur on! we love the bounding
  Of barbs that bear us to the fray;
"The charge" our bugles now are sounding,
  And our bold Stuart leads the way.

Chorus.

The path to honour lies before us,
  Our hated foemen gather fast;
At home bright eyes are sparkling for us;

---

[1] The two Sweeneys were Sam and Dick Sweeney. Writing of Stuart's camp as it was in the fall of 1861, Colonel W. W. Blackford commented: "Stuart had now organized the band of stringed instruments and singers which afterwards became so well known and so associated with him. Sween[e]y, a brother of the celebrated Joe Sween[e]y, who had brought the banjo into European notice by his skill upon it, was one of the band; he played the banjo and sang. . . . [Stuart] collected around him a number of experts, not only in music, but in theatricals and tricks of various kinds, and they added much to the pleasure of camp life. Sween[e]y and his banjo and his negro melodies were the favorites; and Sweeny always carried his instrument slung at his back on marches, and often in long night marches the life of the men was restored by its tinkle." W. W. Blackford, *War Years with Jeb Stuart* (New York, 1945), p. 50–51. These entertainers are the subject of W. E. Hemphill's article, " 'Band Joe' Sweeney and His Banjo," *Virginia Cavalcade,* (Richmond), II (1952), 34–35.

[2] William W. Blackford.

We will defend them to the last.
At home, &c.

Spur on! spur on! we love the rushing
Of steeds that spurn the turf they tread;
We'll through the Northern ranks go crushing,
With our proud battle-flag o'erhead.
The path of honour, &c.

Spur on! spur on! we love the flashing
Of blades that battle to be free;
'Tis for the sunny South they're clashing—
For household gods and liberty.
The path of honour, &c.

Stuart's camp is always one of the jolliest; as the General is very fond of music and singing, and is always gay and in good spirits himself, and when he laughs heartily, as frequently happens, he winds up with a shout very cheering to hear. One of his couriers, Grant,[3] has a magnificent voice.

The couriers, a certain number of whom are attached to every general's staff, do not rank as officers, though they perform pretty much the same duty as is done in European armies by aides-de-camp and galopins. They are usually young fellows of good family, and, of course, provide their own horses.

Stuart gave up his tent and blankets to me when we retired to rest, and the next morning we paid our respects to Mrs Stuart, who was staying at a gentleman's house not far off. Here we were also introduced to "General Jimmy J. E. B. Stuart, junior," as he calls himself, a sturdy young four-year-old, very fond of visiting his father's camp, and running about amongst the horses'

---

[3] Not identified.

legs. Horses never kick in this country, but the same cannot be said of the mules, so this propensity of the young gentleman causes some anxiety.

We went on to visit General Lee. The General, who was just returning from church, welcomed us very kindly, and we sat in his tent and conversed for some time.

General Lee lamented the suffering caused by the war, especially to the poor country-people in this neighbourhood. They have been stripped of everything, he told us, by the Yankees, and their houses often burnt down, for no practical purpose, as this part of the country was far too much exhausted to extract any supplies from. But it appeared to be part of the war policy of the enemy to devastate the whole country wherever they occupied it.

When I began to mention the way his own property had been treated at Arlington, he interrupted me at once, saying, "That I can easily understand, and for that I don't care; but I do feel sorry for the poor creatures I see here starved and driven from their homes for no reason whatever."

General Lee pressed us to remain and partake of his Christmas fare, but we were obliged to decline the honour, as we were already engaged to General Stuart. Just as we had started on our return, however, a messenger came galloping up to advise us, if we were invited to dinner, to accept by all means, as the turkey and ducks and other delicacies had not arrived. But it was too late. We got a pretty good dinner notwithstanding.

The amount of good cheer that has been sent up to the army this Christmas by their friends at home is something wonderful. One North Carolina regiment is said to have received two hundred turkeys. Stuart had an enormous box of oysters sent him. They were all hard frozen.

In the evening our amusement was to throw them into the burning embers of our roaring fire, and pick them out roasted. Oysters in this country are rather too large to eat raw, but roasted they are delicious.

A story has gone abroad and been widely circulated, that the General had been in the habit last summer of always decking his horse with garlands of flowers, &c. Stuart had been rather annoyed by it, as not only had all the newspapers abused him for his levity, but many persons had remonstrated with him by letter on the subject, so that he had had no end of worry.

It seems that the only foundation for the story is that one day, as Stuart was riding through a village, a young lady came out and hung a chaplet of flowers over his horse's neck. Of course the General was too polite to take it off as long as the lady was within sight; but although he did so immediately afterwards, several persons had seen him riding with it, and rumour, with her thousand tongues, got hold of the story. So much was this absurd affair exaggerated, that at one time it was seriously injuring his reputation.[4]

A deserter was brought in in the course of the evening.

---

[4] Fremantle had recorded his impression of Stuart after meeting the cavalryman at Hagerstown shortly after the Battle of Gettysburg. The Britisher wrote, "he is a good-looking, jovial character, exactly like his photographs. He has certainly accomplished wonders, and done excellent service in his peculiar style of warfare. He is a good and gallant soldier, though he sometimes incurs ridicule by his harmless affectation and peculiarities. The other day he rode through a Virginian town, his horse covered with garlands of roses. He also departs considerably from the severe simplicity of dress adopted by other Confederate generals; but no one can deny that he is the right man in the right place." Fremantle, p. 293.

He had entered the old army seven years ago, but had never bargained upon fighting against his own countrymen, he said. Till very lately he had been stationed in the Far West, and his company had only just joined the army of the Potomac, where they were very much disgusted with everything they saw—the officers were always drunk—none of them knew their duty. He and all his comrades had made up their minds to quit at the first opportunity, and here he was.

General Stuart is an absolute teetotaller, and never drinks anything stronger than lemonade. He says that if he were to drink any strong liquors at all, he is sure he should be too fond of it, and therefore prefers total abstinence.[5] Nor does he ever smoke. It was, however, imperative that V. and I should have some egg-nogg, a compound which is universally partaken of in Virginia at this season of the year. Accordingly, next morning, we walked over, about a mile, to the Quartermaster's camp, where some of this beverage had been prepared. It is a very nice mixture of rum, sugar, and eggs.

Captain Grattan,[6] the General's ordnance officer, who was with us, told us an anecdote of his political life before the war. He had been a candidate for some county office, for which a number of others had competed. All had to make a stump speech, and when Grattan's turn came his competitors had exhausted most subjects: he thought one piece of spouting would do as well as another, and he gave his audience "My name's M'Gregor, on my

---

[5] John Esten Cooke quoted "Stonewall" Jackson as saying, having been offered whiskey by Dr. Hunter McGuire, "Oh, yes, I like liquor, the taste and the effect—*that's why* I don't drink it." New York *Daily News,* October 24, 1865.

[6] Charles Grattan.

mountain heath," &c., and treated them to a fine piece of ranting. All were delighted, except one old farmer, who had promised him his vote. "What does he say is his name?" he complained. "I thought his name was Grattan; I'm not going to vote for M'Gregor."

The camps in these winter quarters are more regularly laid out than I have seen them before. Each tent has a large chimney, the lower part of stones and brick, with a flue constructed of logs of wood, the interstices filled up with turf or moss.

Colonel St Leger Grenfell's tent and stable are a model to be studied, and worthy of such an old campaigner. The Colonel, who is Inspector-General of Cavalry, has only lately been transferred to this army, and looks back with regret to the stirring and fighting time when he was with Morgan in the West.

He told us some capital stories of his various adventures. Few men can have seen and done more fighting than he has. He at one time commanded the body-guard of Abd-el-Kader. At another he fitted out a privateer, and cruised on his own account against the Riff pirates. He has served in Turkey, India, South America, and I know not how many other places. Morgan's men in the West adored their "fighting old Colonel," and would have followed him anywhere.

Few young men of twenty are as active and full of life as Colonel Grenfell, who is now not far from sixty. One day I rode with the General and Blackford to Clarke's Mountain, whence we could see the position of both armies very clearly. Coming back we went into a farmhouse for some milk. A crazy gentleman sat by the fire apparently in his second childhood, but when we said something about his being old, they exclaimed, "Oh no! he's not old at all; he's only seventy-seven." "Time to lose his body as well as his mind," Stuart remarked after we had left.

Enlivened by our symposium we galloped home merrily, singing the 'Cavalier's Glee,' and many other songs as we rode through the night.

Of course all the scouts report to Stuart, and their adventures were often the theme of conversation in camp. The scouts here are generally young Virginians, who are intimately acquainted with every hole and corner in the country, for Virginians are fond of field-sports, and their old-fashioned slow style of hunting gives them a perfect knowledge of the country.

The other day, or rather night, three young fellows who were reconnoitring had lain down in a wood to sleep under their blankets. Amongst them was one of Stuart's most famous scouts, but I must not mention names. In the night, which was rainy, they were discovered by a party of some half-dozen Yankees. Bringing a lantern to bear upon the sleepers, "Hollo! Rebs," one of them called out—"hollo! Rebs; come along with us, and we'll give you better quarters." "Oh Frank, I do wish you would leave me alone," said ——, pretending to be half asleep; but all the time he was fumbling about under his blanket for his six-shooter, and when he had got it ready he let fly, and shot the Yankee stone dead. Singularly enough, the musket of the man discharged itself as he was falling, and killed one of ——'s companions. The remaining two were on their feet in a trice—bang bang—bang bang—went the six-shooters on either side, and in half a second three more of the Yankees were dead, and the others were off.[7]

---

[7] This story is told in John Esten Cooke's *Wearing of the Gray* (New York, 1867) in the chapter "Hunted Down," pp. 487–99.

The headquarters of the generals, both on the Federal and the Confederate side, are distinguished by a large flag, which is always guarded by a sentinel, and the scout I have been speaking of once brought in the very flag which had been floating before the headquarters of Meade, the Yankee Commander-in-Chief.

An amusing story was told of his disappointment on one occasion when he hoped to capture a Yankee quartermaster, who he knew had a hundred thousand dollars in greenbacks about his person. He rode with him for a long time, pretending to be himself a Yankee, and saying he knew the gentlemen in the neighbourhood were a set of rebel scoundrels whom it would be meritorious to rob, and pointing to one house and another declared there was capital whisky to be found there, and dwelt on the advantage it would be to his quartermaster stores to prig some of it; but it was all in vain. Either the quartermaster was not thirsty, or he had a private bottle, or perhaps he was an honest man; at any rate he resisted every temptation, and thus saved his bacon and his greenbacks.

Stuart accompanied us back to Richmond on the last day of December.

On New Year's Day we paid our respects at court like everybody else. The President looked, and I have no doubt was, very much fatigued with the exertion of shaking hands and exchanging compliments with the multi-

---

This was one of a series about scout life Cooke wrote in 1863, but it did not appear in print during the war. The scout was Frank Stringfellow. Stringfellow did attempt the theft of Meade's flag but did not capture it. See Blackford, p. 244. For an account of Stringfellow, see James W. Peavey's *Confederate Scout: Virginia's Frank Stringfellow* ([Onancock, Va., c. 1956]).

tude of visitors who called upon him on the occasion.[8] Of generals at present in Richmond there are, as they say here, "quite a number,"—Hood, who is fast recovering from the severe wound he received at Chicamauga, A. P. Hill, Buckner, Preston, Williams, Gordon, and others; but the hero of the day is John Morgan. He lately made his escape from prison, having been captured last July during a raid in Ohio. On his coming to Richmond a grand reception was given to him by the city.[9]

I met him often, and one evening had a long conversation with him. He is a very fine fellow, tall and handsome, and his men are devoted to him.

As soon as it was known that he was to take the field

---

[8] Jones did not go to the President's reception of January 1. He did go to a similar affair on January 26 and wrote of it the next day: "Last night, the weather being very pleasant, the President's house was pretty well filled with gentlemen and ladies. I cannot imagine how they continue to dress so magnificently, unless it be their old finery, which looks well amid the general aspect of shabby mendicity. But the statures of the men, and the beauty and grace of the ladies, surpass any I have seen elsewhere, in America or Europe. There is high character in almost every face, and fixed resolve in every eye." Jones, II, 136.

[9] The Richmond correspondent of *The Index* had written on December 5, "The escape of John Morgan from the Ohio penitentiary caused a thrill of joy throughout the Confederate States. His arrival is anxiously looked for in this city. . . ." *The Index,* IV (1864), 28. On January 1 Jones wrote, "The City Councils have voted the hospitalities of the city to Brig.-Gen. J. H. Morgan, whose arrival is expected. If he comes, he will be the hero, and will have a larger crowd of admirers around him than the President." On January 7 he noted, "Gen. Jno. H. Morgan arrived this evening, and enjoyed a fine reception, as a multitude of admirers were at the depot." And on the eighth he added: "Gen. Morgan received the congratulations of a vast multitude to-day." Jones, II, 122, 125, 126.

again with a separate command, every one was anxious to join him, and his adjutant-general told me afterwards that within three weeks he had answered above fourteen thousand applications. But none are allowed to join Morgan except native Kentuckians.

As Morgan's men are always called guerillas by the Yankees, it may be as well to say here that they are regular soldiers.

Guerillas are civilians who take up arms on an emergency to defend their homes and property, but who resume their peaceful pursuits as soon as the enemy has left their own immediate neighbourhood.

Morgan's command consists, and always did consist, almost exclusively of young Kentuckians, sons of country gentlemen in that State, who have voluntarily taken up arms and regularly enlisted in the Confederate service. Kentucky being still nominally a Yankee State, they could not now, if they wished it, return to their home.

That the Yankees, when they captured Morgan and a large part of his command last summer, should have confined them in a penitentiary, and subjected them to all manner of indignities, is a disgrace to them, and not to Morgan and his brave followers. If they had been accused of anything contrary to the rules of war, they ought to have been tried by a court-martial, but such a pretence was never set up. They simply treated them as malefactors because they chose to do so, and when the Confederate authorities demanded an explanation and threatened them with retaliation, it was found that no one was responsible for the outrage.

Nothing would be easier than for the Confederates to confine an equal number of prisoners in a penitentiary and shave their heads in retaliation, but they have not done so.

Congress, in both houses, has been voting thanks to the generals and armies, and, what we all thought an especially graceful act, both houses gave a particular vote of thanks to Major Von Borcke, a Prussian officer who has done gallant service under General Stuart, and was very severely wounded during the Pennsylvania campaign.[10] A similar compliment was paid during the revolutionary war to Lafayette.

There are very few foreigners in the Confederate service. As President Davis said to Captain Feilden at Charleston a short time ago—"Our service offers but little inducement to the soldier of fortune, but a great deal to the man of principle." The few who have entered the Confederate service have, almost without exception, distinguished themselves highly.

---

[10] The Confederate Congress approved the following resolution January 30:

"Whereas Major Heros von Borcke, of Prussia, adjutant and inspector general of the cavalry corps of the Army of Northern Virginia, having left his own country to assist in securing the independence of ours, and by his personal gallantry in the field having won the admiration of his comrades as well as that of his commanding general, all of whom deeply sympathize with him in his present sufferings from the wounds received in battle: *Therefore*

"Resolved by the Congress of the Confederate States of America, That the thanks of Congress are due, and the same are hereby tendered, to Major von Borcke for his self-sacrificing devotion to our Confederacy and for his distinguished services in support of its cause.

"Resolved, That a copy of the foregoing resolution be transmitted to Major von Borcke by the President of the Confederate States." *Official Records of the Union and Confederate Navies in the War of the Rebellion* (Washington, 1894–1922), Ser. II, III, 158.

The Yankee service, on the other hand, is crowded with adventurers. Not only was the North easy of access, but, from having been for a long time the receptacle of the "scum and refuse of Europe," most of the revolutionary heroes of 1848 and later, such as Blenker, were there already.

In European armies numberless officers are obliged to quit their profession, mostly from having been extravagant; and to these "soldiers of fortune" the American war has been a perfect godsend. They have all espoused the Northern cause, not because it was dearest, but because it was nearest to them. Many of them are excellent officers. The Southern Confederacy being very difficult of access, the foreigners who have taken service here have all been impelled to do so by their sympathy with the cause, which is in truth a noble one. Very few foreign officers even visit the Southern States now, which surprises me, for nothing could exceed the courtesy and kindness with which strangers are received; and so interesting a period of seeing the country can hardly be expected to occur again. At present, there is a young English officer of engineers here, who, with but a very short leave of absence, crossed the lines on foot with a small kit, saw the army in Northern Virginia, visited Charleston, Wilmington, &c., and is now going to walk across the lines again on his return. With the exception of Colonel F., no other "tourist," as far as I am aware, has visited the country since I have been here. I attended the sittings of Congress on several occasions, and was struck with the fluency of the members and the general excellence of the speeches made.

I was surprised to find from conversation with politicians here, how very little it had been expected in the South that secession would have been followed by war.

When South Carolina, thirty years ago, "nullified"—that is, refused to carry out a law which had been passed by the Federal Congress—the argument against her was that she had *no right to remain in the Union,* if she would not accept the laws passed in Congress. When Texas was received into the Union as a slave State, the Legislature of Massachusetts actually passed an ordinance of secession; but as no other State followed the example, no further action was taken in the matter. No one would have dreamt of coercion if Massachusetts had persisted in her resolution. At the election of Buchanan there was a great outcry in the North for secession; but when Hill of New Hampshire introduced a motion into the Senate that the Union should be dissolved, he found only two supporters. Their names were *Seward* and *Chase,* both now the most prominent supporters of the Union. As to the doctrine of sovereign states' rights, the Northern States were formerly the great supporters of it. During the war of 1812, the New England States refused to allow their troops to be used beyond the borders of their own respective States, on the ground that the Federal Government had no business to interfere with their sovereign rights; and it is not thirty years now since the State of New York very nearly engaged in a war with England upon her own responsibility, by refusing, at the demand of the Federal Government, to release a British subject who had been arrested by the New York State authorities on suspicion of having been concerned in the destruction of the Caroline, a steamer fitted out by American sympathisers in aid of the rebellion in Canada.

On the 9th of January I accompanied General Stuart on a tour of inspection to see some of his brigades near Fredericksburg. We got out of the cars at Hamilton's

Crossing, and visited General Young's brigade, and then proceeded to Fredericksburg. The two Generals drove in a sledge, whilst I rode with an orderly, who was to take care of my horse, and who was a very communicative fellow. He gave me lots of information on their cavalry matters, which I need not repeat.

The Mayor of Fredericksburg—who possesses, what is remarkable since the battles last year, an entire house, with furniture in it—entertained us hospitably, and in the evening we went to a ball.

Fredericksburg, which, before the war, is said to have been a delightful residence, has undergone manifold misfortunes in the last two years. After having been in Yankee hands in the summer of 1862, it suffered a terrible ordeal in December of that year, when the battle took place to which it gives its name. It was bombarded for hours together, after which the Yankees took possession; and finally, before leaving, they totally pillaged it. Again, during the battle of Chancellorsville, the enemy got possession, and again they pillaged it. It is still so near the Yankee lines that, although safe at present, it may at any moment be subjected to the tender mercies of their armies. Consequently, although the inhabitants have returned to their homes, they are by no means as particular as they used to be about having good furniture, and everything nice and stylish about them. In the ball-room, at the private house where we danced, there was very little furniture besides the piano, and it was illuminated by tallow-candles stuck into empty black bottles. Perhaps some of the ladies may have been dressed in homespun instead of silks and satins—but it was too dark to see. For all that, we had as pleasant a party as could possibly be; and were very sorry when twelve o'clock came and put an end to the ball, as the next day was Sunday.

On leaving—there had been none but young ladies there, no chaperones—every young lady paired off with a gentleman who accompanied her to her home. Unacquainted with the customs of the country, I was left out in the cold without a partner, much to Stuart's amusement. This was a new experience, although I had seen and admired before the independence which young ladies are allowed in America.

I rode over the battle-field of Fredericksburg with General Stuart, who described the battle and pointed out the different positions to me. Fredericksburg is on the right bank of the Rappahannock, close to the river. The Stafford Heights, which Burnside occupied, rise immediately on the other side. They were covered with heavy guns, which not only commanded the city, which they bombarded for several hours to clear it of the Confederates, but could also sweep the plains beyond; and it was under cover of these guns that, after effecting the passage of the river, the Federals advanced against the position occupied by Lee. This was by no means as formidable a one as I had always before imagined.

About three-quarters of a mile from the city there are some low hills. Marye's Height, on Lee's left centre, is in itself very insignificant; but it happened that just below it there was a road, which for a few hundred yards was sunk about five feet lower than the open plain which intervenes between Fredericksburg and the hills.

Thus a most formidable natural breastwork was formed, out of which, even if there had been faint hearts amongst the gallant troops who lined it, no one could retreat without exchanging comparative safety for great exposure and danger.

It struck me, as I looked at this, that a line of defence might be made much more formidable by digging deep ditches, than by throwing up breastworks, from which men are often driven by a panic. Two lines, a hundred yards apart, like this sunken road—they of course need not be made so broad—would be an awkward thing to storm.

Meagher's Irish brigade attacked Marye's Hill with a gallantry which was the admiration of all who beheld it, but they were literally annihilated by the Confederates lining the road, who themselves suffered hardly any loss. Fourteen hundred and sixty Irish were buried, who in this attack had fallen on a piece of ground about forty yards deep and three hundred broad. As is well known, the Yankees were everywhere repulsed, and next day retired across the river under cover of the guns on the Stafford Heights.

Some surprise, I remember, was expressed, when the news of Burnside's defeat reached Europe, that Lee had not pressed his retreat; but as any advance of the Confederates over the open plain which intervened between them and the Rappahannock would have exposed them to the sweep of the Federal artillery on the high hills which rise abruptly on the northern bank, it would not have been easy to do so.

A more favourable place for crossing a river in the face of the enemy than at Fredericksburg could not well be found; that is to say, by an army coming from the north, and being consequently in possession of the Stafford Heights. To force a passage there from the south in the face of those heights would be simply out of the question.

The position on the northern bank of the river is entirely impregnable; and in comparing it with that on the southern side in the early part of the war, and long before the battle, one of the Southern Generals—I think, Joe Johnston—is reported to have said that there was as much difference between the two positions as between a horse chestnut and a chestnut horse.

We returned in time for church, where Dr Moore [11] of Richmond, a celebrated preacher, gave us an excellent sermon. The clergyman was a Presbyterian, but the congregation was almost entirely Episcopalian. In Virginia all the old families are Episcopalians, and it seemed to me that the higher classes were universally so in the South. In country places, I understand that many, though professing themselves Christians, and attending some service regularly, are of no particular denomination, but frequent any church that may be most convenient to them.

The next day we drove to Hamilton's Crossing, and met there General Wade Hampton, who commands one of Stuart's divisions of cavalry. General Hampton is a gentleman of very large landed property in South Carolina, and was not a professional soldier before the war. At its commencement, however, he raised a "legion," and equipped it at his own expense, and is now very highly thought of as a cavalry general. He was severely wounded at Gettysburg both by sabre and bullet, but seems to have perfectly recovered.

From Hamilton's Crossing we took the cars to Guiness [Guinea or Guinea's] Station, whence we proceeded to General Gordon's camp, and reviewed his brigade of North Carolinians. It was too cold for the men to turn out

[11] Thomas Verner Moore.

regularly, but we rode and walked about through the camp, and saw how they were getting on. The horses were in good condition in spite of the severe weather; of course they were as shaggy as bears.

We spent a pleasant evening at the house of a Mr Coleman,[12] where we slept, and next day we returned to Richmond.

On the 14th of January a grand dinner was given at the Oriental to L., who is returning to England, much to the regret of his many friends here. Some excellent speeches were made on the occasion.[13]

---

[12] Probably Clayton G. Coleman of Louisa County.

[13] Lawley carried with him to England a letter to Fremantle from a friend on Longstreet's staff which brought the British officer news of happenings since his visit to the Confederacy. The letter (with its address, signature, and a few personal references deleted) was published in *The Index,* IV (1864), 188:

"As our mutual friend L. is about to cross the water, I thought I would trouble you with a line, to inform you of the progress of affairs here.

"We are carrying on the war as when you were with us, hopefully, though under many difficulties, but the fact is that we know full well that we must win our independence after a while, and with this consciousness impressed upon our officers and men, sacrifices are borne with comparative indifference. The end must come, and when it does come, we will reap our full reward in being free from the despicable race to whom we have heretofore been bound. If a truthful history of this war could be written, with all its details, what an amount of human suffering it would unfold! You saw nothing of it in the Pennsylvania campaign. Think of an army of 25,000, 800 of them cavalry, sent to drive back an enemy numerically stronger, and provided with all the appliances of war, while we were without efficient transportation, without any supplies, except the beef we could drive up within our lines, and the wheat we could haul and grind at mills from which we could expel the enemy. Our railroad communications entirely cut off by the defeat of poor unfortunate Bragg at Missionary Ridge, our very horse-shoes had to be made of old iron picked up in the country, and when that gave out we had to draw the spikes out of the railroad iron in order to shoe our wagon horses, that they might haul wheat to mills ten or fifteen miles, and then haul flour from ten to thirty miles to the troops. No ammunition, except a limited supply in the reserve ordnance trains: we had to economise even the lives of the enemy to protect our own. Without ambulances for the wounded, I have seen men carried on litters, through mud and rain, 23 miles to a hospital. And yet, under all these circumstances, we have held our position until the rail-road communication to Richmond is nearly completed. We are now trying to build a pontoon bridge across the French Broad to forage with our cavalry, and we have to send 80 miles by wagon road for nails and axes. No one but a military man can appreciate these difficulties; and if you add to them a scarcity of shoes, clothes, and blankets, with winter snows, and a scarcity of supplies to be collected, you can then appreciate the leading difficulties overcome by General Longstreet in holding his portion of East Tennessee. We could hardly bear up but for the assistance given us by the Federals, but the fact is, wherever they get a foothold their atrocities are so great, and their tyranny so unlimited, that they teach us that these sacrifices are light to the humiliation and suffering we should have to bear if they were our masters. We have nothing left us but to fight on, fight ever, rather than wear the chains which they would forge for us; but now [how] we shall bless the day of honourable peace; how sweet will be the quiet of home and the restoration of law and order! May "Merrie England" never bear the sorrow that she may feel the joyous change. Dr.—— has just passed out and desires to be remembered to you; —— is in Richmond, where he is no doubt at present 'over all the ills of life victorious.' —— is under the weather, having been cut off from spirituous supplies, but he is at present running a distillery on his own account, and expects in a few days to revel in rye. The General is wrapped up in his own thoughts, and looks as if he would give his kingdom for horseshoes, as that is what he chiefly lacks to make a forward movement. I am kept pretty busy devising ways and means to spread a daily repast to my hungry family, and when bad weather drives me to shelter I luxuriate in your india-rubber overcoat which [Ross] very kindly gave me."

CHAPTER XII

After spending six weeks very pleasantly at Richmond, I decided to visit Mobile and the army of the Mississippi. A journey of such length by rail in the present state of the cars is rather an undertaking, but I was fortunate in having two very pleasant travelling companions, Colonel Walton and Colonel Deas.[1]

We started about the end of January, and slept the first night at Petersburg. Here we spent the evening with Captain Dunne, aide-de-camp to General Longstreet, who, having been wounded at Knoxville, was now staying with his wife and family at his home in the city. Here too we met Captain Winthrop [2] again, an Englishman, who was badly wounded at Bean's Station, where he distinguished himself very highly.

---

[1] George Deas.

[2] Stephen Winthrop.

At Wilmington we made a longer stay. V. left us, going by the Hansa to Nassau, and thence to Europe.[3] General Whiting took us down one day, and we went over all the fortifications at the mouth of the river. Fort Caswell, and the other works at the south outlet of the river, I had not seen before. They are exceedingly strong. "Not fortifications," says Colonel Deas, but "fiftyfications at least."

Another day there was a review. The garrison here is numerous, and the regiments more complete than is usual. They were more uniformly dressed, too, than I had seen any Confederate troops before. The men—chiefly North Carolinians—are a fine-looking race, and went through their evolutions unexceptionably. General Whiting, who, at West Point, graduated No. 1 in everything, is an excellent soldier, and had evidently taken a great deal of pains with his division. A brigade of his about this time went on an expedition against the Yankees, near Newbern, in this State, North Carolina, and gained much success and credit. As we were not pressed for time, we determined to avoid the main thoroughfare by Atlanta, which was sure to be excessively crowded, and to travel by Charleston and Savannah.

Colonel Gordon, an Englishman in the Confederate

---

[3] Vizetelly wrote of his journey through the blockade: "The voyage from the Confederate States averages about fifty hours; but then these fifty hours are fraught with an excitement that a voyage of fifty days would fail in producing. From the time of leaving Cape Fear River, Wilmington, to the time of sighting Nassau and getting into British waters, these adventurous crafts are never safe from being overhauled by a Northern man-of-war." *Illustrated London News,* XLIV (1864), 366.

service, and C.,[4] accompanied us as far as Savannah, so we were "quite a party."

At Charleston we remained for two days. The Yankees had recommenced shelling the city some time before, but comparatively little mischief was being done. Few shells fall beyond the part of the town which was destroyed by fire previous to the first bombardment, and the houses of Charleston, as in most cities of the Southern States, are very much scattered, except in two or three business streets, each one standing in a large courtyard, and having besides a garden of shrubs and "shade trees." Thus nine out of ten shells fall harmless; and the hope of the Yankees to set fire to the city or to batter it down has been hitherto entirely disappointed.

The district nearest the bay, which is most exposed to the shelling, is nearly deserted by the inhabitants, but still ladies enter it without hesitation to visit their houses; and a friend of mine, Captain Mordecai,[5] told me that he had in vain attempted to prevail on his old negro housekeeper to evacuate his premises. "Them shells never do nobody any harm," she argued.

In walking through this part of the city, the only observable results of the bombardment are the broken windows in houses where shells have exploded; and General Jordan never even hinted the possibility of its being an objection to our visiting the Battery and other exposed places to have a look at Fort Sumter, the Blakely guns, and other objects of curiosity, and he and several of his fellow-officers accompanied us on the expedition.

Various individuals were lounging about in the streets

---

[4] Alexander Collie.

[5] J. Randolph Mordecai.

and on the Battery, which Battery, I think I have mentioned before, is not a battery, but a promenade from whence there is a beautiful view of the harbour and bay. Of the row of fine houses here—the best in Charleston—fronting the bay, only one has been struck by a shell.

In the "safe district" we visited the "Soldiers' Home," where every soldier, whether wounded or sick, or travelling on furlough to visit his friends, is provided with board and lodging. Everything was admirably clean and well kept, and the dinner, which was just being served, appeared excellent. In almost every town in the South there is an establishment of the same description generally close to the railway station. They are supported by the surrounding country, and in many of them the ladies of the neighbourhood take it by turns to wait upon their guests.

The establishment at Charleston is extensive, and we were shown over it by Mr Gibbs,[6] a wealthy Charlestonian, who has remained in the beleaguered city, determined to abide by his native place in its dark hour; and he makes this "Home" an object of his chief care and solicitude.

We had a very pleasant journey to Savannah. The weather was delightful; indeed, from the time we reached Wilmington we had found the climate entirely different from that we had left at Richmond. A Mr B——n [7] had joined our party,—a New Orleans gentleman, and a friend of Colonel Deas, who was very amusing.

Savannah is the largest city of Georgia, on the south bank of the Savannah river, eighteen miles from the sea,

---

[6] Probably Robert Wilson Gibbes.

[7] Not identified.

and has a population of about 16,000 whites and 12,000 blacks.

A city with less than 30,000 inhabitants in the Northern and North-Western States of America is at the utmost considered a rising and promising young place; but it is different in the South, where population does not congregate at commercial centres, and the comparatively ancient town of Savannah is an important city. It was founded by General Oglethorpe in 1732 [1733], and, like most of the seaboard towns, was in the hands of the British during almost the whole of the Revolutionary War. It is a beautiful place, and, to quote an American guide-book, "regularly built, with streets so wide and so unpaved, so densely shaded with trees, and so full of little parks, that but for the extent and elegance of its public edifices, it might seem to be a score of villages rolled into one. There are no less than twenty-four little green squares scattered through the city, and most of the streets are lined with the fragrant flowering China tree, or the Pride of India, while some of them have four grand rows of trees, there being a double carriage-way, with broad walks on the outer sides, and a promenade between." The neighbourhood is exceedingly pretty, with drives on the banks of the river, and avenues of live oaks, bay-trees, magnolias, and orange-trees. A favourite drive is to the Cemetery of Bonaventure, which was originally a private estate, laid out in broad avenues; and these avenues of live oak, now grown to an immense size, with their huge branches sweeping the ground, and carrying heavy festoons of the hanging Spanish moss, are magnificent. We were at the Pulaski House, which is a capital hotel. General Beauregard was staying there, and we paid our respects to him the morning after our arrival.

He was looking remarkably well, and said he had never in his life been in better health, which was the more gratifying to hear, as it was from ill health that the General had been obliged to give up his command in the field two years ago.

General Beauregard repeated what General Jordan had told us at Charleston, that he considered Fort Sumter stronger now for internal defence than it had ever been before.

At the railway station we parted with our friends Gordon and C., and proceeded on our journey to Mobile. It was long and tedious, but we got on pretty well. Some time before this we had discovered the dodge of fraternising with the conductor as soon as he came round to collect tickets, and the result was that we were generally introduced by him to his private box or to the mail-room, where there were always chairs and plenty of space for making ourselves comfortable.

Between Columbus and Montgomery General Bragg entered the cars and travelled with us some distance. He told us that he had just been all through south-western Georgia and eastern Alabama, and had found surprising abundance everywhere. The tax in kind which was now being levied by the Government was working exceedingly well, and provisions had already been collected amply sufficient to supply the armies in the west till the next harvest.

An old farmer in the car became intensely excited when he heard what an illustrious passenger he was travelling with, and rushed up saying, "Are you Mr Bragg? are you General Bragg? Give us your paw!" and the General very good-naturedly shook hands with him. Then he sat down and stared in mute admiration; but when the General had left he attacked Colonel Deas: "What big ears you've got! Why, you've got ears like a mule!—haw! haw! haw! You mustn't mind me,—I'm an old fool,—haw! haw! But I've shook hands with Mr Bragg anyhow,—haw! haw! haw!" And so he went on like a maniac, much to our amusement.

We stopped a few hours at Montgomery, and reached Mobile after a journey from Savannah of a little more than two days and two nights.

CHAPTER XIII

Mobile had suffered very little from the war, and still carried on a brisk commerce with the outer world in spite of the blockade. It is pleasantly situated on a broad plain, and has a beautiful prospect of the bay, from which it receives refreshing breezes. Large vessels cannot come directly to the city, but pass up Spanish River six miles round a marshy island into Mobile river, and then drop down to Mobile.

We took up our quarters at the Battle House,[1] an enormous caravanserai; and after a refreshing bath, and a capital

[1] "I put up at the principal hotel at Mobile —viz., the 'Battlehouse' [Battle House]. The living appeared to be very good by comparison and cost $8 a-day. In consequence of the fabulous value of boots, they must not be left outside the door of one's room, from danger of annexation by a needy and unscrupulous warrior." Fremantle, p. 129.

breakfast at a French restaurant, we sallied forth for a walk in the city.

Colonels Walton and Deas, who are well known here, were greeted by friends almost at every step and we presently adjourned to the Manassas Club, where our arrival was celebrated with a "cocktail." We then paid our respects to Admiral Buchanan and to General Maury, who commands the military department of the Gulf.

In the evening we went to a grand wedding-party and ball, where all the beauty of Mobile was assembled; and the reports I had heard of the charms of the fair sex at Mobile I found to be not at all exaggerated. This was the last ball of the season, as Lent was about to commence, but they had been very gay here during the carnival.[2] There is always a great deal of social intercourse at Mobile, and I shall ever cherish amongst my most agreeable recollections of the South the pleasant hours spent with the genial inhabitants of that city. It is usual to pay visits in the evening between seven and ten o'clock.

We were not much pleased with our accommodation at the hotel, and were removing to a boarding-house; but Colonel Scheliha, now Chief Engineer of the Department of the Gulf, whom I had met in the West, insisted upon my taking up my quarters with him, which I accordingly

[2] Kate Cumming, a Confederate hospital matron (i.e., nurse) in the Army of Tennessee, wrote in her journal March 3, 1864, shortly after her return to Newnan, Georgia, from a visit to her home in Mobile: "I had quite a pleasant time in Mobile; I found it gayer than ever. The excuse is there are so many soldiers there away from their homes, and the ladies say they must do what they can to entertain them. Quite a plausible reason!" Kate Cumming, *A Journal of Hospital Life in the Confederate Army of Tennessee from the Battle of Shiloh to the End of the War. . . .* (Louisville, Ky., c. 1866), p. 122.

did. He also placed his horses at my disposal, and we had many rides together. The Colonel is engaged in erecting a new line of forts round Mobile, which are perfect models of strength and judicious arrangement. They are built entirely of sand, with revetments of turf alone.[3] The turf on the embankments is fastened down to the sand by slips of the Cherokee rose, an exceedingly prickly shrub, which when grown will become a very disagreeable obstacle to a storming party. Though I must not say much more about them, I may mention, as a proof of the solidity of these works, that the parapets are 25 feet wide, the traverses against splinters of shell are 18 feet wide, against enfilading fire, 32 feet wide. Besides these forts there are two other lines of defence at Mobile, which will soon be one of the most strongly fortified places in the world.[4] The forts in the harbour, which are built on artificial islands, were being much strengthened; and everything was being done now with great energy, as it was reported that the Yankees designed to attack the city.

Sherman had advanced upon Jackson, but it was not supposed that an attack by land would be made from that quarter, as the country through which the Yankees would have to pass was poor and thinly populated, so that they

---

[3] The New Orleans correspondent of *The Index* wrote of preparations at Mobile against a Federal offensive. He quoted a Yankee officer in the blockading squadron as saying of the forts in Mobile Bay: "The walls are now concealed and protected by a heavy embankment of sand, against which shot and shell vainly pound." *The Index,* IV (1864), 108.

[4] The Legislature of Alabama had, in November, 1862, resolved that "The city of Mobile shall never be surrendered; that it should be defended from street to street, from house to house, and inch by inch, until, if taken, the victors' spoils should be alone a heap of ashes." *The Index,* IV (1864), 182.

would find it difficult to obtain supplies.[5] To attack Mobile by land they would have to make Pascacoula [Pascagoula] their base.

One day we went down the bay to visit the outer defences in a magnificent river-steamer. The Governor of Alabama, Admiral Buchanan, General Maury, and other gentlemen and ladies, were of the party. A very good band of music from one of the regiments of the garrison played, and dancing was soon got up in the splendid saloon. They dance the "finale" of the quadrille here with all sorts of figures—one of them like the last figure in the Lancers, walking round and giving the right and left hand alternately. Admiral Buchanan, who was looking on, joined in this, and naturally by doing so created a great deal of confusion and merriment, at which he was in high glee. He is immensely popular, and the young ladies all call him a charming old gentleman, although he is at least ten years too young to be an admiral in England.

We landed at Fort Morgan and went over the place. I confess I did not like it at all. It is built in the old style, with bricks here, there, and everywhere.

Now when bricks begin to fly about violently by tons'

---

[5] On February 16 Jones wrote: "The Federal General Sherman, with 30,000 men, was, at the last dates, still marching southeast of Jackson, Miss. It is predicted that he is rushing on his destruction." The next day he recorded: "Gen. Sherman, with 30,000 or 40,000 men, is still advancing deeper into Mississippi, and the Governor of Alabama has ordered the non-combatants to leave Mobile, announcing that it is to be attacked. If Sherman *should go on,* and succeed, it would be the most brilliant operation of the war. If he goes on and fails, it will be the most disastrous—and his surrender would be, probably, like the surrender of Lord Cornwallis at Yorktown. He ought certainly to be annihilated." Jones, II, 151, 151–52.

weight at a time, which is the case when they come in contact with 15-inch shells, they make themselves very unpleasant to those who have trusted to them for protection. This was conclusively shown at Fort Sumter.[6]

Fort Gaines, which we did not visit, was, they told me, a much better place, lately finished and strengthened on newer principles; but all agreed that these two forts were a very inadequate defence for the bay, into which the Yankees might enter whenever they chose to make the attempt.

Governor Ward made a speech to the garrison, and complimented the men who had lately re-enlisted for the war. At the commencement of the present struggle the soldiers only enlisted for three years, and in the whole army the term of enlistment was now drawing to a close. This was very awkward, as these men could not be dispensed with, and Congress would have been obliged to pass some law on the subject. But it was spared all trouble. The men knew as well as the Government that they were "bound to fight it out," and came forward voluntarily, re-enlisting with great enthusiasm for "ten years," "forty years," some even for "ninety-nine years," or "the war."[7] The alacrity with which the army has come for-

---

[6] "There are several batteries contiguous to Fort Morgan, the whereabouts of which the Yankee will never know until with hostile intent he comes in range of their fire. The battered walls of Fort Sumter have taught a lesson which the Confederates have not been slow to improve. Forts Morgan and Gaines are now in condition to 'laugh a siege to scorn,' at least such a one as the Yankee monitors might attempt." *The Index,* IV (1864), 108.

[7] "Everywhere our troops are re-enlisting for the war; one regiment re-enlisted, the other day, for forty years!" Jones, II, 152. In an address to the "Soldiers of the Armies of the Confederate States" February 9, President Davis expressed his appreciation for the re-enlistments. "I would," he wrote, "in vain attempt

ward on this occasion has caused much good feeling, and the few who before were inclined to croak and despond are now again as confident as ever of ultimate success.

From Fort Morgan we went on to Fort Powell, a beautiful little sandwork in Grant's Pass. This is an inlet to the bay, through which, in former days, steamers used to take a short cut to New Orleans, paying a toll to a Mr Grant, who had deepened the channel for them, and who was rewarded by a large fortune for his enterprise. Fort Powell, which was only just being completed, had six guns, Fort Morgan about fifty. There were still strong rumours of a contemplated attack upon Mobile, but General Maury told me he did not believe in them.[8]

A gentleman on board the steamer gave the General and myself a touching description of a melancholy journey he had made to the battle-field of Chicamauga, in search of the body of his son who was killed there. Ultimately, after great trouble and difficulty, he had succeeded in his

---

adequately to express the emotions with which I received the testimonials of confidence and regard which you have recently addressed to me. To some of those first received separate acknowledgments were returned. But it is now apparent that a like generous enthusiasm pervades the whole Army, and that the only exception to such magnanimous tender will be of those who, having originally entered for the war, can not display anew their zeal in public service." *Official Records* (Navy), Ser. II, 3, 162. A series of resolutions of thanks for re-enlistments passed by the Confederate Congress appear in the same volume, pp. 164–171.

[8] "Gen. Maury writes from Mobile that he cannot be able to obtain any information leading to the belief of an intention on the part of the enemy to attack Mobile. He says it would require 40,000 men, after three months' preparation, to take it," wrote Jones on February 8. But on February 23 the diarist noted, "A letter from Gen. Maury indicates now that Mobile is surely to be attacked." Jones, II, 145, 156.

object. The General suggested that after all a soldier could hardly find a better resting-place than where he had fallen in battle, and the father said, "Yes, he had always thought and said so himself, and his wife had agreed with him; but when the blow really came they had both felt that they could never be happy again, until their son's body had been found and laid near the place where they themselves would one day rest." I could not help thinking of the heartless indifference to similar feelings in the North which had been shown by the Yankee commander after Chicamauga, and I shuddered at the recollection of what I had seen on the battle-field there.

The tide was low at the Dog River bar when we returned, and although our river-steamer drew but little water, we were detained a couple of hours.

Whilst at Mobile we visited the men-of-war in the harbour, of which the Tennessee was the most formidable.[9] The great difficulty is how to get this ship over the Dog River bar, which has never more than nine feet of water, whilst the Tennessee draws full thirteen. They have therefore to raise her four feet by *"camels,"* which with the dearth of mechanical appliances in the South is a very difficult operation, and Admiral Buchanan almost despaired of succeeding.

---

[9] Miss Cumming gave a woman's view: "I also visited a very fine gun-boat—the *Tennessee*—said to be one of the largest afloat. Lieutenant Jordan, one of the officers, kindly showed us all over. It is a ram, and has many a dark-looking corner, where the men are to be stowed away in case of a battle. All looked very mysterious. I certainly felt I should not like to be one of the crew. There were a few more gun-boats nearly completed, but we did not go on board of them." Cumming, p. 123.

Apropos of the detention of the rams in England, Admiral Buchanan told me that during the war between the Brazils and Buenos Ayres, some sixteen years ago, he himself commanded and took out to Rio Janeiro one of two ships of war which were built at Baltimore for the Brazilians. He had given a grand entertainment—I think he said to 500 persons—on board his ship, before leaving Baltimore, and no secret was made of his destination. The Minister of Buenos Ayres at Washington was perfectly aware of what was going on, but never dreamed of making a complaint to the United States Government, and had he done so it would most certainly have been disregarded.

Another American, of the name of Chase, was in the service of Buenos Ayres, and in command of a little fleet of smaller vessels than the one Buchanan took out, and he told Buchanan afterwards that he had been on the look-out for him, and had orders to capture him on the way if he could; in which case, the Admiral said, there would very likely have been a row between Buenos Ayres and Uncle Sam.

Again, during the insurrection of Texas against Mexico, ships of war were openly built, and sent to the assistance of the insurgents, yet the Mexican Minister never thought of complaining, and if he had it would have been of no avail.

Were it not for the friendly neutrality of the British Government towards the North, the Confederates would have had a fleet, and the war in consequence would have been over long ago.

Although the Confederates think that they have been very unhandsomely and unfairly treated by the British Government, and comment freely upon the "extraordinary conduct" of Earl Russell, I may say here that they appreciate very highly the sympathy of Englishmen, which they believe to be entirely with them; and I never in the South heard an unpleasant remark made about the people of England, whom they believe to be misrepresented by their present Foreign Secretary.

A few days after our excursion down the bay, Fort Powell was attacked by a fleet of gunboats, and underwent some shelling; but after a day or two, finding they could make no impression, the Yankees retired.

There is a capital hard "shell road," so called from being made of oyster-shells, which runs alongside the bay for some seven miles. It is the favourite drive for carriages at Mobile. At the end is a house where refreshments are taken. We drove there one day, and were in the house whilst the firing at Fort Powell was going on. When the heavy Brooks [Brooke] gun in the fort was fired, it shook the windows so as to make them jingle, although the distance was near thirty miles. Owing to scarcity of stone, there are very few good roads in the Southern States, except near the mountains. The sand is often so deep that horses can hardly get along. For traffic they have railways, and as Southerners, male and female, prefer riding to driving, they care little for their roads. The shell road at Mobile, however, is excellent, and at New Orleans I am told they have some equally good made of the shell of the coquille.

I met a gentleman here, the fidelity of whose negro servant (slave) deserves to be put on record. He had had to fly in haste from Natchez on the Mississippi, when that place was occupied by the Yankees, and had left very important papers and a large sum of money securely hidden at his house there. Not being able to return himself to his home, he sent his negro servant, who, with a good deal of trouble, dodged his way in and out of the Federal lines, and brought his master all his important papers and ten thousand dollars in gold (two thousand pounds). How many white servants could be trusted with a similar mission?

I have said before that Southerners are the reverse of severe with their servants. Sometimes, however, they show a refinement of ingenuity in correcting them which is remarkable.

A lady here told me of a little boy about ten years old, whom I saw about the house, that he had been an incorrigibly wicked little rascal, whom no correction could improve, till she hit on the following mode of punishing him. She got another child of about the same age, and treated him to sweetmeats, whilst the naughty boy had to look on and got none. The moral affliction was intense, but it proved "a perfect cure."

I was present at Mobile at two weddings; one was that of General Tom Taylor, and the other of my friend Colonel Von Scheliha with Miss Williams, upon which occasion I officiated as groomsman. On the day this ceremony took place, we heard that nine other couples had been wedded. The happy men were all officers in the army. They say that marriages were never more frequent in the South than now. General Stuart was a great promoter of matches. He used to tell his officers that now was their time; they could marry without any questions being asked as to how they could support their wives, who would naturally remain at their homes and be taken care of by their parents. If they waited till the war was over it would be different. It was, to be sure, shockingly improvident, but seeing difficulties far ahead was not a foible of Stuart's. I believe his advice was frequently acted upon.

I was disappointed of my trip to the army in Mississippi, as it had fallen back from Meridian, and Sherman advancing had cut the railroad. I did not know exactly where I should find General Polk's headquarters, and delayed my excursion till it was too late to undertake it at all.

We had decided to return by steamer up the Alabama river as far as Montgomery, as it was a much pleasanter mode of travelling than by rail. The steamers all over this continent are splendid vessels, and we were very comfortable on board our boat. The country through which we passed was fertile and cultivated, and produces much cotton.

The cultivation of cotton in America is of comparatively recent date. Colonel Deas told me, that in 1774 his grandfather, who then resided in England, wrote out to his agents in Charleston, and directed them to attempt the cultivation of a sufficient amount of cotton to supply the negroes on his plantation with homespun. At that time the great staple in the Southern States was indigo, the cultivation of which is now so entirely discontinued that they were not able to make the naval uniform in the Confederacy blue, as every one knows a naval uniform ought to be. It is now the same colour as the military uniform. I believe the reason that seamen dress in blue, is because it is the only colour which is not stained by salt water.

At Selma a large body of soldiers came on board our boat, and for the rest of our journey to Montgomery we were crowded. However, the colonels and myself took refuge in "Texas," a glass shed built high over the centre of every river-steamer, whence the vessel is piloted. The cabins below this, and above the grand saloon, where the officers of the vessel are accommodated, also belong to "Texas." Here we had chairs, plenty of room, and a fine view.

The soldiers belonged to Hardee's corps, which had been sent to reinforce General Polk, but they were now no longer required, as Sherman had retreated. He fortunately never reached the rich country about Demopolis, but the already desolate country his army passed through he devastated in the most frightful manner, both coming and going, and everybody says he deserves to be hanged.

After a short stay at Montgomery we proceeded on our journey and reached Macon the next morning. There is a magnificent railroad station here and a capital hotel, the Brown House, where we breakfasted. At the station there were a large number of Yankee prisoners, who had been picked up during Sherman's retreat.

We slept that night at Savannah and went on to Charleston next morning. Here we made a two days' rest, and I took up my quarters with Mr Ch., finding a dinner-party assembled as usual, and old friends among the guests. One of them, as a parting gift, made me a present of an enormous cigar-case full of Havannah cigars, a princely benefaction under present circumstances in Dixie, when Havannah cigars are not to be purchased at any price.

Soon after we reached Wilmington my two friends and travelling companions returned to Richmond, their leave of absence having expired, whilst I with much regret prepared to say farewell to "the sunny South." A few pleasant days flew quickly by, and then with C., whose business called him to Nassau, I embarked in the Hansa, a noble ship, which was now to run the blockade for the eighteenth time.

It was exhilarating enough when, the moon having set at midnight, we slipped out of Cape Fear river, and dashed at full speed through the blockading fleet. It was pitch dark, and not even a cigar was allowed to be alight on deck. For nearly an hour we kept peering through the night to discover whether any Yankee ship lay in our way, but we passed unobserved, and then all immediate danger was over.

The next day we saw a large number of cotton bales floating in the sea, and on arriving at Nassau we heard that they had been thrown overboard by the Alice, which had left the night before us, and had been chased for a whole day by a Yankee cruiser. A little schooner was engaged in picking them up, and as a single bale is worth £40 she was no doubt making a good thing of it. We performed our voyage to Nassau in about sixty hours, and were loudly cheered as we steamed into the harbour.

Nassau, which before the war was rather an insignificant place, is now a flourishing town, large amounts of money being made and spent there. The island of [New] Providence, of which Nassau is the capital, is very fertile, and used to be a great place for cotton cultivation. It still grows weeds in profusion, but nothing else. Every ounce of butcher-meat, every potato or other vegetable, milk—which comes in tin-cases—in short, every necessary of life, is imported from New York or Havana. Blockade-running has made everything very dear, and the natives complain of being reduced to live upon turtle and pineapples.

The sponges which are picked up near the island are said to be superior to those in the Mediterranean, and conch-shells used in the manufacture of cameos are also an article of export. These shells have given a name to the natives of the Bahamas, who are known in this part of the world as Conchs.

We were invited to a pic-nic and fishing party on the island, about ten miles from Nassau, and spent a pleasant day. Our party was a large one, and consisted of most of the officers of the garrison and a good many gentlemen from Nassau.

We commenced fishing early in the morning and dragged a creek, and we caught amongst other fish a small shark. But the most curious things were the balloon fish; they are very small, but if you tickle them on the stomach they blow themselves up to the size of a football, and I am sorry to say that some of our party were so cruel as to use them as balls. It did them no harm, however. I put several back into the water after they had been flying about in the air, propelled by the boots of some of the company, and they immediately collapsed and swam away merrily.

From Nassau I proceeded to Havana.

CHAPTER XIV

We had a beautifully bright passage, and reached Havana in the morning of the second day after we had left Nassau. The Moro [Morro] at the entrance of the harbour is a fierce-looking fortress, and so is the Punta on the other side of the bay, and they both display an enormous amount of guns; but these are of the description now usually sneered at as "popguns," and I am afraid would be of very little use against a serious attack.

As we ran up towards the city and harbour we disturbed the myriads of flying-fish with which this landlocked bay abounds, and sent them in flocks before us, glittering like diamonds in the morning sunshine. These creatures are as good as they are beautiful—I mean, *to eat*—but they are seldom caught except by accident. One dropped on board the Hansa as we were coming from Wilmington, and I partook of it after it had been cooked, and found its flavour was most delicate.

On landing I was struck by a peculiar monomania of the Havana lower orders. Every one who does you the slightest service immediately asks for two dollars. The boatman who rows you ashore, the porter who carries your portmanteau to the custom-house, the man who takes it to the cab, the man who calls the cab, the cabman himself, each specifies two dollars as the remuneration he expects. It is "dos duros" here, and "dos duros" there, and "dos duros" everywhere. It is, however, least expensive and most amusing to refuse their demand, as they will then run after you for ten minutes together, chattering all the time, and giving you a capital Spanish lesson gratis.

Havana is a very fine city, and the streets are regular, though too narrow for carriages to pass each other, and they have to drive up and down alternate streets to avoid collisions. The houses are built like those in the south of Spain, with no display towards the street, but with *patios,* pillars, marbles, and fountains in the interior.

The suburbs are in more modern style. Between the suburbs and the city there is an *Alameda,* or broad promenade planted with trees, which is crowded in the evenings, and from it the *Paseo de Tacon* leads to the Governor's palace and gardens, a couple of miles from the town. The gardens are remarkably fine, and the vegetation most luxuriant. I was amused to see the pains they were taking to cultivate amongst all their tropical plants our cottage-garden flowers, such as the convolvulus, larkspur, marigold, and single dahlia; but the poor things did not seem to flourish.

Among the peculiarities of this country are the "volantes." They are like the old-fashioned French cabriolets, only with extraordinarily long shafts. The horse is harnessed at least six feet away from the carriage, and is ridden by a postilion; the tail is plaited, adorned with ribbons, and fastened to the saddle, which I thought rather cruel in such a hot country, but was told that flies and other insects do not torment horses here as they do in Europe. Most of the "volantes" have but one horse, and are the "cabs" of Havana; but there are some two-horse private ones which are very gay and stylish.

Havana is a great place for blockade-runners, which make their trips from hence to Mobile, Galveston, and many other points on the Texas and Florida coast. Of course there were many Southerners here; amongst them were officers on their road from Richmond to Texas and *vice versa,* who had preferred the sea route to the long overland journey; and as I had brought letters to the Confederate Government agent as well as to several other gentlemen at Havana, I was in no want of pleasant society. Through the miscarriage of a letter I was, however, prevented from visiting a plantation on the island, which I very much regretted, as I was anxious to see something of negro life in Cuba. At Havana, on all public works, and along the railroad to Matanzas, I saw no negroes at work; all the labourers were Chinese coolies. The system of coolie labour is rapidly increasing in the West Indies, and the philanthropist may hope that it will in time supersede slave labour and the slave trade, as it is much more profitable. The coolie traders will sell a Chinaman (women are not imported) for eight years for 150 dollars, after which he is free to starve, or go home, or to bind himself for another period. Consequently, by taking it out of different individuals, forty of the best years of man's life can be bought for 750 dollars—much less than an able-bodied negro costs, who, besides that you seldom get forty years' work out of him, has to be maintained both when he is too young and when he is too old to work. I have been told by skippers who have been engaged in transporting coolies, that in the East Indies the crimps or dealers sell coolies at five rupees a-head, ready for shipment, so that those engaged in the trade make no small profits. Thus it is satisfactory to all concerned; and at the same time, so as not to offend the sensibilities of philanthropists, the odious terms of buying and selling are never made use of; it is called immigration, hiring, &c. Employers have to be careful how they punish their coolies, as a Chinaman invariably commits suicide if the lash is used upon him. They are not so particular, I am told, about the bamboo.

Although on public works, railroads, &c., and near the large cities, none but Chinamen, as I said before, are to be seen at work, yet, in the interior, I understand that the planters are very unwilling to employ them; the negroes dislike them, and their habits are abominable. They are by no means as lively and fond of amusement as the negroes, but of a sober and rather melancholy disposition.

The opera company had left Havana a few days before my arrival, but I went one evening to the Gran Teatro de Tacon, more for the purpose of seeing the house than the play. It is a very fine theatre, and, the Havanese say, the finest in the world. When the curtain fell after the first act, I was not a little astonished to see staring me in the face, an invitation in enormous capitals to visit the "Cocktail Coffeehouse, Mercaderes, No. 22"; and, on closer inspection, it turned out that the drop-curtain was adorned with a figure of Mercury dancing on tiptoe on a box of cigars, with an anchor leaning against his shin, and a hogshead of molasses in the distance. Around this picture seventy-two advertisements large and small were tastefully arranged.

Havana is one of the last places where I should have expected such an exhibition of commercial enterprise, as its inhabitants have by no means the reputation of being a very go-ahead or commercial race.

There are many Yankees here carrying on business and enterprises with great energy, to the intense disgust of the indolent Havanese. They have paved the city, lighted it with gas, built splendid suburbs with broad streets and modern houses; and now they want to open the bay, which is at present so landlocked that the waters are almost stagnant, and the cause of a great deal of *vomito* and yellow fever in summer.

This could be easily remedied by cutting through to the sea, and then, the place being no longer unhealthy, any amount of strangers would come and reside here, whilst at present they have all to fly from it in the hot season. But the Havanese object decidedly. The climate suits them as it is, and they have quite as many strangers amongst them already as they wish to have.

I gained a good deal of information about cigars whilst at Havana, and went over the celebrated manufactory of Partagas. Some fifty men were at work rolling up cigars, which they do very neatly and slowly, as the quality of a cigar depends in great measure upon its being carefully made. The workmen are not allowed to make more than a certain number—I think one hundred—each day.

When done, they are taken into the sorting-room, and are there divided, according to their careful finish, into firsts, seconds, and thirds—or *flores, superiores,* and *buenos,* as they are generally called. The quality of the tobacco is nearly the same in all cigars which cost more than forty dollars a thousand. The light-coloured cigars are, of course, milder in flavour than the dark ones, and they are classified as *claro, colorado, maduro,* and *oscuro,* with intermediate shades such as *claro-colorado, colorado-oscuro,* &c.

Partagas and del Valle (Cabanas y Carvajal) are the greatest exporters of cigars, and their productions are supposed to be the best, as they certainly are the most expensive; but there are, I believe I may say, hundreds of other manufacturers, some of whom produce a most excellent "weed."

The last steamer which left for Southampton carried with her six millions of cigars, and I was told that was rather under the average. The export of cigars has increased wonderfully during the last few years, and the manufacturers can at present hardly supply the demand. The finest and most expensive go to San Francisco, the next best to England.

A bad cigar is hardly to be found, and smoking is permitted everywhere; even in the cathedral, I saw a man holding a cigar in his hand, and giving a puff every now and then that it might not go out. *Good* cigars are always best when they are fresh; it is only bad ones that improve by age and dryness.

I must not forget the fish-market at Havana, which, as far as the beautiful exterior of the fish goes, is perhaps unrivalled in the world. It reminded one of a jeweller's show-window in the Rue de la Paix, or of one of those stalls in the Lowther Arcade where they sell *papier-maché* portfolios, so brilliant and sparkling were the colours exhibited. It was oppressively hot when we left Havana, but it became colder and colder every day; and when we reached New York we found it quite wintry, although it was the end of April.

I was not molested on landing, as I had half expected, though, of course, as long as I stayed in the Northern States I had to be very careful of getting in the way of the authorities; and, on account of my friends, it will not be prudent for me now to say much about where I stayed, or with whom I associated, during my sojourn in "Yankee-doodledom."

CHAPTER XV

A few extracts from my letters written at the time may perhaps be found not uninteresting, as showing the views taken at that time of passing events by partisans of the South, with whom I almost exclusively associated.

April 25, 1864.—There has been some hard fighting and some very expeditious marching in Louisiana. The Federals, who had advanced on the road to Shreveport as far nearly as Mansfield, which is only forty miles from Shreveport, began to march back again on Friday afternoon at five o'clock, and on Sunday afternoon at two o'clock they had reached Grand Ecore, which is fifty miles from Mansfield, on the road back to New Orleans. They won several glorious victories, too, whilst they were marching in this direction, so I think you will agree with me that they made a pretty good use of their time. I suppose that every one was anxious to bring the first news of the glorious victories to their friends in the gunboats at Grand Ecore.

Besides the killed and wounded, some fifteen thousand men are said to have been left behind, as the pace was too much for them; and the rebels were also kind enough to take charge of all General Banks's trains, leaving him not so much as a tooth-brush, they say; and yet the 'New York Herald' edition for Europe, which leaves with this letter, will contain "a full and detailed report, from our special correspondent, of the three days' fighting and glorious victory of the Union forces in Louisiana."

The 'Evening Post' of to-day thinks that the probable results of the glorious victories will be to clear out the rebels entirely from Louisiana, Arkansas, and the greater part of Texas. Almost all the other newspapers talk pretty much in the same style.

They are a funny people.

General Banks was a blacksmith, a dancing-master, and a lawyer successively, before he took to soldiering; and they say that if he could fight as well as he can dance, he would find few who could beat him. He told —— that he seriously expected to be President of the United States some day; but I am afraid he has not improved his chance by his late victories.

General Grant is said by his former comrades to be a drunken little vagabond; and indeed he had to quit the old army in consequence of his predilection for whisky, and led a very obscure and miserable life for some time near St Louis. He is said, though, to have excellent officers on his Staff.

There was a tremendous excitement in the money

market here the other day, when Mr Chase came over from Washington and sent down the price of gold. Wall Street was quite a sight to see; the "lame ducks," as they call the ruined speculators, were rushing about in a state of frantic excitement quite wonderful to behold.

Never, they say, was New York so gay as it is now: the private carriages and servants in livery have more than doubled, and entertainments are given by the *nouveaux riches* of the most wonderful magnificence.

The New Yorkers assert that their present prosperity is owing to the wonderful development of the trade in corn from the west during the last few years, and that if it were not for the war they would be far more prosperous than they are. They admit, however, that some large fortunes have been made by contractors and stock-jobbers.

One gentleman, who two years ago was not worth a cent, has fitted up a private theatre, costing ten thousand pounds, where five amateur performances are being given for the benefit of wounded soldiers. Every one invited has to pay five dollars for his ticket, and they clear about a thousand dollars a-night. There is nothing like benevolence after all.

. . . .

May 3.—Mr Seward went to Baltimore the other day, and there was a grand *fête* at the Sanitary Fair for the benefit of wounded soldiers. He took nearly all the foreign ministers with him, and showed them off to the public in a way they did not like. The "great lion of his menagerie," as he called him on a similar trip last year, had, however, profited by experience, and was not there; nor, of course, were any decent inhabitants of the city present. The newspapers say that Mr Seward was more tipsy than usual on this festive occasion.

There is to be a convention on the 7th of June at Baltimore to nominate a candidate for the next presidency, and some people say that Grant will not be allowed to fight before that time, as if he wins he will perhaps himself be a candidate, and if he loses, Lincoln most likely loses his chance of re-election too.

. . . .

May 17, 1864.—As yet each army has been giving entire satisfaction to its friends. Every Northern newspaper, almost, is full of accounts of glorious victories, and I daresay the Southern papers are the same; but the authorities here are very careful in preventing them from being brought through the lines, and we have not seen a single Richmond paper since the battles began.

We hear, however, that they claim great successes on the part of Lee, and that Richmond was illuminated in consequence. After the first two days' fighting Grant was entirely cut off from his communications with Washington, and nothing was heard of him for several days. He had to open a new line of communication through Fredericksburg and Acquia [Aquia] Creek, with which he is now so pleased that he says he will fight on that line all the summer.

The loss of the Yankees is said to be frightful: 70,000 killed, wounded, and missing, was stated in yesterday's papers, and is said to be below the mark.

There are more than 27,000 men wounded in the battles of Thursday and Friday, the 5th and 6th of May, in the hospitals of Fredericksburg and Washington, whilst those of the later battles are still in hospital-tents in the field.

Lee, fighting behind intrenchments, lost, comparatively, very few men.

It might, perhaps, be a consolation to the Yankee public, if they cannot take Richmond, to lose 100,000 men, killed and wounded, in the attempt, as it would be "a big thing;" but the soldiers themselves do not like it particularly, and there are symptoms of great discontent, both amongst officers and men, at the way in which they have been handled by Grant.

Lee has been preparing the trap made use of on the present occasion ever since Meade's advance last November, when you may remember Meade bitterly disappointed Lee by going back without fighting.

Intrenchments were being thrown up and plank-roads being made from Orange Court-house, to facilitate the movements of the army, when I was there in December. The wonderful part of this business is, that a commander-in-chief should be found so ignorant and obstinate as Grant, to come and knock his head against these positions.

His army, the finest and best equipped that the Yankees ever put in the field, is now pretty nearly destroyed, and they are scraping together all the men they can to send on reinforcements.

The militia is everywhere being called out to relieve the regular soldiers in the garrisons, and probably very soon Mr Lincoln will have to make another call for 200,000 men at least. Then there will very likely be a row.

At the camp of Confederate prisoners, at Lookout Point, negro soldiers are doing duty, and are said to be very insolent to their prisoners, and to amuse themselves by shooting into their camp.[1] The other day they killed two and wounded four, for what reason nobody knows and nobody cares. These negroes are not naturally vicious, but they are incited to misbehave by their officers, who are a low set of ruffians. I need hardly say that no man of any self-respect in the North would consent to be officer in a negro regiment.

Everybody in this neighbourhood is so anxious about the fighting, that very little else is thought of or talked about.

I understand that, in society in Boston and New York, it is considered very *mauvais genre* to talk about the war, and very unfashionable to know anything about or take any interest in the "latest news."

They told me at New York that politics were entirely tabooed. The only approach to them is to abuse England, which every one is glad to do; and as everybody agrees on this point, there is no difference of opinion, and no one's feelings are hurt.

. . . .

I made a trip to Wilmington (in Delaware) and Philadelphia the other day, and stayed at Philadelphia at the Continental Hotel, a big place, where there are twenty miles of bell-wire, seven miles of gas-pipe, five miles and a half of steam-tubing, and over five acres of carpet, be-

---

[1] A Confederate account of life at Point Lookout is A. M. Keiley's *Prisoner of War; or, Five Months Among the Yankees, Being a Narrative of the Crosses, Calamities, and Consolations of a Petersburg Militiaman During an Enforced Summer Residence North*. By A. Rifleman, Esq., Gent. (Richmond, [1865]). Keiley's narrative was republished after the war as *In Vinculis*.

sides 25,000 square feet of marble pavement in the halls and public rooms.

Philadelphia is a fine city. The inhabitants are a little prim and particular, and in one of the large squares—a sort of park—they have taken up all the benches that used to be there, and have substituted little mushroom-stools, placing them about two yards apart.

Philadelphia propriety is no longer to be shocked by the possibility of young people sitting down together on a bench under a shady tree, and whispering soft nothings into each other's ears.

Philadelphia has a private war-debt of thirty millions of dollars paying interest, as has in the same proportion every county and city in the Union. New York has quite a national debt of its own, incurred since the war began, chiefly for the purchase of substitutes; and this is in addition to the national expenditure of the Union, which people in Europe suppose is to ruin the Americans and eventually stop the war.

May 22, 1864.—Mr Grant, I am happy to say, is making strategic movements, the object of which it would be improper to divulge, says Mr Stanton, Secretary of War.

That is to say, that Lee, having driven him from his first line of communication with Washington by the Rapidan fords, has now driven him from his communication by Fredericksburg, and Grant is in a bad way. Probably he will try and get to Tappahannock or Urbanna, and then most likely back again to where he came from as fast as he can. Grant's soldiers are getting tired of him and call him the butcher, and won't fight.

. . . .

June 6, 1864.—Grant did not go back, as I prophesied he would, after his terrible defeat on Thursday, May 12, though he ought to have done so; and Mr Stanton is reported to have said that every other officer in the United States army would have done so; but it would have been too humiliating.

Lee seems to have it his own way everywhere, though it is impossible to get at the exact truth, as Southern accounts are suppressed with wonderful success; but it is clear that Grant is fighting very hard, and with terrible loss to himself, to get where he could have gone by water without losing a single man.

But it saves appearances, and there are plenty of silly people in the North who applaud and crow over his wonderful "flanking movements." Whenever he has tried to force his way to where he really wants to go, he has been very badly beaten.

. . . .

June 14.—We are kept entirely in the dark about Grant's movements, but it is pretty well understood that his active campaign has come to an end. He has certainly succeeded in spoiling a large army with greater celerity than any other general of modern times.

The other day there was great crowing in the papers, as the Commissary-General Ingalls telegraphed to a friend in the Senate that they had "made a *ten stroke*" (alluding to knocking down all the ten pins at skittles), and "had the rebels '*this pop;*' " and Grant telegraphed that Lee was "in his last ditch," and that he meant "to fight on his present line if it lasted all the summer." It turns out now that they were being more severely handled that day (May 12) than ever they had been before, and, of course, everybody says it was the Commissary's whisky that made them send such boasting telegrams.

. . . .

The Baltimore Convention has nominated Lincoln President, and one Johnson, a tailor, who never learnt to read or write till he was grown up, Vice-President.

CHAPTER XVI

Just at this time, when the North was most loudly proclaiming success, and Southern sympathisers had, on the contrary, become convinced that Grant's campaign was a total failure, a great sensation was caused at New York by a spurious proclamation, purporting to emanate from President Lincoln, appointing a day of fasting and humiliation, and admitting an entire want of success.[1]

---

[1] This fraudulent proclamation was written by Joseph P. Howard of the New York *Times.* Dated May 17, it was printed in the New York *World,* in *The Journal of Commerce,* and a portion of the edition of the New York *Herald* for the morning of May 18 before the hoax was exposed. The proclamation represented President Lincoln as pessimistic about the summer campaign and called for a draft of an additional 400,000 soldiers. It was reprinted in *The Index,*

The Administration was furious, and so were their organs in the press: it was pronounced to be a traitorous device calculated to aid and comfort the enemy; and several of the opposition journals which had published it were seized and suspended. It turned out, however, that the inventor of the hoax was one of their own party, and had not wished to damage the North by his *jeu d'esprit,* but only to make a little money by stockjobbing.

He was imprisoned, but soon released. Curiously enough, this is the same fellow—his name is Howard—who, as correspondent of the 'New York Times' when the Prince of Wales was at Richmond, invented a story about his having been insulted by the mob. There was not the slightest foundation for the tale, which the fellow entirely invented out of revenge for not having been invited to some entertainment given to the Prince; but the idea of there being a ruffianly mob at staid and sober Richmond was much too agreeable to the Yankees not to be eagerly repeated and believed; and although the Richmond people took the trouble afterwards officially to deny the truth of the report—the Duke of Newcastle adding his testimony—the story had been already "thoroughly well authenticated" by frequent repetition, and the Northern newspapers did not, of course, think it their duty to refute a rumour which might damage the slaveholding aristocracy of the South.

Neither people nor papers are particular here on the score of veracity, and there is not the slightest disgrace attached to being found out in a falsehood. Not content

---

IV (1864), 362. The New York correspondent of *The Index* reported the hoax in his regular letter (p. 363), and it was also recounted (with considerable editorial bias) in an additional summary account written in London (pp. 360–61).

sometimes with telling a fib themselves, some people will, without the slightest hesitation, request their friends to tell one for them.

A man who could not tell a lie without blushing would here be considered the reverse of "smart."

When newspapers quarrel and abuse each other, you never find one trying to convict another of an untruth, as they usually do in their quarrels in Europe, simply because such a conviction would be no discredit, but rather the contrary. The consequence of this absence of veracity is, that nobody ever believes anybody; and as to official despatches, they, as Sir Robert Walpole said of history, must be lies. Mr Stanton has over and over again circulated, during this last campaign, statements which he must have known to be untrue, and which were certain to be contradicted in the course of a few days or even hours.*

---

*As for Admiral Porter, whose ridiculous assertions have excited grave attention lately in Europe, he is well known in America to excel even his compeers in flights of fancy.

CHAPTER XVII

Grant's campaign being virtually at an end, in the first days of June I left the neighbourhood of the seat of war, and spent a few weeks at the city of New York, and in visiting some of the famous watering-places of that State.

Rambling about the country, angling and shooting in the vicinity of Saratoga, Sharon Springs, Trenton Falls, &c., we used to make friends with the country-people as much as we could, and try to elicit their political opinions.

At this time everybody was strenuously in favour of peace and McClellan's election to the Presidency, but then the country population of the State of New York has always been *"Democratic."*

The "Democrats," I need hardly say, are the Conservatives here; the "Republicans" are the Radicals.

We met a knot of men one day in a bar-room who were abusing the Administration lustily. One of them, the loudest of the lot, was twitted by his friends as being the assistant provost-marshal for the county, an official whose duty it would properly be to carry out the conscription; but he swore that he had never enlisted a man nor arrested a deserter, and that he never would.

It is the same thing, I am told, all over this State, and very similar in several others, especially in the West. And since I heard this, it has been a mystery to me how the conscription is carried out in Democratic counties.

In Pennsylvania the great increase of mining since the war began has been attributed by some to the number of deserters from the army who have sought for employment under ground.

We found Trenton Falls the most delightful place on our tour. The cascades are beautiful, and it is always shady and cool amongst the rocks, a great luxury in July.

There was a grand gathering on the 4th of July, Declaration of Independence Day, and plenty of fireworks at night. In the South this anniversary is no longer observed, but is considered a Yankee festival. Soon after this we proceeded to Niagara Falls, and got very comfortable quarters at the Clifford House, on the Canadian side. The "season" had hardly yet commenced, but we found here a number of Morgan's men, who were delighted to meet their old colonel [1] again. During Mor-

---

[1] St. Leger Grenfell. Grenfell and Ross travelled together during Ross's visit to the North. The reason Grenfell is not mentioned by name in the narrative is explained in one of Ross's letters to William Blackwood. "I am very sorry to say," he wrote from London February 27, 1865, "that my friend Colonel St. Leger Grenfell has got into trouble and been arrested in the North, probably from having been implicated in the late raids from

gan's late raid in Kentucky, three hundred of his followers had been cut off from his main force, and most of them had now made their way through the Western States into Canada, where they were enjoying "hospitality," for which they paid three dollars a-day in gold, or five in greenbacks, and which they abused by talking Secesh politics and plotting mischief against the Yankees.

They were all nice gentlemanly fellows. There were also other refugees from Kentucky at the Falls; ladies and old gentlemen, who told of the horrible barbarities practised by the Federals in their State. No one's life, honour, or property, not even that of Union men, seemed to be safe now from the fury of such Yankee leaders as Burbridge, Payne,[2] and some others. Besides these there were some prominent politicians from the South staying at the hotel and in the neighbourhood, whose avowed object it was to negotiate with the leaders of the Democratic party in the North and bring all their influence to bear upon a peace "platform" being raised at the coming Presidential election.

We made several excursions in the neighbourhood, and went over several fields of battle where British and Americans fought in their last war; and we heard many traditions concerning them.

Our memories were also refreshed concerning the way our American cousins behaved to our Canadian relations when they had that little difficulty in Lower Canada in 1837.

Canada. Please to scratch the anecdote about Seward's asking him to tell a lie, as it might make them more spiteful against him. Also the mention of him as having travelled with me in the North."

[2] John Payne.

It is rather interesting just now to recall their "strict neutrality."

The "rebellion," it will be remembered, was confined to Lower Canada, and Sir Francis Head, the Governor of Upper Canada, had sent every soldier from his province to the seat of the disturbance; and, moreover, to show his confidence in the loyalty of the Upper Canadians, he had caused 6000 stand of arms to be "committed, free from all military custody or care, to the mayor of Toronto." A certain M'Kenzie did, however, with five hundred followers, raise the flag of insurrection at Montgomerie's tavern, near Toronto, on December 4, 1837. The standard was inscribed, "Bidwell and the glorious minority—1837—and a good beginning." The good beginning consisted in murdering Colonel Moodie, "a distinguished veteran officer, who, passing Montgomerie's tavern accompanied by three gentlemen on horseback, was fired at, wounded in two places, and taken into the tavern, where he died."

M'Kenzie then "committed every description of enormity—robbed the mail, with his own hands set fire to Dr Horne's house, plundered many inoffensive individuals, stole several horses, made a number of respectable persons prisoners," &c. &c., till, on December the 7th, Colonel M'Nab attacked him with some hastily-collected militia, and "a total rout ensued; and, according to Sir Francis Head, 'Mr M'Kenzie, in a state of the greatest agitation, ran away.'" He fled in disguise to Buffalo, in the State of New York.

For the crimes of murder, arson, and robbery, for which there was not the slightest excuse, except that some hundred miles off a rebellion was going on, the extradition of this felon was immediately demanded by the

British, and acceded to be the American authorities? No, indeed.

M'Kenzie, now a great hero and patriot, remained at Buffalo, "enlisting soldiers" and organising fresh raids into Canada. For this purpose "public meetings were convened, volunteers were called for, the very women inciting them to enlist, and arms, ammunition, and provisions were openly contributed. . . . Artillery and munitions of war belonging to the American Government were, in the most public manner, and in the face of the American authorities, employed for the purpose of invading the British territory. . . . At the same time the language, not merely of the journals, but of official men, was such as to lead to the conclusion that the English, and not themselves, were the aggressors." The 'Annual Register' mentions four different raids, in different parts of the country, all organised in the States, and chiefly carried out by Yankee sympathisers. On one occasion a party of Canadians, led by one M'Leod, destroyed a steamer, the Caroline, used by the raiders, whilst it was in American waters. At this the Yankees were so furious that, when some time afterwards another person of the name of M'Leod was travelling in the States, he was seized and tried for his life, and would certainly have been hanged if it had not turned out that he was the wrong man.

There was no "excusable irritation" to be allowed for in those days.

These raids were renewed in the following year; and on one occasion, when a hundred and fifty-nine prisoners were taken, it was found that among them were four Upper Canadians, eight Lower Canadians, five British and Irish, three Poles, five Germans, three French, and a hundred and thirty-one natives of the United States.

The details of these affairs are to be found in the 'Annual Register' for 1838, and I have only mentioned them here to show that the Yankees have not always treated their neighbours as they insist upon being treated themselves.

It may be questioned whether the present submissive policy of the Canadians will prove advantageous to them in the long-run. Intimidated by the threats of Mr Seward and General Dix, as the Yankee newspapers boast, they have already stretched their laws so as virtually to give up the right of asylum to refugees—a right which even the Turks maintained against the threats of Austria and Russia; they have consented to pass a still more stringent "alien law" than they already possessed; and they have even voted an "indemnification of fifty thousand dollars in order to *buy off the Gauls.*" But all this will never appease the "excusable irritation" of which we hear so much, as long as Canada continues to be prosperous, to absorb a large amount of emigration, and to refuse to see the advantage of being under the "best government under the sun."

M'Kenzie would certainly never have been given up to Canada, not if there had been a thousand extradition treaties against him, and the Yankees will only despise the Canadians for stretching and changing their laws at their dictation. They are the last people in the world to give up bullying because they see that it alarms their neighbours; and, after all, the Canadians have no great reason to be afraid of them. Their long frontier is not a bit longer than the opposite one, and quite as easily defended. Indeed the Yankees have so many vulnerable points, in the shape of large commercial cities near their border, that they would probably feel the inconveniences of war much sooner than the Canadians. It is said, in excuse for the Canadians giving up Southern refugees, that these people had no right to plot mischief on neutral territory. If so, the offence they committed was clearly against the neutral territory, and it is there that they ought to be called to account.

From the Falls we went by Lake Ontario and the St Lawrence to Montreal, where we spent a few pleasant days.

The hotels in Canada are all very well managed, but the black servants are perfect idiots compared to the smiling and attentive "boys" in the South. We visited the artillery barracks, and admired the beautiful Armstrong battery, and the magnificent horses—which latter, however, were crowded together in the most execrably bad stables I have ever seen. Part of these were built in two storeys, and the sewage from the upper stables was dripping through the flooring down into the lower one. I could be under no delusion in regard to this, as a drop of filth fell upon my coat. But the Canadians seem to be profoundly indifferent as to how the troops are accommodated, and part of the garrison has already, for want of room, to camp out on an island in the St Lawrence.

When the proposed concentration of all the troops in Canada at Montreal and Quebec is carried out, there will be a squeeze.

At Quebec I only stayed just long enough to see that its present fortifications are "of no account;" indeed, as they consist chiefly of thin stone walls, they would be very disagreeable to their defenders, and to nobody else, in case of a fight.

Our voyage in the Nova Scotian was pleasant and prosperous; indeed, crossing the Atlantic in Canadian boats has a great advantage in being the shortest sea-passage. We were three days on the St Lawrence; and seven days after losing sight of Newfoundland, the green cliffs of old Ireland welcomed us to Europe and home.

APPENDIX

Extract from Appleton's Guide-book

Rambling, once upon a time, through the negro quarters, we amused ourself in studying the varied characters of the slaves, as shown in the style of their cabins, the order in which they kept them, the taste displayed in their gardens, &c.; for every man has all the material and time at his command to make himself and his family as comfortable as he pleases. The huts of some bore as happy an air as one might desire; neat palings enclosed them; the gardens were full of flowers, and blooming vines clambered over the doors and windows. Others, again, had been suffered by the idle occupants to fall into sad decay; no evidence of taste or industry was to be seen in their hingeless doors, their fallen fences, or their weed-grown gardens. These lazy fellows were accustomed even to cut down the shade-trees which had been kindly planted before their homes, rather than walk a few yards farther for other and even better fuel. The more industrious of the negroes here, as elsewhere, employ their leisure hours, which are abundant, in the culture of vegetables and in raising fowls, which they sell to their masters, and thus supply themselves with the means to purchase many little luxuries of life. For necessaries they have no concern, since they are amply and generously provided with all which they can require. Others, who will not thus work for their pin-money, are dependent upon the kindness of their masters, or more frequently upon their ingenuity at thieving. Many of them sell to their master in the morning the produce they have stolen from him the previous night. At least they all manage to keep their purses filled; and we were assured that not one, had he occasion or desire to visit Charleston or Augusta, but could readily produce the means to defray his expenses.

While once visiting some friends in Carolina, we had the pleasure of witnessing the bridal festivities of one of the servants of the family, a girl of some eighteen years. The occasion was one of those pleasant things which hold long place in the memory. For days previous, the young ladies of the household gaily busied themselves in kind preparations for the event; in instructions to the bride,—in the preparation of her white muslin robe, of her head-dress, and other portions of her toilet,—in writing her notes of invitation to her sable friends—Mr Sambo Smith, or Miss Clara Brown, according to the surnames of their respective owners, whose names the negroes of the South always assume. The ceremony took place in the cabin of the bride, and in presence of the whites; and then followed revelry, feasting, and dancing upon the lawn, much to the delight of the happy pair and their dark friends, and scarcely less to the pleasure of the bride's kind mistresses, and of all of us who witnessed their sports from the parlour windows. By the way, when you journey in South, line your pockets with tobacco, dispense it generously to the darkies, and they are your friends for life.

Here the rice plantations abound. Many of them are

of great extent, some of the planters employing several hundred slaves. The white population is thus necessarily thin, but opulent. The cabins of the negroes on these extensive domains, surrounding the mansion and its many outbuildings of the proprietor, give to every settlement the aspect of a large and thriving village. There is something peculiarly fascinating in this species of softened feudal life. The slaves are for the most part warmly attached to their masters, and they watch over their interests as they would their own. Indeed they consider themselves part and parcel of their master's family. They bear his name, they share his bounty; and their fortune depends wholly upon his. Through life they have every comfort; the family physician attends them when sick, and in their old age and imbecility they are well protected. They glory in their master's success and happiness; and their pride is in exact proportion to the rank of the family they serve.

"Go 'way, Sambo," we once heard one of these jovial lads exclaim to another, whose ill-fortune it was to serve a less opulent planter than himself; "go 'way Sambo; your massa only got fifty niggers; my massa got hundred." And he pulled his shirt-collar, and marched pompously off with the step of a millionaire.

The masters themselves, descended from a chevalier stock, and accustomed for many generations to the seclusion of a country life, and that life under Southern skies, and surrounded with all the appliances of wealth and homage, have acquired an ease, a grace, a generosity, and largeness of character, incompatible with the daily routine of the petty occupations, stratagems, and struggles of modern commercial and metropolitan life, be it in the South or the North.

Where the swamps and bayous do not extend, the country, still flat, is mostly of a rich sandy soil, which deeply tinges the waters of all the rivers from the Atlantic to the Mississippi. This is the grand characteristic of the southern portion of all the Gulf States.

ILLUSTRATIONS

The endpapers are reproductions of pages from FitzGerald Ross's original manuscript in the Blackwood correspondence at the National Library of Scotland, Edinburgh. The illustrations following page 26 are from the following sources:

1. Fremantle photograph. Privately owned. Taken on his return to London and sent as a personal memento to General James Longstreet.
2. "Opening Spring Campaign." From an original watercolor by William L. Sheppard. The Confederate Museum, Richmond, Virginia.
3. "Quaker Battery." From an oil painting by Conrad Wise Chapman. Confederate Museum, Richmond, Virginia.
4. "Repairing Damages in the Casemates. . . ." *The Illustrated London News,* June 13, 1863; from a sketch by Frank Vizetelly.
5. "The Interior of Fort Sumter. . . ." *The Illustrated London News,* December 5, 1863; from a sketch by Frank Vizetelly.
6. Longstreet. *The Illustrated London News,* June 11, 1864.
7. Stuart. *The Illustrated London News,* June 18, 1864.
8. "General Stuart's Head-Quarters. . . ." *The Illustrated London News,* April 30, 1864; from a sketch by Frank Vizetelly.
9. "Confederates Sinking Torpedoes. . . ." *The Illustrated London News,* May 16, 1863; from a sketch by Frank Vizetelly.

10. "The Defences of Charleston. . . ." *The Illustrated London News,* April 4, 1863; from a sketch by Frank Vizetelly.
11. "Fort Fisher. . . ." *The Illustrated London News,* January 23, 1864; from a sketch by Frank Vizetelly.
12. "Confederate Sharpshooters. . . ." *The Illustrated London News,* December 5, 1863; from a sketch by Frank Vizetelly.
13. "Unloading Cotton from Blockade-Runners. . . ." *The Illustrated London News,* April 30, 1864; from a sketch by Frank Vizetelly.
14. "Battle of Chicamauga. . . ." *The Illustrated London News,* supplement, December 26, 1863; from a sketch by Frank Vizetelly.
15. "Enlisting Irish and German Emigrants. . . ." *The Illustrated London News,* September 17, 1864.
16. "Camp of Federal Prisoners. . . ." *The Illustrated London News,* April 9, 1864; from a sketch by Frank Vizetelly.
17. Confederate soldiers at Mobile. The Confederate Museum, Richmond, Virginia.
18. "The Federals Shelling the City of Charleston. . . ." *The Illustrated London News,* December 5, 1863; from a sketch by Frank Vizetelly.

INDEX

Alabama, Governor of, 196, 197
Alabama Legion, 122
Alabama Legislature, 195
Alabama River, 203
Alexander, E. Porter, 130–31
Alice (ship), 205
All the Year Round, 9, 16, 23
Allen, Robert C., 38, 56
Ammunition, shortage of, 78, 130, 185
Anderson, Richard H., 43
Anderson, Robert, 114
Andrew (slave), 83
Antietam, Battle of, 43
Appleton's Guide-Book, quoted, 234–37
Aquia Creek, 217
Arlington, 169
Artemus Ward His Book, 13
Artillery, 129–31
Ashley Hall, 101, 102
Ashley River, 146
Athenaeum, The, xii, 84–85
Atlanta, 116–17, 136, 140, 187
Atlantic Monthly, 71

Augusta, Ga., 114–15, 140, 141, 143, 144
Austrian Hussars, xiv–xv
Austrian rifle, 132

Ballard House, Richmond, 94, 156
Baltimore, 77, 216, 217
Baltimore Convention, 1864, 217, 222
Baltimore and Ohio Railroad, 21
" 'Band Joe' Sweeney and His Banjo," 167
Banks, Nathaniel P., 215
Barksdale, Randolph, 47, 61
Barksdale, William, 52, 53
Battery Gregg, 99, 102, 103, 113, 144
Battle House, Mobile, 193
Beall, John Yates, xix–xx
Beauregard, Pierre Gustave Toutant, 26, 100, 102, 107, 108, 190–91
Beecher, Henry Ward, 147
Belle Isle, 70–74, 162
Bendigo (ship), 150
Benjamin, Judah P., 24, 27
Bermuda, 149
Blackford, William Wells, 167, 172, 174
Blackwood, William, xv–xx, 227
Blackwood's Edinburgh Magazine, xvi, xviii–xix, xxi
Blakely, Captain, 142
Blakely guns, 142, 143, 188
Blockade runners and the blockade, 95, 114, 115, 144, 149–51, 187, 205
Boissieux, Captain, 72
Bonaventure Cemetery, Savannah, 190
Bookseller at Augusta, Ga., 143
Boonsboro', Md., 44
Booth, John Wilkes, xx
Borcke, Heros von, xviii–xx, 157, 177
Boston, 219

Braddon, Mary Elizabeth, 71
Bragg, Braxton, 114, 121–27, 137–40, 152, 164, 184, 191–92
Bream's Tavern, 63, 64
Breckinridge, John C., 127, 137
Breech-loading rifles, 132
Brien, L. Tiernan, 157
British, neutrality of the, 200–1
Brooke gun, 26, 201
Brown House, Macon, 204
Browne, Charles Farrar, 13
Brownsville, Tex., xiii
Bruce, Robert V., 107
Buchanan, Franklin, 194, 196, 199–200
Buchanan, President James, 179
Buckner, Billy, 120
Buckner, Simon Bolivar, 122, 123, 125–27, 153, 175
Bull, Colonel, 101
Bull, Sir William, 101
Bunford, Colonel, 142
Burbridge, Stephen Gano, 228
Bürgerkrieg in den Nordamerikanischen Staaten, Der, 38
Burnside, Ambrose E., 164, 181, 182
Butterfield, Daniel, 59
Byrne, C. H., 114, 118, 152

Canada, xv, xvii, xix, 227–32
Canadian rebellion of 1837, 228–31
Cannon foundry, 142
Cape Fear River, 95, 150, 151, 187, 205
Carlisle, Penna., 41, 76, 77
Carrington, Charles S., 27
Casey, Silas, 155
Cashtown, Penna., 63
"Cavalier's Glee, The," 167–68, 173
Cavalry (Confederate), 33, 81, 118, 154, 155
Cavalry (Federal), 81

Cemetery Hill, 49, 57
Ceres (ship), 151
Chambersburg, Penna., 37–44, 56, 77
Chancellorsville, Battle of, 20, 21, 92, 180
Charleston, S. C., xv, 94, 96–98, 100, 102, 105–8, 113, 114, 141, 144, 148, 149, 178, 187–89, 191, 204
Charleston Hotel, 97, 106
Charleston *Mercury,* 103
Chase, Salmon P., 179, 216
Chattanooga, 118, 123–25, 127, 136
Chattanooga, Battle of, 164
Chattanooga Creek, 123
Cherokee Indians, 133, 134
Chesnut, James, 81
Chesnut, Mrs. James (Mary Boykin Chesnut), 124
Chester Gap, Va., 90
Chicamauga, 128, 153, 154
Chicamauga, Battle of, xv, 119, 121, 124, 125, 152
Chicamauga, Battlefield of, 138, 198–99
Chicamauga, Plan of, xvii
Chicamauga Station, 139
Chickasaw Indians, 133
Chilton, R. H., 49
Chinese coolies, 209–10
Choctaw Indians, 133
Cigars, 204, 211–12
Citadel, The, 97
Civil War Prisons, 72
Clarke, John J., 48
Clarke's Mountain, 172
Cleburne, Patrick, 118, 127, 153–55
Cleveland, Tenn., 140
Clifford House, Niagara Falls, 227
Coleman, Clayton G., 184
Collie, Mr., 152, 188, 191, 204
Collie, Alexander, & Co., 152

Columbus, Ga., 191
Confederate arsenal, Augusta, Ga., 141
Confederate Congress, 156, 177, 198
Confederate currency and finances, 40–42, 93–94, 160
Confederate scouts, 173
Confederate Scouts: Virginia's Frank Stringfellow, 174
Connecticut (ship), 151
Conscription, 117
Continental Hotel, Philadelphia, 219
Cooke, John Esten, 171, 173, 174
Cooper, Samuel, 22, 54
Cornhill Magazine, The, 23
Corporal punishment, 156, 157
Cotton, cultivation of, 203
Crane, Mr., 28
Creek Indians, 133
Cullen, J. S. Dorsey, 47, 56, 132–36
Culpeper Courthouse, Va., 89, 93
Cumming, Kate, 194, 199

Dahlgren, Charles Bunker, 143
Dahlgren gun, 99, 142
Dahlgren Shell-Gun and Its Services During the Late Civil War, The, 143
Dalton, Ga., 140, 155
Davis, President Jefferson, xix, 26, 27, 123, 136, 137, 174–75, 177, 197, 198
Dawson, Francis Warrington, 128, 129, 131
Deas, George, 186, 187, 189, 191, 194, 203
Demopolis, Ala., 204
Diary from Dixie, A, 124
Dix, John A., 231
Dog River, 199
Dow, Neal, 163
Draft (U. S.), 223
Drewry's Bluff, 24–26

Drunkenness. *See* Whiskey and drunkenness
Dunne, Captain, 128, 186

Early, Jubal Anderson, 29, 50
Ehrhardt, Captain, 31
Elliott, Stephen, Jr., 145
Enfield rifle, 131, 132
Equipment of Confederate soldiers, 33–34
"Ethiopian serenaders," 112
Everett, Edward, 79
Ewell, Richard Stoddert, 20, 30–32, 47, 53, 54, 57, 58, 60, 65, 66, 68, 77
Exports, 149

Fairfax, John W., 128
Fairfield, Penna., 63
Fairoaks (Fair Oaks), Battle of, xviii
Farrow, Edward S., 143
Farrow's Military Encyclopedia, 143
Faulkner, Charles J., 31, 32, 88
Faulkner, Mrs. Charles J., 32
Fearn, Walker, xvi, 156
Feilden, Henry Wemyss, 101, 177
Female soldier, 116
Finney, R. H., 142
First Blood, 81
Flogging, 156, 157
Fontaine, Felix Gregory, 105
Food, 12, 71, 90, 101, 134, 135, 157–61, 163
Foreigners in Confederate service, 177
Foreigners in Federal service, 177
Forrest, Nathan Bedford, 118
Fort Caswell, 151, 187
Fort Darling. *See* Drewry's Bluff
Fort Delaware, 71, 72
Fort Fisher, 150, 151

Fort Gaines, 197
Fort Johnson, 102
Fort Lafayette, 16
Fort Morgan, 196–98
Fort Moultrie, 103
Fort Pemberton, 100
Fort Powell, 198, 201
Fort Sumter, 26, 79, 98, 102–5, 107, 114, 144, 145, 188, 191, 197
Fort Wagner, 98, 99, 102, 103, 107, 113, 144
Fort Warren, 12
Fortress Monroe, 71
Fourth of July (1864), 227
Franklin, Benjamin, statue of, 39
Franklin Hotel, Chambersburg, 38, 45
Frederick, Md., 35, 43
Fredericksburg, 17, 21, 22, 179, 181, 182, 217, 220
Fredericksburg, Battle of, 181–82
Fredericksburg, Battlefield of, 181
Fredericksburg, Mayor of, 180
Fremantle, Sir Arthur James Lyon, xii–xiv, xxi, 8, 15, 25–27, 35, 38, 40, 44, 45, 48, 52, 55, 57, 58, 61, 62, 65–67, 75, 76, 78, 83, 84, 95, 97, 98, 116, 136, 143, 170, 178, 184, 193
Fremantle Diary, The, xii–xiii
French, Justus C., 114
French Broad River, 185
Front Royal, 90

Gaines's Mill, 44
Galveston, 209
Gambling, 156
Gardner, Mr., 90
Geary, Colonel, 116
Georgetown, D. C., 76
Gettysburg, 41, 44, 47, 49, 57, 58
Gettysburg, Battle of, xiii, xv, 40, 47–60, 68, 78, 79, 170, 183

Gettysburg, Map of, xvii
Gettysburg College, 41
Gibbes, Robert Wilson, 189
Gillmore, Quincy A., 102, 106–8
Glances Back Through History, 97
Gordon, George, 59, 175, 187, 191
Gordon, John B., 183
Gordonsville, Va., 12
Goree, T. J., 119, 128
Göttingen University, xiv
Gracie, Archibald, 122, 127, 137
Grand Ecore, La., 214, 215
Grant (courier), 168
Grant, Mr., 198
Grant, President Ulysses S., 215, 217, 218, 220, 221, 223
Grattan, Charles, 171–72
Greek fire, 107, 108
Greencastle, Penna., 36
Greenville, Ga., 155
Greenwood Mills, Ga., 117
Grenfell, St. Leger, 172, 227–28
Guerillas, 176
Guinea's Station, 33, 183
Guns: 6-pounder, 130; 3-inch rifled, 129, 130

Hagerstown, Md., 32, 35, 43, 44, 66–68, 75, 78, 80, 170
Hamilton's Crossing, Va., 179, 183
Hampton, Wade, 183
Hancock, Md., 75
Hansa (ship), 150, 187, 204, 207
Hardee, William Joseph, 122, 204
Harman, J. A., 31
Harper's Ferry, 43, 44, 92
Harpers Magazine, 71
Harrisburg, 77
Harrison, Burton N., 23, 24, 26
Harrison, Mrs. Burton N. (Constance Cary Harrison), 97

Havana, xvii, 205–12
Heidelberg University, xiv
Hemp, xix
Hemphill, W. E., 167
Hesseltine, William B., 72
Heth, Henry, 48, 50, 57
Heth's Division, 58
Hill, Ambrose Powell, 37, 46–48, 50, 53, 54, 60, 175
Hill, Daniel Harvey, 43, 44
Hill, Isaac, 179
History of the Confederate Powder Works, 143
Hood, John Bell, 48, 53, 55, 121, 175
Hood's Division, 60
Hooker, Joseph, 21, 39, 68, 77, 155
Hoole, W. Stanley, 97
Hotze, Henry, xi
Howard, Joseph P., 223, 224
Howitzers: 12-pound, 130; 24-pound, 130

Illinois Cavalry, Eighth, 18
Illustrated London News, The, 9, 72, 97, 102, 103, 106, 128, 150
In Vinculis, 220
Index, The, xi, xvii, 41, 69, 70, 79, 82, 105, 136, 160, 175, 184–85, 195, 197, 223–24
Indians, 133
Indigo, 203
Inflation, 161
Ingalls, Rufus, 221
Inside the Confederate Government, 24
Ireland, 233
Iron manufacture, 164

Jackson, Miss., 195, 196
Jackson, Thomas Jonathan ("Stonewall"), 21, 32–33, 43, 44, 90, 92, 171
Jacobs, Michael, 41

James Island, 98, 100, 102
James River, 25
Jeff (slave), 82, 83, 134, 137, 138
Jenkins, Micah, 115–17, 126
Johnson, President Andrew, xx, 222
Johnson's Island, xx, 103
Johnston, Joseph E., 152, 183
Johnston, William Y., 127
Jones, John Beauchamp, 17–18, 20–21, 68, 137, 157, 160, 161, 163, 175, 196–98
Jordan, John R., 199
Jordan, Thomas, 100, 188, 191
Journal of Commerce, The, 223
Journal of Hospital Life in the Confederate Army of Tennessee, 194
Joynes, Edward S., 23, 24
Jubiläumserinnerungs-Medaille, xiv

Kean, Robert Garlick Hill, 24, 68
Keiley, Anthony M., 219
Keitt, Lawrence M., 113
Knoxville, Tenn., 124, 152, 153, 164, 186
Krakow, xiv

Lake Ontario, 232
Lamb, William, 150, 151
Land We Love, The, 44
Latrobe, Osman, 56, 58, 76, 128
Law, Evander M., 65
Lawley, Francis, 32–33, 38, 41, 42, 44, 45, 48, 61, 63, 65, 66, 76, 78, 134–36, 139, 140, 144, 166, 184
"Lay of the Last Rebel, The," 82
Lee, George Washington Custis, 137
Lee, Robert Edward, 16, 21, 22, 25, 27, 37, 39, 42–44, 48, 51, 53, 54, 60, 63–65, 67–69, 76–80, 83, 92, 133, 156, 169, 181, 182, 217, 218, 220, 221
Lee, Sydney Smith, 24–26

Leonard's Town, Md., 16
Libby Prison, 69, 71, 72, 74, 162
Liddell, St. John R., 127
Lincoln, President Abraham, xx, 79, 127, 217, 218, 222, 223
Lincoln and the Tools of War, 107
Little Bookham, England, xiv
Locke, John, 147
London, xvi–xx
London *Times,* 38, 70, 140
Longstreet, James, 31, 37, 43, 44, 46–49, 51–58, 60–62, 64, 65, 68, 75, 76, 81, 90, 91, 114, 115, 118, 119, 121, 122, 124, 125, 131, 133, 137, 140, 152, 153, 164, 184–86
Lookout Mountain, 125, 126, 134, 136, 137
Lookout Mountain, Battle of, 153
Lord, Walter, xiii
"Lorena" (song), 51
Lovettsville, Md., 43
Loyal Publication Society, 74
Lucas, J. Jonathan, 100
Lucy (ship), 150

McClellan, George Brinton, 42–44, 226
McGuire, Hunter, 32, 171
Mackall, T. B., 140
Mackall, William W., 127
McLaws, Lafayette, 43, 44, 56, 65, 92, 120, 121, 124
McLaws' Division, 60
Macon, 204
Madeira, 147–48
Madrid, xvii
Manassas, 43
Manning, P. T., 121, 129, 131
Mansfield, La., 214
Marine Corps (Confederate), 25
Marshall, Charles, 42
Martinsburg, Va., 29, 31, 43, 68, 88

Marye's Height, 181, 182
Maryland, Confederate entry into, 23
Maryland, Confederate sympathizers in, 9–15
Matamoros, Tex., 44
Maude Campbell (ship), xvii
Maury, Dabney Herndon, 194, 196, 198, 199
Maury, Thomas F., 47
Maury, William Lewis, 26
Maxwell, Mary Elizabeth (Braddon), 71
Meade, George G., 55, 60, 68, 69, 76–78, 80, 133, 174, 218
Meagher's Irish Brigade, 182
Medical service (Confederate), 132, 133
Meridian, Miss., 203
Merrimac (ship), 26
Michigan Volunteers, Twenty-Fourth, 19
Middleburg, Md., 43
Middleton Place, 146
Military Tourist, A, xiii
Mills House Hotel, Charleston, 96, 108
Milroy, Robert H., 20, 22, 30
Missionary Ridge, 127, 153–55, 185
Missionary Ridge, Battle of, 152
Mississippi rifle, 132
Missouri, xix
Mobile, 161, 186, 192–202, 209
Mobile Bay, 195–99
Mobile River, 193
Monocacy River, 43
Montgomery, 191, 192, 203, 204
"Month's Visit to Confederate Headquarters, A," xvi
Montreal, 232
Moore, Thomas Verner, 183
Mordecai, J. Randolph, 188
Morgan, John Hunt, 172, 175, 176
Morgan, Peter K., 159
Morgan's raid, 175

Morris Island, 98, 99, 102, 144
Morrow, Henry A., 19
Morton, Dr., 126, 127
Moses, R. J., 61, 65
Murfreesboro, Battle of, 116, 123, 124
Music, 40, 112, 167–68, 196

Nantucket, Mass., 111
Napoleon gun, 129, 130, 142
Narrative of Privations and Sufferings of United States Officers & Soldiers While Prisoners of War, 74
Nashville, 125, 134
Nassau, xv, 149, 187, 204–6
Natchez, 201
Negro labor in Missouri, xix
Negro labor at Mobile, 162
Negro servants in Canada, 231
Negro soldiers, 165, 218–19
Negroes in the Confederacy. *See* Slaves and slavery
Neutrality, British, 200–1
New Bedford, Mass., 111
New Ironsides (ship), 99, 103
New Orleans, 214
New Providence, 205
New York, 205, 213, 216, 219, 220, 223, 226
New York *Daily News,* 171
New York *Evening Post,* 215
New York *Herald,* 215, 223
New York *Times,* 223, 224
New York *World,* 223
Newbern, N. C., 187
Newburyport, Mass., 111
Newnan, Ga., 194
Niagara Falls, 227, 232
Nocquet, James, 123
Norfolk, 117

Norris, William, 23, 24, 27, 88, 92, 164
Northrop, L. B., 163
Notes on the Rebel Invasion of Maryland and Pennsylvania and the Battle of Gettysburg, July 1, 2 and 3, 1863, 41
Nova Scotian (ship), 233

Official Records (Army), 18, 20, 31, 54, 90, 108
Official Records (Navy), 177, 197–98
Orange Courthouse, 166, 218
Ordnance, manufacture of, 26
Ordnance service (Confederate), 131
Oriental Saloon, Richmond, 157–59, 184
Owens, William M., 51, 135

Parrott guns, 99, 129, 130, 143, 145
Pascagoula, Miss., 196
Patrick Henry (Confederate schoolship), 25
Payne, John, 228
Pearson, driver, 166
Peavey, James, 174
Pegram, John, 125
Pendleton, William N., 62
Pennsylvania Dutch, 37
Percussion-caps, 141
"Perfect Cure, The," (song), 128
Perryville, Battle of, 116
Petersburg, Va., 95, 117, 131, 186
Pettigrew, J. Johnston, 58, 80–81
Philadelphia, 77, 219, 220
Photographs used for introductions, 23
Pickett, George E., 58, 59
Pickett's Division, 56, 58–60, 68, 117
Planters' Hotel, Augusta, 115, 141, 143
Pleasonton, Alfred, 18
Point Lookout, xx, 218, 219
Polk, Leonidas, 122, 124, 125, 137, 203, 204

Pope, John, 42, 122
Porter, David Dixon, 225
Potomac River, 80
Powder mills, 142
Preston, William B., 79, 122, 125, 127, 128, 135, 175
Price, Sterling, xix
Pringle, Motte A., 144
Prisoner of War, 219
Prisoners and prisons, xx, 69–74, 120, 154, 162–64, 176, 204, 218–19
Pulaski House, Savannah, 190

Quebec, 232

Rains, George W., 141–43
Randolph, George Wythe, 79
Randolph, Innes, 82
Rapidan fords, 220
Rapidan River, 21
Rappahannock River, 181, 182
Rations for laborers, 162
Rebel War Clerk's Diary at the Confederate States Capital, A, 18
Rebel yell, 39–40, 89
Recollections Grave and Gay, 97
Record, The, 23
Re-enlistments, 197–98
Reminiscences of Confederate Service, 1861–1865, 129
Reynolds, John F., 47
Rhett, Alfred, 99, 105
Richmond, 21, 23, 26, 27, 93–95, 117, 136, 141, 144, 156–64, 174–77, 186, 204, 217, 218
Richmond (ship), 26
Richmond *Examiner,* 69, 157
"Richmond and Washington During the War," 23
Richmond *Whig,* 17, 19

Ringgold, Ga., 117, 118, 154, 155
Ripley, Roswell S., 98
Rosecrans, W. S., 114, 122, 124
Ross, FitzGerald: as propagandist, xi; comments of *The Athenaeum* on his book, xii; appraisal of his book by *The Saturday Review,* xii; his book compared to Fremantle's, xii–xiv; biographical material on, xiv–xv; publishing record of his book, xv–xviii; in Spain, xvii; in London, xviii–xx; excerpts from his letters to Blackwood, xix–xxi; reception of his book, xxi–xxii; in Maryland, 9–16; crosses Potomac to Virginia, 16; lands in Virginia, 16; first days in Virginia, 16–20; hears news of Battle of Winchester, 20; arrives in Richmond, 21; summarizes spring campaign of 1863, 21–23; in Richmond, 23–27; interviews Secretary Benjamin, 24; visits Drewry's Bluff, 24–26; interviews President Davis, 26; travels to Staunton, 27; at Woodstock, 28–29; comments on Battle of Winchester, 29–30; travels to join army in Pennsylvania, 31–36; crosses into Maryland, 33; at Hagerstown, 35; reaches Pennsylvania, 36; comments on Pennsylvania Dutch, 37; reaches Chambersburg, 37; on Rebel yell, 39–40; meets General Lee, 42; on "lost order," 42–44; camps near Gettysburg, 44; meets Fremantle, 44–45; at Battle of Gettysburg, 46–62; breakfast with General Longstreet, 48; describes town of Gettysburg, 49; on character of Confederate soldiers, 49–50; describes charge, 52–53; on wounding of Hood, 53; quotes Lee's report, 53–54; quotes Longstreet, 55; on Pickett's charge, 56; rides into Gettysburg with Fremantle, 57; on repulse of Pickett, 58–59; talks with Longstreet and General Pendleton, 61; at Bream's Tavern, 63–64; meets General Stuart, 64; at Hagerstown, 66–68, 80; on prisoners and prisons, 69–74; notes Fremantle's departure for England, 75; visits with Lee, 76; comments on Gettysburg campaign, 76–78; told of interview with President Lincoln, 78–79; comments on cavalry services, 81; describes Negroes in camp, 82–84; on the term "Yankee," 87–88; camps with Confederate

Army, 88–89; at Chester Gap, 90–91; on Confederate Signal Corps, 91–92; at Richmond, 93–94; leaves for Charleston, 94; reaches Charleston, 96; in Charleston, 96–114; meets Vizetelly, 97; visits Fort Sumter, 98; visits Ashley Hall, 101; describes attack of August 23, 103; describes shelling of Charleston, 105–8; comments on slavery, 109–12; arrives at Augusta, 114; at Augusta, 114–15; travels to battle area, 115–18; describes female soldier, 116; at Atlanta, 116–17; reaches Longstreet's headquarters, 118; in Chicamauga area, 118–34; describes Battle of Chicamauga, 121–22; comments on Chattanooga, 123–25; climbs Lookout Mountain, 125–26; meets von Scheliha, 126; meets generals of Confederate Army, 127; makes notes on Confederate ordnance and artillery, 129–32; describes medical service of the Confederacy, 132–33; describes camp life, 134–35; reports visit to camp by President Davis, 136–37; rides over battlefield at Chicamauga, 138; leaves camp, 139; describes ordnance works at Augusta, 141–43; returns to Charleston, 144; visits Fort Sumter, 144–45; visits Summerville and Middleton Place, 146; on slavery, 146–47; describes social life in Charleston, 147–48; travels to Wilmington, 148–49; at Wilmington, 149; visits Fort Fisher, 150–52; quotes letter from friend in Bragg's army, 152–55; arrives at Richmond, 156; on gambling, 156; on flogging, 156–57; describes fare at the Oriental Saloon, 157–59; on reported starvation, 160; on food supply, 160–62; visits Libby Prison, 162–63; visits Tredegar Ironworks, 164; visits Stuart's camp, 166–74; quotes "Cavalier's Glee," 167–68; visits Lee, 169; on Stuart, 170–71; on St. Leger Grenfell, 172; remarks on Stuart's scouts, 173–74; returns to Richmond, 174; attends President's reception, 174–75; meets General Morgan, 175; comments on Morgan, 175–76; mentions foreigners in Confederate and Federal armies, 177–78; accompanies Stuart to Fredericksburg, 179; at Fredericksburg, 180–83; describes Battle of Fredericksburg, 181–83; leaves for Mobile, 186; at Petersburg, 186;

at Wilmington, 187; at Charleston, 188–89; at Savannah, 189–90; visits General Beauregard, 190–91; reaches Mobile, 192; at Mobile, 193–203; on social life in Mobile, 194; describes defenses in Mobile Bay, 196–99; visits aboard the *Tennessee,* 199; on slavery, 201–2; leaves Mobile, 203; travels to Selma and Montgomery, 203; reaches Macon, 204; sails from Wilmington through blockade, 204; describes trip through blockade, 204–5; arrives at Nassau, 205; proceeds to Havana, 206; at Havana, 207–12; reaches New York, 213; quotes extracts from letters, 214–22; on General Banks, 215; on General Grant, 215; comments on Negro soldiers, 218–19; visits Wilmington, Del., and Philadelphia, 219–20; reports spurious proclamation, 223–24; on reliability of newspapers, 224–25; visits in New York City and New York State, 226–27; describes Independence Day celebration, 227; at Niagara Falls, 227–28; comments on Canadian rebellion of 1837, 228–32; travels to Montreal and Quebec, 232; leaves for home, 232

Mentioned, xi–xxii, 13, 17, 19, 20, 35, 44, 45, 48, 54, 70, 74, 81, 84, 85, 97, 129, 163, 185, 227

Ross, John, 134
Rossville, Ga., 134
Russell, Lord John, first earl, 139, 201
Russell, Sir William Howard, 140

St. Lawrence River, 232, 233
St. Michael's Church, Charleston, 108
Sanitary Fair, Baltimore, 216
Saratoga, N. Y., 226
Saturday Review, The, xii, xxi–xxii, 85, 86
Savannah, 187–92, 204
Savannah River, 114
Scheibert, Justus, 38, 48, 94, 101, 106
Scheliha, Victor von, 126, 162, 194, 195, 202
Scouts, Confederate, 173

Secession, 178–79
Second Report of a Board of Artillery Officers, 143
Seddon, James A., 27, 32
Sedgwick, John, 55
Selma, Ala., 203
Semmes, Paul J., 55
Seven Days, Battle of the, 44, 117
Seward, William H., 74, 179, 216, 217, 228, 231
Sharon Springs, N. Y., 226
Sharpsburg, Battle of, 43
Sharpsburg, Md., 43
Sharpshooters, 132
Shenandoah Valley, 22, 29
Sherman, William Tecumseh, xx, 154, 195, 196, 203, 204
Short, Leir, 107
Shreveport, La., 214
Signal Corps (Confederate), 91–92, 125
Slaves and slavery, xii, 32, 82–86, 109–12, 120, 121, 137, 146, 147, 161, 201–2, 234–36
Small-arms, 131, 132, 142
Smooth-bore muskets, 131, 132
Soldiers of fortune, 178
Soldiers' Home, Charleston, 189
Sorrel, G. Moxley, 48, 128
Sothern, Colonel, 164, 165
Sothern, Mr., 165
South Mountains, 46–47
Southern Historical Society Papers, 44
Southern Illustrated News, The, 68
Southern yell. *See* Rebel yell
Spain, xvii, xviii
Spanish River, 193
Spencer rifles, 132
Springfield rifle, 131, 132
Stafford Heights, 181–83

Stanton, Edwin McMasters, xx, 220, 221, 225
Staunton, Va., 27, 28
Stevenson, Carter L., 153
Stoneman, George, 20
Stoneman's cavalry, 20
Stringfellow, Frank, 173–74
Stuart, Alexander Hugh Holmes, 79
Stuart, James Ewell Brown, 64, 66, 76, 166–74, 177, 179–81, 183, 202–3
Stuart, Mrs. James Ewell Brown (Flora Cooke Stuart), 168
Stuart, James Ewell Brown, Jr. (Jimmy), 168
Summerville, S. C., 146
Sumter, Ga., *Republican,* 82
Susquehanna River, 76
"Swamp Angel" (gun), 106, 108
Swanberg, W. A., 81
Sweeney, Dick, 166–67
Sweeney, Joe, 167
Sweeney, Sam, 166–67

Tappahannock, Va., 220
Tax in kind, 191
Taylor, Thomas H., 202
Taylor's Gap, Ga., 155
Taylor's Ridge, Ga., 155
Tennessee (ship), 199
Texas, xx
Theatre at Augusta, 143
Thomas, George H., 138
Thompson, John Reuben, xvii–xx, 70, 136
Thomson, Captain, 28
Three Months in the Southern States, April–June 1863, xii–xiv, 15, 25
Timrod, Henry, 148
Toombs, Robert, 82
Traveling in the Confederacy: by rail, 27, 94, 115, 148, 149, 156, 191; by stage, 28; by steamer, 203

Tredegar Ironworks, 23, 129, 164
Trenton Falls, N. Y., 226, 227
Trimble, Isaac R., 59
Trip of the Steamer Oceanus to Fort Sumter and Charleston, S. C., 114
Trollope, Anthony, 71
Tunnel Hill, Ga., 152, 155

Urbanna, Va., 220

Van Dorn, Earl, xx
Vienna, xiv
Virginia (ship). *See Merrimac* (ship)
Virginia, secession of, 78
Virginia Cavalcade, 167
Virginia Legislature, 156
Visit to the Cities and Camps of the Confederate States, A, xi, xii, xv–xviii, xx–xxii, 84–86
Vizetelly, Frank, 9, 16, 23, 70, 72, 97, 102, 103, 106, 107, 114, 118, 125, 139, 140, 143, 144, 149, 150, 163, 166, 167, 187
Vizetelly, Henry, 97
Vizetelly Covers the Confederacy, 97

Walker, H. Pinckney, 101, 148
Walker, W. H. T., 43, 44, 127
Walton, J. B., 50, 51, 56, 128, 129, 131, 135, 186, 194
Walton, Thomas, 47, 48
War of the Rebellion: Official Records. See Official Records
War Years with Jeb Stuart, 167
Ward, Artemus (pseudonym of Charles Farrar Browne), 13
Ward, Governor of Alabama, 196, 197
Warner, Captain, 163
Washington, D. C., 76, 77, 217, 220
Washington Artillery (of New Orleans), 51
Washington Hotel, Hagerstown, 67, 80
Watkins' House, 119, 123
Wearing of the Gray, 173

West Point (military academy), 97, 187
Westmoreland County, Va., 17–19
Wheeler, Joseph, 122, 123
Whiskey and drunkenness, 10, 11, 15, 16, 34–35, 171
White, Ebenezer, 165
Whiting, William H. C., 149, 187
Whitworth guns, 130, 132, 151
Wickham, Williams C., 78, 79
Williams, John S., 175
Williamsport, Md., 33, 34
Wilmington, Del., 219
Wilmington, N. C., 95, 114, 148–50, 152, 156, 178, 187, 189, 204, 207
Winchester, Battle of, 29–30
Winchester, Va., 20–22, 27, 28, 31
Winthrop, Stephen, 186
Wofford, William T., 91
Wolseley, Garnet, xvi
Woodstock, Va., 28

"Yankee" (as epithet), 87–88
York, Penna., 76
Young, P. M. B., 180